History Comes Alive

History Comes Alive

Public History and Popular Culture in the 1970s

M. J. Rymsza-Pawlowska

The University of North Carolina Press CHAPEL HILL

This book was published with the assistance of the Authors Fund of the University of North Carolina Press.

© 2017 The University of North Carolina Press
All rights reserved
Set in Espinosa Nova by Westchester Publishing Services
Manufactured in the United States of America
The University of North Carolina Press has been a member of the Green Press
Initiative since 2003.

Library of Congress Cataloging-in-Publication Data
Names: Rymsza-Pawlowska, M. J., author.
Title: History comes alive : public history and popular culture in the 1970s /
    M.J. Rymsza-Pawlowska.
Other titles: Studies in United States culture.
Description: Chapel Hill : University of North Carolina Press, [2017] |
    Series: Studies in United States culture | Includes bibliographical
    references and index.
Identifiers: LCCN 2016050514 | ISBN 9781469633855 (cloth : alk. paper) |
    ISBN 9781469633862 (pbk : alk. paper) | ISBN 9781469633879 (ebook)
Subjects: LCSH: United States—History—Historiography. | United States—
    History—Public opinion. | History in mass media. | Nineteen seventies. |
    Historical reenactments—Psychological aspects.
Classification: LCC E175 .R96 2017 | DDC 973—dc23
    LC record available at https://lccn.loc.gov/2016050514

Chapter 1 was published in an abbreviated form as "Broadcasting the Past: History Television, 'Nostalgia Culture,' and the Emergence of the Miniseries in the 1970s United States," *Journal of Popular Film and Television* 42 (Spring 2014): 81–90. Used here with permission.

For my mother,
Elzbieta Rymsza-Pawlowska,
and in memory of my father,
Wojciech Rymsza-Pawlowski

Contents

Illustrations

Acknowledgments

In both spatial aspects and temporal ones, this book exceeds far beyond a couple hundred pages. It's been an active part of my life for several years, and as a set of ideas and questions, for much longer. And so, the people who I wish to thank have been involved both explicitly and implicitly in its—and in my—development.

Foremost, I would like to thank Susan Smulyan and Steven Lubar, whose intellect and generosity have been models to aspire to, as scholars, teachers, and colleagues. I have also benefitted from the wisdom of several careful and rigorous readers and interlocutors who have pushed me to continuously rethink this project in new ways. These include Lynne Joyrich, Alison Landsberg, Ralph E. Rodriguez, Sandy Zipp, Douglas Nickel, Gillian Frank, Matthew Delmont, Matthew Pratt Guterl, Richard Rabinowitz, Pamela Henson, Peter Liebhold, Nora Pat Small, Debra Reid, Terry Barnhart, Lynne Curry, Sace Elder, Charles Foy, Newton Key, Dan Kerr, and the two anonymous readers engaged by the University of North Carolina Press.

Many others have listened, read, questioned, and commented on my work in ways that have been incredibly helpful. My gratitude extends to co-panelists and respondents at annual meetings of the American Studies Association, the American Historical Association, the Organization for American Historians, and the Society for Cinema and Media Studies. I would also like to thank participants in the Mellon-sponsored workshop Affect Unbounded, weekly seminars at the Cogut Center for the Humanities, colloquia at the National Museum of American History and the National Air and Space Museum, the Museums at the Crossroads Summer Institute at the Mathers Museum of World Cultures, the Women's Studies Brown Bag series at Eastern Illinois University, a seminar at the Cité des Télécoms, and the Modern Culture Workshop at Brown University.

I am grateful to Mark Simpson-Vos, Lucas Church, Jessica Newman, and others at the University of North Carolina Press, who have worked with me on developing the ideas and words that follow. I would also like to thank Grace Hale and the other series editors for Studies in United States Culture.

My work has been supported through fellowships from the Cogut Center for the Humanities at Brown University and the Smithsonian Institution. Likewise, I have found encouragement and community in the Departments of American Studies, Modern Culture and Media, and Theatre Arts and Performance Studies at Brown University, the Department of History and Graduate Program in Historical Administration, and Center for the Humanities at Eastern Illinois University, and, most recently, the Department of History and Graduate Program in Public History at American University. Anita Shelton, Donna Nichols, and Jeff Cabral are just a few of the people who have helped make institutional homes feel like real ones. For several summers, I have been lucky enough to work on this manuscript at the John Nicholas Brown Center for Public Humanities and Cultural Heritage in Providence, Rhode Island, for which I thank— again (and always!)—Susan Smulyan.

Some of my favorite moments working on this project have happened in the archive. I would like to thank archivists and librarians at the National Archives in College Park, the Boston Public Library, the City of Boston Archives, the Rhode Island Historical Society Library, Independence Historical National Park in Pennsylvania, the State Archive of Pennsylvania, the David L. Wolper Archive at the University of Southern California, the University of Pennsylvania Architectural Archives, the Gerald R. Ford Presidential Library and Museum, the Richard Nixon Presidential Library and Museum, the Colonial Williamsburg Foundation, the Shippensburg Historical Society, the Massachusetts Institute of Technology Special Collections, and the Smithsonian Institution Archives. I am also grateful to friends who have been generous with their spare rooms and their company, making research trips fun as well as edifying. This list includes Stephen Groening and Andrea Christy, Dawne Langford, Nicole Restaino, and Matthew, Adam, and Kayako Abrams. A special thanks also to Katelyn Dickerson, who, as a graduate assistant at Eastern Illinois University, helped me to secure images and permissions for this text.

I have been fortunate to be a part of communities that have been nurturing, inspiring, and, when needed, distracting. Most especially, Sarah Seidman has been a fantastic colleague and friend since almost the very first day of graduate school. Thanks also to Bonnie Laughlin-Schultz, Brian Mann, Charlotte Pence, Suzie Park, C. C. Wharram, Michelle Liu Carriger, Pooja Rangan, Josh Guilford, Sarah Osment, David Fresko, Sean Dinces, Erin Curtis, Jonathan Olly, and Miel Wilson. My newest community, in the History Department at American University, has been a wonderful place to finish the very last stages of this project.

My last and greatest thanks go to the people whose love and care have helped see this—and me—through. My stepfather, Andrzej Rogalski, and my mother, Elzbieta Rymsza-Pawlowska, have supported me and my work in more ways than I can count. Nathan Conroy is my best sounding board, my most thorough editor, my favorite research assistant, my most rigorous interlocutor, and so much more. Without his encouragement and patience, this would not have been possible.

History Comes Alive

Introduction
The Historical, Transformed

> While professional historians may continue to regard themselves as custodians of the nation's past, the average person's awareness of his own history and the history of the United States has come from a number of influences and has intensified in the last two decades. Some history is learned in schools and universities, to be sure, but some through motion pictures and television as well. One cannot always vouch for the authenticity of such history, or indeed, measure how it is perceived and how much the viewer absorbs. But it cannot be denied that such influences have been considerable.
>
> —JOHN HOPE FRANKLIN, from *The Past Before Us*, 1980

> We mark out lives in memory, but we do not live there. I don't like the way America is opening its attic, dragging out all kinds of junk and dressing up as if it could be young again just by playing the old songs. When the kids do that, I'm afraid they're afraid, and a sense of future doom is moving them rather than a sense of history. When middle-agers try it, they look as desperately foolish as the fat drunk at the fraternity.... Nostalgia, I think, should be folded carefully in the gut and carried quietly for comfort. It wears quite poorly in the street.
>
> —ART SEIDENBAUM, "No More Nostalgia," *Los Angeles Times*, May 10, 1971

To even the most casual observer, American culture in the 1970s was flooded with history. Television viewers could tune into *Happy Days*, *The Waltons*, and *Laverne and Shirley*, or to historical miniseries like *Roots* and *Eleanor and Franklin*. Blockbusters like *The Great Gatsby* and *American Graffiti* were accompanied by trends like the bell-bottom pant and platform shoe, which, when they first appeared, were deemed to be 1920s and 1930s throwbacks.[1] The Gibson Girl, the Victorian Christmas, and other nineteenth-century motifs all enjoyed a certain standing in the 1970s aesthetic imagination and in the popularity of books such as E. L. Doctorow's *Ragtime*, which seamlessly mixed historical figures like Harry Houdini and Emma Goldman with fictional characters.² Men cultivated handlebar mustaches and sideburns, while the advent of the maxi skirt as an alternative to the sixties-era miniskirt was often characterized as suggestive of residual Victorian modesty.³ A reprint of the 1897 Sears catalog was a surprise entry on the bestseller lists, prompting the subsequent reissues of the 1902 and 1927 editions as well as catalogs from retailers Montgomery Ward and Johnson Smith, the venerable 1893 travel guide *Baedeker's United States*, and even the 1907 *Temperance Songbook*.⁴ Readers could flip through newsprint pages that advertised everything from farm machinery to corsets. But they could also order and wear more recent versions of yesteryear's clothing from the newest Sears or Montgomery Ward catalogs, which featured takes on prairie, World War II, and flapper fashion.⁵ Clearly, the historical—in many shapes and forms— mattered deeply to American culture.⁶

The degree to which the past had become central to contemporary culture was particularly striking because in prior decades, Americans had been inspired by the future, not the past. From the early twentieth century through the postwar period, the apex of what some critics have called "the project of modernity," Americans had been looking forward; optimistic faith in the progressive promise of tomorrow influenced not only political and technological priorities like space exploration but also popular culture. Think, for example, about the series of World's Fairs that occurred in the early to mid-twentieth century, each showcasing and promising technological innovation paired with increasing standards of living. Think also of aesthetic style: from the clean lines of 1930s Art Deco to the modernist designs of Charles and Ray Eames, the structures that Americans built, the way they designed their interiors, and the new consumer goods that they purchased all imagined a future that was simultaneously fantastic and assured.⁷ But by the 1970s, American culture seemed quite suddenly to be fixated not on the future, but the past.

This new predilection was not lost on cultural critics, who noticed these developments and worried about them. *Time, Life*, and *Newsweek* all ran cover stories on what they characterized as a cultural phenomenon, deeming it "the nostalgia trend," and later, "nostalgia culture." These articles attributed this "new nostalgia" to the various upheavals and social unrest of the 1960s and the disappointments of Vietnam, which had given rise to a widespread fear or disenchantment with the present.⁸ The events of that decade, commentators speculated, had made Americans fearful of looking into the future and led to heightened interest in the historical.⁹ As the work of social critics shifted from relatively tame critiques of postwar conformity (typified by books like *Organization Man* and *The Feminine Mystique*) toward the more ominous (*Beyond Belief, The Population Bomb*), the future began to be imagined as a decline—as opposed to a realization—of progress.[10]

Other critics portrayed the new penchant for the past as inertia, reflecting Americans' inability to deal with the present, maligning the nostalgic impulse as escapist and unproductive. For instance, in a column entitled "No More Nostalgia," *Los Angeles Times* editor Art Seidenbaum bemoaned what he considered to be a new and dangerous cultural obsession, "I don't like the way America is opening its attic, dragging out all kinds of junk and dressing up as if it could be young again just by playing the old songs," Seidenbaum wrote.[11] The representation of "nostalgia" here and elsewhere in 1970s commentary suggested an emotional yearning for an inaccessible and irrecoverable past, one that was both futile and unproductive.

A range of commentators characterized 1970s popular culture as paradoxically both overly concerned with history *and* prone to rendering an unrealistic version of it.[12] Journalist and writer Tom Wolfe noted in the 1976 essay that famously anointed the 1970s as the "Me Decade," that the current generation had no connection to either the past or the future.[13] The historian Christopher Lasch expanded upon this diagnosis a few years later in *The Culture of Narcissism*. Echoing Wolfe and others, he described "a collapse of historical faith" and "the waning of the sense of historical time." For Lasch, this erosion meant the emergence of a cultural persona that was at once self-obsessed and insecure, a generation that was completely unable to relate to either its past or its future.[14] In a society that had been accustomed to looking forward with optimism, popular culture's infatuation with history signaled a dramatic rupture, and one that both worried its contemporaries and that continued to inform later critical assessment of the decade.[15]

But looking backward in times of rapid change was itself not new or unique to the 1970s. As Karal Ann Marling has observed, "Throughout history, revivalism has always been a response to the irritant of time."[16] In the last decades of the nineteenth century, faced with growing cities, massive immigration, and all of the confusion that accompanied large-scale industrialization, Americans became fascinated with the Early Republic, immersing themselves in a colonial revival that lasted through the 1920s. Honoring figures like George Washington and collecting art and antiques from the eighteenth century (or mass-produced replicas thereof) were ways for Americans to find sanctuary from the upheavals of rapid modernization.

American history, during this period, inspired furniture and decorative goods in the colonial style, films and plays about people from the great American past, and thousands of pageants staged in towns and cities across the country. Model villages like Colonial Williamsburg and Greenfield Village, developed in the years before World War II, likewise presented Americans with tangible representations of the past. Then, as in the 1970s, commentators and critics attributed this cultural preoccupation to a reaction to and rejection of the problems of modern life.[17]

While 1970s "nostalgia culture" appeared to resemble its predecessors in both cause and content, the *way* that Americans were thinking about and using the historical was very different. During the earlier colonial revival, Americans had expressed their interest in the past through relics and replicas of colonial goods, through spectacular performances of noteworthy historical events, and by memorializing and raising monuments to the lives and experiences of significant personages. In short, the majority of these engagements with the past concentrated on visual and material forms, encouraging reverence for and reflection upon august periods in American history, which were understood to be both distant *and* different (and thus, a contrast to modern times). But in the 1970s, something changed. Popular engagements with the past were increasingly interactive, encouraging not reflection, but contemplation.

The prevalent diagnoses of the 1970s, as before, styled the nostalgic impulse as a search for a safe space that was secure from the ills of the times. But looking more closely, we can see that Americans in the 1970s were doing more than longing for bygone eras or shrinking from the conflicts of the present. Instead, they were relating to and identifying with particular expressions of history in novel ways, looking to place themselves directly into the past, to know and feel the experiences of historical individuals as well as to see them. By paging through a historical catalog or wearing clothing associated with a different era, one makes meaning not only by thinking, but also by doing.[18] By visiting a museum exhibit that positions visitors emotionally or bodily proximate to the past, or by talking with interpreters of a different era, one learns about and considers the past from the vantage point of "being there." This kind of historic engagement is immersive and interactive; it emphasizes personalized and individual connections with the past.

Today, we are used to thinking about history in these terms. We expect personalized and absorbing historical experiences not only in museums, but also in video games, and on the Internet. Scholars working across a variety of fields have begun studying experiential knowledge production, taking account of the processes of embodied engagement. Work by Alison Landsberg, Diana Taylor, Scott Magelssen, Vanessa Agnew, and others foregrounds affective or empathetic rapport: a perception of commonality of feelings or experience that can bridge radically different historical circumstances.[19] These interpretations of the complex relations of present-day historical thinking more closely reflect the cultural activity that emerged and was consolidated in the 1970s. What was described by some as the "nostalgic impulse" actually bound up diverse perspectives and resulted in multiple types of historymaking that cannot be defined simply as wistfulness for a lost past.[20] Critics writing against nostalgia culture in the 1970s and thereafter were reacting to the change, but did not fully account for how or why this unfolded.

History-based cultural production can take many forms: museum exhibitions, living history, building preservation, and oral history, to name just a few. But we also learn about the past from film, television, novels, fashion, and music: history is, for better or worse, all around us, and all of these forms influence how we imagine and understand the past. I begin with examples from wider popular culture to illustrate how far-reaching American interest in the past was by the 1970s, but the best instances with which to examine and understand this development are those that are more self-consciously "historical." In the following pages, I introduce a series of case studies loosely organized around the 1976 American Revolution Bicentennial, a national commemoration that came at precisely the moment that engagement with and use of the past was changing and which served as both site and vehicle for many encounters and projects that reflected these changes.

In this moment, popular and public history across multiple fields shifted from instructive, reflective, or visual efforts to represent the past to ones that encouraged emotional, as opposed to informational, production of historical knowledge. History came alive: it moved from the past into the present. It became as much about feeling as about thinking, about being inside the past instead of looking upon it. Numerous individuals, groups, and institutions created projects and programs around the Bicentennial in the context of a larger cultural preoccupation with the past, seeking to experience and empathize with the lives of historic individuals as a means to reevaluate the past, to reconsider contemporary events, and most importantly, to learn about themselves.

Changes within popular historymaking (to use a term borrowed from Roy Rosenzweig and David Thelen's landmark study) came alongside and were informed by significant developments in scholarly practice, which too reflected the revolutions of the 1960s.[21] Academic historians were placing more emphasis on social history, or "history from the bottom up," looking to study and describe the experiences of people of color, women, working individuals, and other previously marginalized groups by using new methods borrowed from quantitative or demographic study and analyzing new kinds of evidence, for example, folk ephemera and material culture.[22] This "new history" (which was also inspired by work by the "Progressive" school of historians of the early twentieth century, themselves reacting to the changes of that era) was accompanied by several other transformations across the field, including parallel shifts in the field of American Studies, new attention to historical archaeology, and the newly forming field of public history.[23] Popular and scholarly history had then—and continues to have—a complex relationship, but overlapped and intersected in significant ways, as professional historians also used new evidence and new approaches to expand their fields of inquiry and to forge important connections between the study of the past and the evaluation of the present. Like more popular historymaking, academic historical scholarship was influenced by larger social and cultural factors and, as the 1960s progressed into the 1970s, took on new subjects and revealed new forms.

This decade saw a change in—and a transition away from—what I call a *logic of preservation*, an understanding of history underwritten by material evidence and expressed by a sense of the past as spectacular, monumental, and foundational to—yet still distant from—the present. Preservation, both as a set of specific practices and, as I discuss it here, a way of *knowing* as well as a way of doing, locates the subject outside of the historical narrative and relies on stable and uncontested material evidence (usually produced by those who hold power or embody the dominant ideology) for the representation and articulation of that narrative. Yet in the 1970s, alongside the weakening of the Cold War–era "consensus," or "top-down" history, via social movements and the emergence of social and cultural history, many Americans questioned these traditional interpretations, a development that resulted in new forms of preservation, as well as a different set of relationships and impulses around the collection and display of material artifacts.[24] In the context of these changes, a *logic of reenactment* replaced preservation as the dominant mode of historical consciousness.

Reenactive engagement privileges an affective and experiential production of historic knowledge, placing the subject *within* the past and sometimes even *between* the past and the present. Reenactment is interesting because it is unpredictable; not only because, as scholars of performance emphasize, bodies always exceed their own meanings, but also because bodies are always already imbued with prior experience, what performance theorist Jeff Friedman calls a kind of "muscle memory."[25] This is one reason why immersive or reenactive knowledge production is often more personalized, because it both stems from and makes meaning around the body of the individual: that body, which comes into the encounter bearing its own history, becomes the site at which the lived experience of the past and the present meet.

The case studies considered in the following pages illustrate how changes in practice in actual preservations and reenactments reflect the movement over these broad cultural logics. While new objects (vernacular buildings, the memories and experiences of "ordinary people," mass-produced commodities, the ephemeral) were selected for preservation, reenactive practices and experiential engagements with history (immersion and first-person interpretation at history museums, the surge of embodied historical activity) grew in number. This was by no means a uniform or total development; preservations and reenactments have existed and continue to exist in various forms.[26] Yet, in the 1970s, Americans took up both practices in order to gain knowledge about and create connections with everyday people of the past. Because the past came to be a site for negotiating contemporary identities and ideologies, reenactment, as a strategy of historical thinking and meaning making, came to overtake preservation as the foremost mode of historical activity. By describing how these changes unfolded across multiple fronts through the late 1960s and the early 1970s, and by attending to the continuum of production and reception that informed historical cultural productions during this decade, I hope to put pressure on contentions that these activities represented a misunderstanding or a misconstrual of history, instead demonstrating how new engagements with the past authorized and produced a range of meanings.

Different individuals, institutions, and modes of popular historymaking both responded to and further articulated larger shifts within popular culture. By widening the lens of inquiry across many forms of historical practice and knowledge production, by examining the myriad ways that Americans were encountering history, we can see a perceptible change. This book is arranged thematically, but it is also true that some practices emerged or changed before others, so it is possible to read a chronology that underlies these larger transitions. That said, this is more a chronology of tendencies, as opposed to one of developments. Separate changes also intersected with one another in surprising ways: they were underwritten by precisely some of the large-scale assumptions that I am trying to unpack. Likewise, there are recurring actors, practitioners who appear across a number of initiatives or projects, but it would be a mistake to assume that the larger transformation in historical thought and practice was propelled by individuals. Rather, certain people perhaps sensed and acted within this shift, making them central players: Alex Haley, Richard Rabinowitz, James Deetz, Esther Hall Mumford, and others were then, and continue to be, "early adopters" of the larger-scale changes I describe.

The first chapter examines the way that commercial television represented the historical in the postwar period, showing how the medium both reflected and revealed the terms of 1970s nostalgia culture. In the forward-thinking 1950s and 1960s, the historical was almost absent from television. What shows did consider the past (for example, *You Are There*, *I Remember Mama*) used framing devices, narrators, and other intermediaries to portray the past as foundational to, but separate and distant from, the viewer. Other programming, like *The Twilight Zone*, depicted the past in a pathological manner: as a dangerous and spatially distinct milieu where one could become trapped. The 1970s saw a proliferation of historical programming (for example, *The Waltons*, *Little House on the Prairie*) that invited the viewer to identify directly with historical characters and advanced storylines that underscored commonality and closeness between the past and present. Most significantly, a new genre, the miniseries, appeared: shows like *Eleanor and Franklin* and *Roots* promoted emotional identification with past people and events.

While these programs were helping Americans rethink history, the nation was preparing for a large-scale commemoration: the two-hundredth anniversary of its founding. The second chapter traces ten years of federal planning of the Bicentennial, examining how federal interests organized the commemoration in order to accommodate the rapidly changing perception of history that accompanied the breakdown of consensus culture. What began in the mid-1960s as a plan for an international exposition celebrating the present and future of the nation had become, by the mid-1970s, a decentralized array of history-based commemoration projects undertaken by states, communities, and individuals. This rapid reversal, and the ways in which planners attempted to adapt and control the changing commemoration, demonstrates not only the shifting position of the historical at that moment, but also the continued commitment on the part of the state—an understanding, that is, of the importance of commemoration and of a shared sense of the past in the encouragement of normative patriotic identity. The different tactics with which presidential administrations sought to orchestrate the commemoration testify to the state's continued investment in the historical as a site of ideological production. Yet this effort had to be continuously realigned as a progress-based Cold War consensus fractured in the face of political, social, and economic turmoil throughout the decade.

Moving from large-scale organization to individual efforts, chapter 3 chronicles changing relationships with material evidence of the past. Building preservation, an early beneficiary of federal and state funding of history initiatives, began as an activity of the upper classes and was initially concerned with saving individual historically significant specimens and showcasing noteworthy architectural detail. By the late 1960s and early 1970s, preservation had become a widespread community activity, with new emphases on vernacular buildings and the creation of historical ambiance through preserved groups of structures of all kinds. In other words, the rationale for preservation changed from reverence to experience. Similarly, transformations in institutional collection practice also reflected a more democratic and inclusive historical inquiry. I examine a number of projects, including a National Trust initiative called "Meeting Houses 1976" and the activities of the Providence Preservation Society, the Weeksville Society in Brooklyn, and the Afro-American Bicentennial Corporation, a DC-based organization that aimed to preserve buildings associated with African American history. Together, these show the different ways in which communities began engaging with the historical built environment. They also serve as the framework for a larger investigation of "preservation" as an activity of historymaking that is a central theme of this book—What kinds of assumptions about the past and what we want from it undergird practices of collecting and saving? How do these practices then change?

The fourth chapter analyzes other "spaces" of history: the museum, the exhibition, and the living history site. Museums, perhaps the most prominent example of historical interpretation done explicitly for the public, were transformed in the early to mid-1970s. In exhibits like the Smithsonian's "1876," historical objects, previously used as evidence of the past, were instead put into the service of creating immersive environments in which audiences could experience history firsthand. Other exhibitions, like Boston's "The Revolution" and Philadelphia's Franklin Court, eschewed artifacts completely, instead using a combination of spatial immersion and new media to place viewers directly in the past. Finally, living history sites like Plimoth Plantation and Colonial Williamsburg moved from third-person to first-person interpretation as guides began engaging visitors in the personas of historical figures. The decisions made around the development of exhibitions across these spaces of history reflected a heightened cultural concern with the everyday experience of the past as well as the beginnings of a recognition of a desire to act directly within, as opposed to outside of, the historical moment. Historical knowledge production at this moment ceased to be informational and became affective. Slowly, the site of this knowledge production shifted from the artifact to the body. Put another way, reenactment overtook preservation as a primary mode of interacting with the past.

Reenactment—namely, embodied engagement with history—is the subject of the fifth chapter. A wide variety of institutions, groups, and individuals took up reenactive practices in the 1970s, generating historical knowledge and consciousness that sometimes reinforced and sometimes disturbed traditional or mainstream narratives of history. Nineteen-seventies reenactments differed from previous initiatives like the tableau vivant, the historical pageant, and the battle reenactment both because they encompassed audiences as well as reenactors, and because participants looked to build affective connections with historic individuals, wanting to understand their feelings and experiences. I examine evidence from a number of 1970s reenactments, most prominently the Bicentennial Wagon Train, in which over a thousand participants traveled in a backward reenactment of the settlement of the frontier. Even though stage agencies organized the Wagon Train to elicit patriotic feelings in participants and spectators, because reenactment makes historical meaning on the individual, not the collective, level, the historical knowledge generated by both participants and audiences was actually much more unpredictable and held the possibility of new identifications and awareness. The different stories told through official records, participant reflections, and media coverage demonstrate both the difference and the potential of embodied engagement with the past.

The final chapter returns to the politicized context of chapter 2, not from the perspective of state articulation of history and commemoration in the interest of maintaining hegemonic power, but from that of resistance and refusal from groups outside of the mainstream who made explicit connections between historical conception and concrete action. New forms of historical consciousness were articulated in politicized activity during the Bicentennial. The People's Bicentennial Commission (PBC) claimed to be the "true heirs" of the Revolution, and attacked Nixon, Ford, and the federal Bicentennial planning body, charging that they had co-opted American history. The PBC invited Americans to look for commonalities between past and present and to identify closely with the original revolutionaries. Other groups disavowed the entire celebration as a commemoration of past and present exploitation. The Black Panther Party and other members of the Bicentennial Without Colonies movement questioned the celebratory tone of commemoration, calling attention to the long history of inequality that most Bicentennial efforts ignored. Meanwhile, activists used interest and funding created by the federal celebration to work to introduce evidence and accounts of the African American experience into mainstream accounts of history. For a range of different groups with varying opinions, the historical became the terrain upon which to marshal progressive political positions; the past became a site of both inspiration and identification.

The ultimate stake of the book is this: historical consciousness—not only *what* we think of the past, but *how* we think of it and *for what purpose*—is inextricable from its cultural context. The changes that I detail in the following pages—from a kind of historical consciousness that saw the past as formative but distant to one that sought affective understanding of and close identifications with people from the past—continue to have vast import today. Historical knowledge and understanding inform how we think of ourselves and of the world around us. For this reason, looking at how this came to be becomes imperative.

CHAPTER ONE

Past as Present

History on Television from the 1950s to the 1970s

> Every day for the next two years—July 4, 1974 through July 4,
> 1976—CBS will unfold another chapter in the momentous story of
> our nation's struggle for independence. Exactly as it happened
> "200 years ago today." These "Bicentennial Minutes," 732 one-minute
> programs in all, are unique in broadcasting history. Tremendous in
> scope, authentic in every detail, the series is a special part of CBS's
> salute to the Bicentennial celebration.
>
> Notables from every walk of American life will participate,
> bringing you both great moments and little known incidents in
> America's surge toward freedom. The brave acts of heroes . . . the
> impassioned words of statesmen . . . the everyday lives of citizens
> caught in the steadily mounting tide—all are brought thrillingly
> to life in a gigantic historical mosaic that encompasses the full
> drama of our nation's birth.
>
> —Advertisement for *Bicentennial Minutes*, July 2, 1974

On the evening of July 4, 1974, CBS concluded its nightly news broadcast
with the inaugural installment of a new program entitled *Bicentennial Minutes*.[1] In this sixty-second segment, the first of more than seven hundred that
would be aired nightly through 1976, a celebrity narrator, accompanied
by a montage of illustrations, detailed an event that had happened exactly
two hundred years prior. The subject matter was diverse; some *Minutes*
described occurrences that led directly to the Revolution; other segments
addressed developments in medicine, technology, or the arts.[2] Narrators
ranged from actors like Lucille Ball, Jessica Tandy, and Leonard Nimoy
to political figures like Senators Joseph Montoya and Robert P. Griffin.
The *Bicentennial Minutes* were well received by the press and the public,
generating local and regional versions as well as parodies on programs like
All in the Family, *The Sonny and Cher Show*, and *Hee Haw*.[3] The popularity
of the *Bicentennial Minutes* demonstrated the growing position of television as a source of historical information: an association that was activated
and undergirded by the larger ways in which conceptions of the past, the

present, and the relationship between the two were changing during this period.

This chapter examines history on television: from the moment of the medium's origin during the high tide of cultural investment in progress and modernity in the 1950s and 1960s, through the 1970s, the moment at which, in the midst of social, political, and economic turmoil, this investment began to weaken as Americans stopped envisioning and anticipating the future and began looking toward the past.[4] Responding to these developments, television generated historical programming that reconciled and reconnected past and present, modeling new ways for audiences to think about history. Where once the past had been imagined and shown as unfolding logically and rationally into the present and then the future, television programming now put forth a more complex model. Historical television in the 1970s made use of the medium's generic traits (seriality, characterization, and immediacy) to call attention to repetitions, parallels, and similarities between past and present and to forge empathetic commonalities between characters and with viewers.

Throughout the 1950s and 1960s, television depicted the past as distant from and inferior to the present: important to know about, but not worth contemplating deeply. But by the 1970s, history on television was both more common and markedly different, reflecting a new sense of history that was coming to dominate popular engagement with the past across many different forms and formats. In family dramas like *Little House on the Prairie* and miniseries like *Eleanor and Franklin* and *Roots*, "realistic" portrayals of historical events and periods hinged not on an informational depiction of the past, but on an affective identification between audiences and historical figures on television. By the 1970s, television not only exemplified new cultural attitudes toward the past, but also was instrumental in extending these perceptions. While television is often said to be a major site of formation and articulation of culture in the United States, looking closely at how the medium turned to the historical in the 1970s helps to identify larger-scale transformations in American culture.[5]

I begin with the *Bicentennial Minutes* because they aptly illustrate how Americans were now thinking about and engaging with the past, and why commercial television programming is so central to understanding these changes. As they charted colonial life day by day, the *Bicentennial Minutes* performed the passage of historical time as analogous and synchronous to contemporary time, reflecting and advancing a new and closer association between the past and the present. With this, the *Minutes* also created a space for active viewer identification with, and participation in, the "making" of history. In publicity interviews, *Bicentennial Minutes* producer Lewis Freedman noted the particular relationship between time, history, and television: "It seemed to me that television is an ideal medium to handle history because like history, it goes on every day very slowly. We decided to do a minute a day to show the process of history."[6] Freedman's statement helps us to understand and underscore the association between certain properties of television (immediacy, flow between programming, continuity between distinct episodes) and this new conception of history.[7] In their adherence to a systematic calendar and their news-like format, the *Bicentennial Minutes* took advantage of television's sense of "presentness" and instantaneousness and sutured it onto a new understanding of the progression of history.[8] The past had become connected to the present, and history was something to experience empathetically rather than to observe from a distance. A parody *Bicentennial Minute* that appeared on *The Carol Burnett Show* in 1975 made this connection literal: as an announcer stood next to a framed painting of a Revolutionary War battle and described its events, a drummer in the painting (actually an elevated stage) moved, reacted, and, finally, reached out from behind the frame and hit the announcer over the head.[9] History had come out of the past, and into the present. As advertisements for the *Bicentennial Minutes* claimed, it was "brought to life."

The *Bicentennial Minutes*, in their insistence on moving through Revolutionary history in "real time," presented a novel mode of engagement with the past. They produced a slowly progressing account of events that were sometimes unrelated and seemingly random (i.e., a segment about political history would be followed by one about technological innovation) but that introduced important information that could eventually be put together to help viewers understand the larger cultural context of the American Revolution. Offered diverse strands of knowledge, viewers were placed into history as it was happening and asked to do their own historical work, explaining and connecting for themselves the events leading up to the Revolution of 1776.

Because it is not likely that any one viewer would see all of the *Minutes*, the way individual audience members assembled this information varied. The *Bicentennial Minutes* produced a history that was flexible and depended on one's own investments (e.g., while some viewers might be drawn to segments concerning scientific advance, others might change the channel at those times) and on the happenstance of watching the news on a particular evening. The segments demonstrate several qualities of historical consciousness that developed in the 1970s: a sense of the past as somehow *present* in the contemporary; more attention to the everyday life of earlier times; and a sense of history as contingent, flexible, and permeable. All of these transformations were animated and reproduced by television's expressions of both history and the passage of time.

Television programs like the *Bicentennial Minutes* and the miniseries that emerged during the same period were critical sites for cultural negotiation of these larger changes, mirroring and ultimately helping to form new relationships with the American past. The medium's affinity for the historical might have been kindled by its generic and institutional qualities, but this connection was further consolidated when American society became more interested in history and, specifically, in thinking about the past in relational and empathetic terms. In response, television developed formats and genres that explicitly attended to these interests.

The Pedagogical and the Pathological: History on Television in the 1950s and 1960s

To examine the evolution of television's representation of the past, we must begin in the earliest days of the medium. In the forward-oriented 1950s and 1960s, television fare echoed American culture at large, which was more interested in the present and the future than the past.[10] Popular culture reflected this tendency, from modernist architecture of the period to projects like Walt Disney's utopian Tomorrowland and initiatives like the space program.[11] Mirroring these broad cultural sentiments, television typically presented history using two modes: the "pedagogical": detailing well-known occurrences and persons who shaped the present; and the "pathological": staging extreme and usually traumatic encounters that stressed the inflexible nature of linear time and the inferiority of the past to the present. Both pedagogical and pathological programming relied on formal devices like framing and contemporary narrators to keep the past separate from the present. Likewise, temporal distance was often underscored through spatial metaphors, casting the past as a remote and often frightening, yet contained, place.

In a similar vein as the educational television documentaries that were popular during this period, pedagogical history television taught viewers about important events in the American past.[12] From 1953 to 1957, CBS aired *You Are There*, in which the newscaster Walter Cronkite and his correspondents simulated broadcasting from politically momentous occurrences, like the Boston Massacre, the impeachment of Andrew Johnson, or the assassination of Julius Caesar. Typically, an episode began with Cronkite describing the significance of the event and then cut to interviews between unseen correspondents and actors portraying the key figures.[13] The interview format of the program foregrounded the agency of singular actors like Thomas Jefferson or Abraham Lincoln in precipitating important events—in these narratives, historical change was not the result of combinations of political, cultural, or social factors, but propelled by individuals, usually powerful white men. *You Are There* can be described as pedagogical in two different ways: first, the program educated the viewing public about significant events spearheaded by great men in American history. Second, *You Are There* taught viewers about the value of the new medium, establishing the standing of television newscasters at a time when television news was still relatively new and had not yet reached the levels of prominence that it would gain by the 1960s. Steve Anderson has observed that *You Are There* used the feelings of immediacy and journalistic integrity associated with news broadcasts to its advantage: on the one hand, working to legitimate television news by placing CBS reporters at all important points in history and, on the other, presenting a seemingly "objective" version of history that was as authentic (i.e., documentary) and impartial as the news itself.[14]

Pedagogical television programs depended on perceptions of both distance and difference between the present and the past, underscoring this through narrators and other intermediaries. The visual contrast between Cronkite's modern CBS studio and the historic milieus in the broadcasts reinforced the gulf between past and present. *You Are There*'s reporters mediated each interaction, keeping the presented historical moments discreet from their audiences. The viewer was therefore positioned as an eyewitness to history, but not as part of it. Through this relationship of exposition and separation, *You Are There* taught Americans about their national past in a straightforward or conventional manner, inviting learning and reflection, but not active contemplation. Shows like *You Are There* and *Profiles in Courage*, another program highlighting the role of the individual actor in history, were typical of the dominant mode of historical programming in the 1950s and 1960s.[15]

Although the narrator is a hallmark of programming that purports to describe "real" events, it is noteworthy that this device was also used in television shows that related fictionalized accounts of the past, which likewise emphasized distance and difference between past and present.[16] *I Remember Mama*, on the air from 1949 to 1957, drew inspiration from the family sitcoms that dominated network television at the time. The show concerned an immigrant family living in San Francisco at the turn of the century.[17] Each episode began with an overhead shot of a photographic album, accompanied by a voiceover from Mama's grown daughter Katrin, talking about her memories of her family as a hand flipped slowly through the pages in the album. Pedagogical history television stressed and validated the medium's visual expositive properties. Television was put forth as an ideal medium for the historical because it could "show" as well as "tell." *I Remember Mama* (and by extension, television) was *like* a photograph, but even better (that is, more able to document and faithfully represent bygone times). Katrin's voiceover appeared again at strategic moments in each episode, again emphasizing distance between the present moment and the action being portrayed on television.[18] Pedagogical programs of the era, casting the past as precedent to the superior present, assumed a teleological position, adhering to the always-progressive rhetoric of modernity.

If pedagogical programs depicted the past as foundational to the present by emphasizing how long-ago events and people had impacted and defined the present, then storylines found on science fiction shows like *The Twilight Zone* and *Star Trek* made the past strange, presenting the historical as a threatening milieu. Overwhelmingly, these were the two dominant narratives available for history television during this period. The science fiction programs' characterization of history worked from many of the same assumptions as the pedagogical program, but it articulated the present's correlation to the past in a pathological, or phobic, as opposed to a pedagogical, or expository, way. Science fiction shows frequently introduced storylines involving accidental or planned bodily travel to the past. Time travel has long been a trope of science fiction, but in the 1950s and 1960s, generic conventions supported modernist notions of temporality: the narratives suggested that the stable, linear development of time is best left alone, that history *and* its interpretation are fixed and immovable, and that the present is infinitely better (and safer) than the past.

In "Walking Distance," an episode of *The Twilight Zone* that aired in 1959 during the show's first season, businessman Martin Sloane is driving through his hometown and finds that, within its boundaries, it is twenty-five years earlier.[19] Sloane is at first excited and anticipates a joyful reunion with his family. But instead, he frightens his parents, who initially do not recognize him and, finally, implore him to return to his own present. Later, Sloane sees his younger self riding a carousel and approaches the child, who is so frightened that he falls off. Once the adult Sloane leaves the town and returns to the present, he finds that he now walks with a limp—the injury that the boy Sloane sustained during the carousel scene remains as a bodily reminder of the adult Sloane's unsuccessful and highly traumatic visit to the past. By the logic of the episode, then, encounters with the past are painful and have a lasting impact. Martin Sloane's parents not only fail to identify their son (a failure that perhaps is contrary to the recognizability and innate belonging emblematic of the logic of family that dominated television and popular culture at the time), but they actively fear him.[20] Although Sloane is eventually able to leave the past—which, in pathological or phobic programming, is geographically specific in that it is always bounded by and associated with an explicit location—and return to his own time, he does not escape unscathed; his permanent injury signifies the enduring damage that preoccupation with the past might enact. As this episode indicates, in the forward-looking early 1960s, the historical past is something to be left behind. The nostalgic impulse, the desire to return to a time and place in the past, is recognized, but rejected.

In subsequent episodes of *The Twilight Zone*, characters who, like Martin Sloane, view the past as idyllic are soon proved wrong. In "A Stop at Willoughby," aired in 1960, Gart Williams, an advertising executive, is under pressure at work from his demanding boss and at home from his critical wife.[21] Several times during his daily commute, he falls asleep and dreams of a train station called "Willoughby," a peaceful town that appears to be stuck in the year 1888. With each occurrence of the dream, Williams attempts to disembark at Willoughby, but finds that he cannot. He becomes fascinated by the town, asking his regular conductor about it. He tells his wife that he would like to live there and swears that "next time," he will get off the train. After a particularly stressful day at work, Williams is finally successful in exiting the train at Willoughby, intending to make the bucolic village his refuge. As a band plays in the town center, Williams is welcomed by Willoughby's residents and invited to accompany a group of young boys going fishing. But in the next scene, it is revealed that in reality, the anxious man has thrown himself from the train and "Willoughby and Sons" is the name of the funeral home that comes to collect his body.

Instead of the tranquil and timeless village, "Willoughby" becomes a hallucination that ultimately drives the harassed protagonist of the episode to suicide and perhaps even a premonition naming the hearse that will be the material sign of his passing.[22] Preoccupation with history here signals mental instability. The past, then, and especially the nostalgic past of Willoughby, is—quite literally—death. Like in "Walking Distance," in "A Stop at Willoughby," those who long to escape into history are punished or exposed as delusional. While the episode acknowledges the hectic nature of modern life (it is not insignificant that both Sloane and Williams work in advertising, a profession long associated with the anxieties of modernity), it cautions against dealing with this pressure through nostalgic escapism.[23] Again, we see the association between the dangerous past and a specific locale, emphasizing clear, territorial distinctions between the past and the present and reproducing the Cold War doctrines of containment that also operated through metaphors that clearly distinguished between "safe" and "unsafe" spaces.[24]

In another common science fiction storyline in 1960s television, characters returned to the past and attempted to change history. *The Twilight Zone* presented several of these episodes, the first of which, "Back There," aired in 1961 and featured a man who tries unsuccessfully to stop Abraham Lincoln's assassination.[25] Physicist Paul Driscoll, the protagonist of "No Time Like the Past," broadcast two years later, is dismayed by what he calls the "bedlam" of the present times and, using a time machine, seeks to avert the bombing of Hiroshima, the ascendance of Adolf Hitler, and the sinking of the *Lusitania*.[26] In each encounter, Driscoll is marked as an interloper: he makes no attempt to disguise his status as a time traveler, he wears a 1960s-style "organization man" suit and hat, and, in conversation with, respectively, a Japanese police officer and the captain of the *Lusitania*, makes references to the events as if they have already happened. When Driscoll returns to his present, he is told by his colleague Harvey that "the past is inviolate." Driscoll accepts this, remarking finally, "I believe that it's not possible to alter the past. And it follows that because of that impossibility, there isn't anything we can do about the present, or the future."

However, like Gart Williams, Driscoll remains fixated on the past, resolving to travel to 1881 Homeville, Indiana (a town that, with its iconic bandstand and soda fountain, resembles Williams's Willoughby), and simply live there. But for Driscoll, the temptation to tamper with history is too great: while trying to prevent an upcoming schoolhouse fire, he instead inadvertently causes it. As in the case of Martin Sloane, Driscoll's interference with the past has a permanent effect, and the lesson is finally learned. In the last scene of the episode, Driscoll tells Harvey, "I'm leaving yesterday alone. To do something about the tomorrows. They're the ones that count, the tomorrows." Again, this episode reinforces a linear and deterministic conception of the progression of history. As the protagonists of these

In a 1963 episode of *The Twilight Zone*, protagonist Paul Driscoll tries to warn the crew of the *Lusitania* of imminent danger. Notice Driscoll's suit and hat, which is typical of the 1960s, helps emphasize his status as an interloper.

episodes find out, history should not and *cannot* be changed, looking forward is always preferable to looking back.

Because *The Twilight Zone*'s address is that of the narrated cautionary tale, the audience is positioned, as in *You Are There*, as witnessing, not enacting, the historical interaction. Close-up shots are used, not to form identification between character and viewer, but for dramatic emphasis (for example, when Driscoll realizes that the schoolhouse will burn), and Rod Sterling, as narrator, is shown, like Walter Cronkite, in a sterile studio environment, directly addressing the audience in the beginning and end of each episode, creating further distance from the diegetic action of the program. Not only are the protagonists of each episode taught that the past must be kept apart, but viewers themselves are kept removed (and ostensibly safe) from actions in the past.

History television programming of the 1950s and 1960s represented the past and present as at once spatially and temporally distinct. Both the pedagogical and pathological programs that characterized postwar television's engagement with the historical rested on affirmations of causality and teleology; that the past led directly and logically to the future. The strength of these assumptions can be seen in "The City on the Edge of Forever," an episode of *Star Trek* that aired in 1967. In this episode, members of the crew of the starship *Enterprise* travel to New York in the 1930s. Captain Kirk meets and falls in love with an idealistic social worker named Edith, who is fated to die in a traffic accident. Kirk's comrade Spock discovers that if Edith does not die, she will begin an antiwar movement that will delay U.S. entry into World War II long enough for Nazi Germany to develop a nuclear weapon. Although Kirk has strong feelings for Edith, he must allow her to perish so that history can run its familiar and "natural" course and the United States can discover nuclear power and establish postwar dominance.[27] The message here, as in other programs, is self-evident: looking backward (much less trying to interact with the past), except as a way to explain or consider the trajectory toward the present, is considered abnormal and even dangerous. The logic of historical programming during this time, then, was that the past was at once remote and foundational—worth remembering and reflecting upon, but necessarily kept apart from, and ultimately in service to, the present. This logic extended over different genres of programming, echoing the commitment to technology, modernization, and progress that characterized the postwar period.

Even the "fantastic" sitcoms of the period, which accepted supernatural activity like ghosts and magic as common and normative fare, warned against interacting with or within the past.[28] A *Bewitched* storyline that was repeated more than once during the program's eight-year run concerned its protagonist, modern-day witch Samantha Stephens, journeying back to seventeenth-century Salem, Massachusetts, only to be found out there as a witch (usually not as the result of her use of magic, but of a presentist slip-up, such as being in possession of a ballpoint pen) and put on trial.[29] In other episodes, figures from the distant past, like Paul Revere or a Civil War general, were inadvertently called into the present, wreaking havoc and upsetting the Stephens' idyllic suburban existence. Here again, the past and its inhabitants were shown as a threat to the domestic ideal that dominated American culture during the postwar period and which was often expressed in sitcoms like *Bewitched*.

Bewitched used the unaging figure of Samantha, a witch who, according to the premise, has existed unchanged for over three hundred years, to reiterate the superiority of the present to the past. In "Eye of the Beholder," from 1965, a seventeenth-century painting of a young woman closely resembling Samantha is found and eventually determined to be of Samantha herself. Upon this discovery, Samantha's husband Darrin, who disapproves of witchcraft, becomes upset at the idea that his wife will remain young as he ages. Over and over again, in this episode and others, this conflict arises and then resolves itself with Samantha assuring Darrin that she has chosen to remain with him, and that her present life as a suburban housewife in the 1960s is preferable to her previous supernatural lifestyle.[30] As in other television programs of the period, Samantha's choice reaffirms both the progressive path of history and of the singularity of the present moment. However, this modernist assertion of progress would change drastically by the next decade.

Feeling the Past: History Television in the 1970s

While programs like *Bewitched*, *The Lucy Show*, and *The Beverly Hillbillies* had dominated entertainment television during the 1960s, by the 1973–74 television season, a sizeable portion of network prime time was occupied by shows set in the American past, a development that responded to as well as helped to constitute the terms of nostalgia culture at large. In 1976 and 1977 the top programs were *Happy Days* and *Laverne and Shirley*, both set in the 1950s. Equally popular were *Little House on the Prairie* and *The Waltons*, shows about families living, respectively, in the 1870s and the Great Depression.[31] In contrast to the shows of the 1960s, these programs portrayed the past as normal and everyday, a source of interest, not fear.

Television's absorption of widespread attention to history was so prevalent in the 1970s that even programs that were set in then-current times introduced storylines that involved the past. In a two-part episode of *The Brady Bunch* that aired in 1971, the Brady family, on a vacation trip to the Grand Canyon, stops to tour an abandoned ghost town. There, the Bradys meet a crazed prospector who, fearing that they are after his gold, locks the family in the town jail, from which they must stage a dramatic escape.[32] The episode places what would have been read as a traumatic supernatural event on 1960s television into the banal context of a suburban family's vacation. The ghost town becomes an immersive and entertaining locale in which the Brady family is able to live out their own historical adventure. In their escapade with the deranged prospector, the Bradys are presented with a genuine historical experience. Like the episodes of *The Twilight Zone*, a connection between past and place is established, but this time without the associated emotional disturbance. The repetitive conventions of the sitcom genre also ensure viewers that, even at the initial, potentially dangerous stages, the family will be intact and unscarred by the commencement of the next episode.[33] This safeguard allows the encounter with American history to be read from the start as exciting, entertaining, and even comedic. The Bradys' understanding of the Old West becomes lived rather than imagined: through their interactions with the figure of the miner, who acts and reacts presumably as an 1840s prospector would (and seems to be of indeterminate origin: his presence in the town is never fully explained), the family can directly commune with history. This episode teaches the Bradys, and, by extension, their audience, about life in frontier times. The availability of the historical for interaction in the present is made literal, thus illustrating the new characteristics that marked historical consciousness and engagement by the 1970s.

In contrast to the 1950s and 1960s shows, television programs in the 1970s emphasized permeability between the past and the present, introducing scenarios that brought the two into contact in new and compelling ways. *Meeting of Minds*, a public television program created in 1976 by Steve Allen, the first host of the *Tonight* show, demonstrated this new relationship in a spectacular fashion, staging a roundtable discussion among historical figures.[34] The first episode introduced a panel of actors playing Theodore Roosevelt, Cleopatra, Thomas Aquinas, and Thomas Paine. Subsequent episodes would pair Charles Darwin with Attila the Hun, or Karl Marx and Ulysses S. Grant. In comparison to *You Are There*, which had presented a predictable and closed narrative of occurrences based on already-established historical interpretation, a strikingly different sense of history underwrote *Meeting of Minds*. Historical characters could travel into the present without consequence, knew about and debated current events (for example, Grant and Marx discussed communism in China), and were familiar with individuals who followed them chronologically or who had lived in different parts of the world.[35] Historical figures interacted across time and space, using their own experiences and expertise to provide commentary on the present— sometimes, as in the case of Marx, on their own legacies. Most fascinatingly, panelists were aware of the medium of television itself—they spoke directly to the television audience and occasionally referred to being able to converse with "millions." In *Meeting of Minds*, history became an active agent in the contemporary, and historical events were perceived as parallel and relevant rather than foundational to the present. *Meeting of Minds* demonstrated and exaggerated television's capacity for history: putting it forward as the ideal medium for the depiction of the new centrality of the historical.

As this suggests, television benefitted from and even exploited American culture's fascination with the past, with producers emphasizing the medium's representational ability and introducing programming that purported historical authenticity in its costumes, sets, and characterizations. NBC's *Little House on the Prairie*, one of the most popular programs of the decade, was based on a series of autobiographical children's books by Laura Ingalls Wilder that told the story of her pioneer childhood.[36] In media interviews, producers asserted the show's historical accuracy in two ways: by detailing their extensive research in re-creating the look and feel of Minnesota in the 1870s, and by reinforcing the real, historical status of Wilder and her family.[37] Although *Little House* was a fictional drama, its basis in tangible historical events gave it currency as a faithful representation of the past. The "reality" of the characters and the sets, and the way that producers of the show insisted on their accuracy, supported television's growing reputation as a conduit to the past.

Little House bolstered its assertions of historical authenticity by presenting storylines that invited in viewers' close identification to its characters. The show was influenced by a concurrent development in network television: programs that addressed current political and social issues and emphasized characterization to introduce relatable protagonists. The most prevalent of these were Norman Lear's *All In the Family* and its multiple spin-offs, including *Good Times*, *Maude*, and *The Jeffersons*, and James L. Brooks's and Allan Burns's *The Mary Tyler Moore Show*. Critics described Lear's shows as "relevance" programming because of the way that plotlines took on some of the realities of life in the 1970s. Audiences and critics considered these shows to be "realistic" not only because they addressed contemporary values, but also because they used these issues to promote identification and emotional affinity between audiences and fictional but realistic plotlines and characters.[38]

If relevance programming sought to advance television's position by emphasizing the medium's ability to attend to and represent current social issues, shows like *Little House* took the additional step of placing these issues within a historical milieu—putting forth television as a source of historical knowledge. *Little House*'s authenticity was two-pronged: it was based on historical events and people but made relatable to its contemporary audiences. Unlike the programs of the 1960s, there was no voice over or CBS news team mediating viewers' encounters with the past; instead audiences were invited into the world of *Little House* and asked to empathize with characters and events *as they happened*, as opposed to treating them as history long past. While the 1960s shows underscored distance, *Little House* foregrounded identification, which, along with the historical accuracy of the characters and props, worked to cement the show's claim to truthful history. In *Little House*'s emotional realism, the program's historicity acted as a substrate upon which viewers could make identifications between featured storylines and similar situations in their own daily lives.[39] As one critic observed, the show "dishes up today's hardships as 1870s hardships."[40]

In *Little House*'s reorientation of frontier life, emotional concerns took precedence over material ones. Wilder's *Little House* books had been written in the 1930s for a juvenile audience and reflected the scarcity of resources faced by many Americans at that time. The books played down characters' personalities and internal thoughts in favor of describing life on the frontier—entire chapters were devoted to detailed inventories of farming, cooking, and sewing techniques employed by the Ingalls family.[41] As a television program, *Little House on the Prairie* introduced storylines and characters that dealt less with material than social issues, focusing, for example, on racial and gender inequality, class difference, and political concerns. Producer and star Michael Landon insisted that the emotional complexity made the show realistic, noting, "Our show is hardly a kid's show. We're much more adult."[42] In fact, both the book series and television program dispelled idealized images of frontier life: Wilder's books complicated notions of the American West as a land of plenty, rich in material resources, while the televised version presented many social problems that 1970s audiences viewed as modern or contemporary. Indeed, the televised *Little House*'s simultaneous attestations to social relevance and historical accuracy extended a portrayal of the past that was markedly different from older depictions of the frontier. On one hand, viewers saw a chronicle of frontier life that seemed familiar, yet that was packaged as a faithful account of history. On the other, *Little House* storylines addressed current problems. By maintaining this dialectic, the program asserted history's ability to serve as a site for contemplation and identification in the present.

By incorporating contemporary topics into the frontier past, *Little House on the Prairie* created a way for viewers to work through present-day issues by viewing them as a part of a longer historical trajectory. For example, in a 1976 episode of *Little House* entitled "Soldier's Return," a Civil War veteran named Granville Whipple comes back to the Ingalls' Walnut Grove, Minnesota, community after a prolonged absence. Although the character seems sympathetic and friendly, it quickly becomes apparent that he is haunted by memories of the war. Whipple cannot sleep and is plagued by flashbacks to a combat incident in which he was lost in a forest during battle and abandoned his best friend to die. In attempting to cope with his complicated emotions, Whipple has become dependent upon morphine.[43] Even though the Ingalls family and other town residents are accepting and supportive, Whipple is unable to overcome his addiction and eventually robs the town pharmacy and commits suicide by overdose. The episode is ostensibly about Civil War veterans; however, the reference to the growing problems of alienation and addiction among returning Vietnam veterans is unmistakable.[44] In the flashback scenes, the soldier Whipple is shown amid dense, disorienting vegetation, a type of landscape more associated with the jungles of Vietnam than the open battlefields of the Civil War. His posttraumatic stress disorder is a hallmark of the Vietnam experience, as is the fact that he chooses to deal with it through narcotics. Particularly grim is what seems to be the ultimate message of the episode: that the (Vietnam) veteran cannot be reintegrated into society. While Martin Sloane's traumatic encounter in *The Twilight Zone* seemed to have little bearing on current events, here Granville Whipple's situation certainly does. His painful ordeal becomes a way to complicate the history of the Civil War as well as to comment upon the ongoing effects of the Vietnam conflict, addressing viewers who might be dealing with similar problems in their own contemporary lives.

At the same time, however, *Little House*'s storylines also contained an ideological charge. Michael Landon, who starred on *Little House* as patriarch Charles Ingalls, was a veteran of *Bonanza* and other television programs, and was very aware of television's growing influence on society. In addition to his role in front of the camera, Landon served as executive producer and, more often than not, writer and director, effectively singlehandedly controlling the show.[45] Landon was also an early supporter of the growing New Right—in 1980, he would campaign for Ronald Reagan—and many of *Little House*'s "relevance" storylines promoted the movement's traditionalist, antigovernment messages.[46] In this respect, they built upon the original book series: Laura Ingalls Wilder had been opposed to the interventionism of New Deal legislation, and in her writing had highlighted her family's self-sufficiency in the face of hardship. In the television program, as in the books, the Ingalls are a self-reliant family and one that embodies traditional values.[47] Landon's Charles Ingalls is the unquestioned leader of the family, although his wife Caroline is the moral and spiritual center.[48] In several instances over *Little House*'s long run, Ingalls, a sustenance farmer, and other residents of Walnut Grove are shown to be in conflict with the U.S. government. In an episode from the fourth season, entitled "Times of Change," Charles Ingalls travels to Chicago for a meeting of the Grange—the populist agricultural movement—and is disappointed to find that the corrupt movement leaders are in league with railroad interests, the enemy of the independent farmer.[49] The message of the episode is clear in its echo of the values of the New Right: morality and the merit of hardworking individualism, and suspicion toward both the government and labor organizations such as the Grange. Even Roger MacBride, Laura Ingalls Wilder's adopted grandson and the executor of her estate, who often criticized Landon over the show's fictionalized portrayal of the Ingalls family, acknowledged and praised the show's mistrust of the government, calling his grandmother "the first libertarian."[50] While history has long been politicized, and memories of the past have been used to justify or critique present actions and circumstances, *Little House* made its appeal in personalized, affective terms, putting forth Landon's political views by introducing storylines that encouraged viewers to learn about the past by identifying with it, to make historical comparisons by weighing emotional reactions.

History showed up on television in many different ways in the 1970s, but all of the new programming demonstrated the medium's ability to adapt and animate the new historical consciousness, which increasingly necessitated visual representation and emotive identification. Both critics and audiences noticed and frequently commented upon television's new capacity to present relatable historicized storylines. This notice was extended to shows more rooted in fiction than *Little House on the Prairie. The Waltons*, which aired from 1971 through 1981, was another popular program concerning family life in the past, this time, during the Great Depression and World War II.[51] Like *Little House*, storylines on *The Waltons* centered upon family togetherness, but also addressed issues of poverty, class difference, racism, and misogyny. Although we now think of the show as saccharine, contemporary critical reception to *The Waltons* did not paint it as naïve or escapist. Instead, contemporary reviews tended to emphasize that the emotions and relationships on the show were convincing and genuine.[52] Historically based television put forth modes of engagement that, on the one hand, advanced television as a prominent site of historical cultural production and, on the other, modeled new possibilities for identification with the past. In this way, television, as it often does, revealed and helped to perpetrate larger shifts in American historical consciousness.

Introducing the Miniseries

In the wake of the enormous success of *Little House on the Prairie* and other historical shows, television introduced a new genre that both engaged and expressed American interest in history.[53] In 1974, ABC announced the introduction of "Novels for Television," which, according to ABC executive Martin Starger, showed the network's commitment "to pioneering a new dramatic form for television," one that would exclusively deal with historical narratives.[54] The miniseries foregrounded particular characteristics of the novel: narrative immersion, characterization, and change over time. These traits were becoming increasingly present in commercial television, but were intensified in this new format. In the press, television executives discussed an intrinsic link between the two mediums, "The novel . . . is a natural source of material for television, which could make for superior programming."[55] The novel was also considered to be a higher cultural form, and thus an opportunity for television, which was still dealing with its "vast wasteland" problem, to profess a gravitas that rested on its new attention to character development and its new ability to present realistic historical narratives.

Miniseries like *Sandburg's Lincoln* and *Eleanor and Franklin* recast political events as personal dramas, connecting the historical with individual transformation and accentuating the ways in which noteworthy figures negotiated their private and public lives.[56] The miniseries was a new format but borrowed many of its generic conventions from the soap opera, one of the oldest and most established genres on television. Like the soap opera, the miniseries employed melodrama in its focus on interpersonal and familial relationships. The miniseries also utilized the soap opera's serial form, that is, relationships and events unfolded and developed over several episodes.[57] However, while the soap opera was then and continues to be denigrated as low culture, the miniseries, because of its historic content, was seen as "upscale" television. But like soap operas, miniseries concentrated on the private experiences and emotions of famous historical persons, the sentiments that might have influenced their historic actions, and how in turn they were emotionally defined by historical events. While the soap opera's appeal to affect signaled fantasy and escapism, in the miniseries, affect added to historical authenticity, advancing a new definition of "real" as *emotionally* real, a project already begun by programs like *Little House on the Prairie*.[58]

While *Little House* used the characteristics of relevance programming to express historical authenticity, the miniseries employed seriality to link character development with historical change over time, underscoring that personal growth in the characters could be connected to larger historical events. *Eleanor and Franklin* traced the life of Eleanor Roosevelt from an awkward girl to a leader in her own right through an investigation of her marriage to Franklin. The plot emphasized how the discovery of Franklin's infidelities made Eleanor a more independent person, which, in turn, had consequences for her public presentation and actions. By concentrating on Eleanor's inner life, the show made the historical figure accessible to audiences who might not have been able to place themselves within her impressive career but could empathize with her reactions to significant events and the feelings that underpinned the choices that she made. *Eleanor and Franklin* centered upon the Roosevelts' private lives but showed its impact on their public lives and, ultimately, their legacies. At the same time, it introduced a new interpretation of the couple, one that placed their marriage at the center of their actions within large-scale historical events.

In its exploration of the public and the private, the miniseries highlighted the development of personal identity. In programs that traced a familial line like *Rich Man, Poor Man* and, later, *Roots*, participation in events like wars and migrations defined and impacted the succession of protagonists.[59] This emphasized the importance of the historical on the formation of individual identity, as opposed to the effects of character or identity on historical change. In 1960s shows like *Profiles in Courage* and *You Are There*, exceptional people had a profound effect on historical events, yet their private or inner lives were rarely probed. By the 1970s, even "great men" like Abraham Lincoln were portrayed in ways that foregrounded the interplay between public and private lives.[60] Like other historical fare, the miniseries proved to be popular with audiences who, in the context of the Bicentennial and nostalgia culture at large, enjoyed new perspectives on historical figures.[61]

The new miniseries also linked seriality to larger ideas of history. Like the soap opera, in the miniseries, the passage of time itself became an important focus of the show; the serial nature of the miniseries helped to reinscribe a sense of temporal progression as history. As one reviewer stated of the promise of the miniseries, "they realize that there exists in the country a great hunger for the continuity of narrative."[62] On one hand, the miniseries was

In the 1976 miniseries *Eleanor and Franklin*, the audience is given firsthand glimpses into private moments between the Roosevelts, like Franklin's marriage proposal to Eleanor.

organized around narratives of change over time, but on the other, these stories often showed succeeding generations of family members grappling with the same personality traits, scenarios, and situations. The miniseries demonstrated historical development through the individual and the family unit. In its appeal to the personal, television's rearticulation of historical identification rested on a new emphasis on individual agency in understanding and formulating interpretations of the past.

The *Roots* Phenomenon

No miniseries made a more meaningful cultural impact than *Roots*, the adaptation of journalist and author Alex Haley's book about the lives of his ancestors in Africa and in the antebellum South. *Roots*, broadcast over eight consecutive nights in January of 1977, was an immediate sensation, setting ratings records and generating enthusiastic responses from the media and the public.[63] By the time that *Roots* aired, television was well established as a premier source for historical fare. *Roots* drew upon this already-present connection and expanded it by underscoring the importance of history and family to personal identity in the present and by introducing a model of historical activity for audiences who were eager to look to their own familial pasts. The adaptation of Haley's novel took the miniseries' capacity to convey a new form of history to its fullest potential, putting forth an account of life under slavery that, in its depiction of the unfolding of generations and its appeal to the emotional, was different and more compelling than any popular history that came before it.

Part of *Roots'* appeal was that Haley's book both represented a new perception of the past and argued that this perception was critical to identity and consciousness in the present. *Roots* was the culmination of twelve years of research. Using "African" terms that had been handed down through his family as a beginning point, Haley worked with historians and linguists to identify the likely origin of his ancestors, searching archives in the United States and in England to find evidence of the slave ship that had transported his forebear to America. Haley's research culminated with a trip to the Gambian village of that ancestor, Kunta Kinte, and a moving reunion with his African "family."[64] Haley's emotional attachment to his research material extended to an empathetic affinity with his ancestor—again and again, Haley avowed a profound affective connection to Kinte, striving to discover how he might have felt during his captivity. Haley famously crossed the Atlantic in the dark cargo hold of an ocean liner in an attempt to replicate the emotional conditions of a slave ship, and he often spoke of Kinte's spirit dictating his writing of *Roots*.[65] In his explanations of the research and writing process, and in the book itself, Haley conflated personal with familial identity. In this construction, the past and the present worked in tandem, creating identifications across time and informing identity and actions in the present. Haley took as his central principle that people could not understand themselves until they understood their familial history. *Roots* was a book about the process of discovery as much as it was about the history that it recounted.

But *Roots* must also be read within the cultural context of the African American freedom struggle during this period. Although Haley wrote for magazines like *Playboy* and *Reader's Digest*, he was also conscious of and in conversation with the many strands of African American cultural nationalism that were flowering during the 1960s and 1970s. Political and cultural leaders like Stokely Carmichael, Amiri Baraka, and Malcolm X (who had collaborated with Haley on his autobiography in 1965) spoke of the unique historical experience of African Americans and the association between social movements in the United States and the struggles for independence from colonialism abroad, emphasizing self-determination, self-empowerment, and identity formation. *Roots* was one of many cultural productions that affirmed the connections between history and collective identity and expressed a set of ideas that, by the 1970s, were firmly ensconced within African American popular consciousness.[66] In *Reader's Digest* in 1974, Haley wrote that his book "not only tells the story of a family, my own, but also symbolizes the history of millions of American blacks of African descent. I intend my book to be a buoy of black self-esteem—and a reminder of the universal truth that we are all descendants of the same creator."[67] Two years later, in an interview with *The Black Scholar*, Haley put this sentiment into more explicit terms: "Every single one of us ancestrally goes back to some one of those villages, someone captured in some way put on some one of those slave ships brought across the same ocean, into some succession of plantations, to the Civil War, Reconstruction and from that day to this day, struggling for freedom. That is my story and that is your story and every black person's story."[68] In interviews and in the book itself, Haley discussed this research in affective, personalized terms, connecting knowledge of the past to political consciousness.

Roots presented a new and different perspective on the history of African Americans. The long civil rights movement and new scholarly and popular interest in documenting the lives of enslaved people provided a context for new academic books like Herbert Gutman's *The Black Family in Slavery and Freedom* and Eugene Genovese's *Roll, Jordan, Roll*, which used the slave narratives collected though the Works Progress Administration in the 1930s to reconstruct day-to-day life in bondage. Haley's book took as an imperative the same urgency of discovery but highlighted the personal and individual as opposed to the social and collective, emphasizing the emotional impact of slavery. Haley wrote in novelistic form, introducing historical information through character and plot development, yet also purporting to tell an accurate and truthful history. In response to scholars and journalists who questioned the veracity of his research and even the originality of his writing, Haley eventually coined the term "faction" to differentiate this new form, but it is significant that, despite ongoing criticism, the public continued to see *Roots* as an accurate and rigorous history.[69] This was, in large part, a result of the expanding scope of the historical to encompass the importance of emotion and personal transformation, aspects that could be traced through research but were best shown in narrative form. Both in its background and its investments, *Roots* exemplified and constructed emerging attitudes about historical knowledge and understanding that flowed across scholarly and popular engagements with history. Haley's approach as well as the enormous response to his work foregrounded the new stakes of the historical: the past's ability to effect change in the present though emotional appeal.[70]

Haley's innovative research methods had garnered notice long before either the novel or the miniseries entered the public sphere. Even before Haley finished his manuscript, Roots was a popular property—at multiple points during his decade-long process, Haley presold rights to different versions (serial, paperback) in order to subsidize his research.[71] As his project grew more lengthy and unwieldy, Haley found new sources of funding, one of which was a series of lecture tours in which he discussed the process of the discovery of his familial lines. These lecture tours were so exhaustive that by 1972 and 1973, executives at Reader's Digest, who had offered Haley an advance for the rights to publish excerpts from the book, worried that Haley would never finish the project.[72] However, Haley's time on the speaking circuit and the publicity his story brought paid off in May of 1974, when Reader's Digest finally published a serialized version of the "African" chapters of Roots, prefaced by an introduction by Haley. Thus, many readers were already drawn to, and familiar with, Haley and his story.

Haley's personal popularity caught the attention of network executives who were looking for properties well suited to television adaptation. As early as December of 1974, only a few months after the publication of the Reader's Digest chapters and just as Novels for Television was being announced, ABC and David Wolper, a producer who had previously worked on Sandburg's Lincoln and many television documentaries, began publicly discussing the possibility of a television program based on Roots.[73] The television adaptation of Roots began before the book was finished, and it can be said that the story of Roots is almost without medium: that its written serialized form influenced its televisual form and vice versa.[74] The final chapters of the book and the miniseries script were written almost concurrently, with Haley passing rough drafts and galley prints to the screenwriters.[75] This close back and forth between Haley and scriptwriters ensured that Roots was not only a novelistic miniseries but also perhaps a uniquely televisual novel, as at least parts of it were written with this adaptation in mind.

From the beginning, producers framed Roots as a new kind of history. In interviews, Wolper declared that the television miniseries was superior to the television documentary, which, he explained, was "the creative interpretation of reality, not reality."[76] The miniseries, on the other hand, was "real," especially *Roots*, which was the result of extensive archival research, and, like *Little House on the Prairie* and *Eleanor and Franklin* before it, documented the lives and experiences of real historical figures. At one point during production, Wolper proposed a disclaimer to *Roots* that would read: "What you are about to see is a recreation of a segment of the past. It is as authentic as years of research can make it. It is harsh; as harsh as the world it depicts. It has not been sensationalized nor has it been sterilized."[77] While this preamble was ultimately not used, it illustrates the terms of television's privileged stake in history: authenticity supported by research, accuracy, and, most of all, emotional realism.

To reinforce the status of *Roots* as a new and important historical document, ABC licensed video distribution rights to a company that specialized in educational programming and worked with Miami Dade Community College to create a course around the program.[78] Two years later, for *Roots: The Next Generation*, the National Council of Churches sent out 100,000 copies of a six-page Interfaith Discussion Guide, and Prime Time School Television released a sixteen-page color teacher's guide. In publicity, ABC executives also emphasized that press kits were mailed to the press and to local affiliates, as well as to librarians and schools.[79] The marketing of *Roots* as an academic resource is noteworthy because it shows that television had begun to expand its assertion of effective and "real" representation of the past and, moreover, advanced the idea that television was the *best expression* of the historical, one that was on par with scholarly treatments and texts.

In interviews, both Haley and Wolper discussed the benefits of television history, and many audience members shared their positive view.[80] Numerous letters written to ABC and Wolper by viewers were emphatic about the effectiveness of this "new history." For example, a viewer wrote from California: "*Roots*, in my opinion, must be somehow preserved, not only as a monument to art, but as a monument to history as well. It is evident now, that history, when combined with art, drama, color, and acting talent, can be realigned by the use of television."[81] A student from Bergenfield, New Jersey, put it more bluntly: "Learning history from television is better than learning about it in school. Are there going to be more shows like *Roots?* I hope so!"[82] As these comments suggest, audience members considered television history to be a truthful representation of the past and, furthermore, a superior account, one that itself was a historical record that "must somehow be preserved."

In the era before cable television and the home video recorder, large segments of the population regularly watched the same television programming, and, for the eight nights that *Roots* aired, it seemed as if everyone in America was watching it. *Roots* was what has been called by Daniel Dayan and Elihu Katz a "media event," a program that interrupted the schedule and flow of broadcast television, and one that viewers watched in an almost ceremonial fashion.[83] Newspapers reported on riveted audiences; on empty stores, bars, and restaurants every evening; and of impassioned water cooler conversations each morning.[84] Several schoolyard fights broke out over *Roots*. The *Cincinnati Post* reported on one man who had put a baby up for adoption twenty years earlier driving from Detroit to a halfway house in Cincinnati and holding workers hostage, hoping to gain information about his son. When interviewed later, the man said that he had been inspired by *Roots* and had hoped to reunite with his son and together take a trip to Rhodesia.[85] Even in its extremity, this incident demonstrates how *Roots*' account of history moved viewers to reconsider present situations and to take action. The enthusiastic reactions to the miniseries and their simultaneity pointed to television's other claim to the historical: not only was the miniseries an important expression of the past, but its airing itself was a historical event, a transformation in popular ideas about the power of television and American ideas about race.[86]

Several hundred viewers immediately wrote to Wolper and ABC, and from these letters we can begin to understand more of how 1970s audiences made sense of *Roots*. Letter writers linked the emotional identifications generated by the miniseries to contemporary problems, particularly racial conflict.[87] Some writers accused Wolper and Haley of inciting racial hatred, while others used *Roots* to discuss their own beliefs about current issues in the continuous push for civil rights and equality. A letter signed "the Concerned Public" referred to "more bad feelings between the blacks and whites." The correspondent enclosed a clipping about a fight at a high school in Hot Springs, Arkansas, that was apparently instigated by remarks about *Roots*.[88] A different anonymous commentator, this one from Columbus, Indiana, wrote, "It was the same old story looking for pity and also sympathy for something three or four hundred years ago. And they are still looking for someone to cry over it. What they are looking for is more food stamps, welfare and handouts."[89] Another writer emphasized television's social impact: "What a crime for the network to stir up so very much hatred of blacks against whites—to completely undo the good that has taken 100 years to come about. How can you ever undo the harm that this has caused?"[90] These letters took for granted that television was an important source of history and extended that position to another longtime worry, that of television's undue influence on society. Television's ability to make emotional connections between racist injustices of the past and those of the present was seen as threatening by these viewers, pointing to some of the potential of the new historical consciousness. For individuals who were invested in maintaining white supremacy, the power of *Roots* to bring the past into the present by relating the experience of slavery to the current situation was alarming. Audiences understood *Roots* as an important historical intervention, but also linked its narrative and its circulation as a media text to contemporary contexts.

In addition to the program's connection of past to present, many viewers commented upon its ability to depict "realistic" history. Significantly, audience letters defined "realistic" as emotional, further conveying the elision that had begun earlier with programs like *Little House on the Prairie*, and which was coming to characterize the majority of cultural engagement with the past. *Roots'* impact as "truthful" history rested on its ability to portray feelings in its characters on one hand, and elicit them from audiences on the other. A woman from Eldridge, Iowa, wrote: "I'm a student of history myself and yet none of the books I've read managed to bring home the reality of the 'black experience' as well as *Roots*. I cried every night. It was simply incredible."[91] A homemaker from Omaha, Nebraska, shared a similar sentiment: "It almost made us ashamed to think anything so cruel could have taken place in our country and yet it brought back true history to us."[92] Other correspondents sent moving letters, several pages long, describing in detail their reactions to the miniseries. An African American woman living in Los Angeles wrote, "Watching *Roots* is such a frightening experience that I have decided to let the past remain the past—to let the 'dead bury the dead,' so to speak." Yet she also recounted bigoted white coworkers stopping to speak to her about the impact the program had on them.[93] All of these letters spoke of emotional reactions: pride, shame, sadness, fright. At least in part, it was television's ability to engender these feelings that made *Roots* so powerful.

Some of *Roots'* emotional impact came from its ability to place viewers directly into the narrative. A viewer from Jamaica, New York, wrote to Wolper upon the 1979 re-airing of the miniseries, "I have never cried over a picture before, like I did when I saw the ending of *Roots*. After all those years this man finally reunited with his true family. I felt like I was right there in that scene when it happened."[94] These senses of immersion and identification extended to the actors who played Haley's ancestors.[95] Reflecting upon a scene in which Kunta Kinte is whipped, LeVar Burton, who played the younger Kinte, recalled that during filming, "I went somewhere else, that's how I dealt with it. All of my ancestors came forward and . . . held me up. It was brutal recreating that whipping sequence. LeVar left and someone else came in, that's how I survived it."[96] Burton's memory parallels Haley's own experience in writing the book but also models the way that many viewers were thinking about and experiencing *Roots* in particular, and history in general. *Roots* was—and, in some ways, remains—television's most successful response to, and adaptation of, new relationships with the American past.

Everybody's Roots

One of the more remarkable effects of the *Roots* phenomenon was that it precipitated a surge in genealogical research. Stories of Haley's research underscored the importance of "finding oneself" and called attention to the availability of materials in repositories such as the National Archives.[97] Thousands of people, both as a result of the program and as part of what Matthew Frye Jacobson has identified as a larger revival in ethic identification during this period, sought to discover their own roots by researching their own families.[98] After the airing of *Roots*, the National Archives reported record numbers of visitors searching for traces of their forbears, while local genealogical and historical societies likewise saw a surge in patronage.[99]

Part of the reason for *Roots*' influence on popular historical practice is that both the book and the miniseries suggested that the individual was the agent of historymaking and discovery, ideas that had been highlighted more generally in the way that television's engagement with the past emphasized personalized meaning making on the part of both historical figures and television audiences. This, in turn, reflected a historical consciousness that rested upon an understanding of the historical past as directly relevant to the present and, further, a feeling that history itself was malleable, as opposed to static, which was the way it had been perceived in earlier decades. The genealogy impetus worked in two directions: the past could influence the present, but the present could also act upon the past. Genealogical research could discover new histories and thereby change assumptions. The genealogy boom must be read in the context of two related developments: the new sense of history, which led to new types of identifications with the past, and, as we shall see, an expansion of what was recognized as historical evidence. New artifacts, documents, and narratives came to be seen as making up the archive that constitutes American history. The practice of genealogy was energized by *Roots*, but it was also a sign that added investment in knowing history was also an investment in rewriting history.

The prevalence of historical programming on television at this time, as well as the way that the form would evolve, point to the centrality of history in the 1970s. While television has long been considered an index of American culture, it is a particularly apt site for the consideration of the transformation of popular historical consciousness, not only because many changes emerged in televisual terms but also because television itself was a central part of these shifts. The popularity of historical television programming in the 1970s and the miniseries in particular attest to this close relationship. New understandings of the relationship of the past to the present alongside new cultural interest in the historical—particularly the personalized, identificatory historical—led to a large-scale reevaluation of the national past in the context of the 1976 Bicentennial celebration. It is this reevaluation that is the subject of the next chapter.

CHAPTER TWO

The Commemoration Revolution

Planning the Federal Bicentennial

> The American Revolution is unfinished business with important
> roles still open for each of us to play.
>
> —RICHARD M. NIXON, 1971

On July 4, 1971, in a televised appearance from the National Archives in Washington, DC, President Richard Nixon declared the inauguration of the "Bicentennial Era." In his speech, Nixon invoked the importance of America's past to its present, emphasizing a link between the two.[1] It is no coincidence that Nixon chose to make his proclamation from the U.S. repository for the official records of its own existence. Archives, through collecting and exhibiting evidence, visibly articulate and celebrate the stability and resources needed to preserve and safeguard documents and artifacts. Like official commemorations, national archives validate the present state by evoking its past. In the United States, the Declaration of Independence and the Constitution—the artifacts that are the cornerstones of the National Archives—are evidence from the American past *and* are simultaneously "living documents." The mandates of their authors (who are called "founders," underscoring the connection between these written documents and the continued existence of the nation-state) are often interpreted literally. Our understandings of "democracy," "freedom," and "liberty" continue to be undergirded by the conditions of their original establishment. As an inscription on one of the statues flanking the National Archives building makes explicit, "what is past is prologue."[2] And so, Nixon's presence in close proximity to these documents was meant to illustrate the terms of the commemoration he was announcing: the visible progression from the past to the present.

National commemorations like the Bicentennial traditionally observe events that are best demonstrated and narrated by archival materials held by the state (like legal documents) or material representations of state actions like wars or colonization (for example, monuments).[3] Historians have shown how commemorations are used by democratic nation-states (those, like the United States, that rest on representational and participatory citizenship) as a periodic form of spectacular legitimization. Through partaking, subjects are inspired by a communal sense of pride and patriotism.[4] When a commemoration expresses a history informed by an accord about a linear progression from past to present, it typically focuses on the present and the future. History is used as a motif but is not itself under question—what is actually being underscored in the celebration is the current state's embodiment of mythic past ideals. And so, Nixon and other agents of hegemonic power saw the Bicentennial as an opportunity to consolidate citizen support for an increasingly fractured United States by evoking patriotic feelings for the nation's monumental history, which the Bicentennial would then connect to the contemporary. Nixon's 1971 proclamation reflected foundational ideas about the triangulated relationship between archives, commemoration, and power, but at a moment when this relationship was in the process of transforming.

Over the decade preceding the commemoration, federal government interests attempted to plan and manage the 1976 Bicentennial in ways that sought to reconcile the imperatives of the past with the initiatives of the present. But by the late 1960s, the senses of stability and endurance that characterized America in the years following World War II were faltering. Between the Vietnam conflict abroad and ongoing domestic upheavals, the United States was undergoing a particularly turbulent period. By the time of the Bicentennial Era, the type of forward progress that commemorations usually honor was no longer assured, as Americans neither believed in a present that emerged logically and systematically from the past, nor looked forward to a future that could guarantee the same. If commemorations, by their very association with the passage of time through their status as "anniversaries," represent an ordered and uncomplicated celebration of the past realized in the present, the Bicentennial came at a moment at which this could not be the case.

Observing and reacting to hiccups and failures in Bicentennial planning became a way for Americans to articulate political, economic, and social frustrations. Continuing debate about the status and the meaning of the celebration opened up spaces of reflection that shifted the concrete political issues surrounding the Bicentennial into a symbolic realm. In the ways in which they understood (or didn't understand) the purpose of the commemoration, how they discussed (or didn't discuss) its planning, and in the kinds of Bicentennial projects they organized, the American people addressed fundamental questions of nation, belonging, and governance, expressing changing ideas about national identity, commemoration, and the links between the two. The Bicentennial remained, on one hand, a way for the federal government to encourage normative patriotic behavior in citizens. But it also became a means for Americans to voice their own discontent with the way that the current state failed to live up to its legacy and, ultimately, to make their own meaning from the history of the United States. Through the decade-long history of its planning, the Bicentennial provided a central site at which to consider the connections between nation and commemoration and between past and present.

Celebrating the Great Society

Government interests began contemplating the upcoming Bicentennial as early as 1963, when John O. Marsh, a Democratic representative from Virginia, made a speech before Congress. Marsh noted, "The purpose of a Bicentennial Commission is to observe the events of 1776 as not primarily a historical commemoration but rather a reexamination of the issues and idea forces which produced the American Revolution."[5] Marsh characterized the Bicentennial as an opportunity for a "renaissance of the concepts and ideas of the American Revolution and the application of the same to the problems of a changing world," most notably communism and its "lamentable" cooptation of the "ideas and ideals of our revolutionary past." Downplaying the actual history of the Revolution, Marsh instead spoke of an ideological tradition that was most clearly alive in the present. "After all," he pointed out, "the words 'liberty,' 'freedom,' and 'justice,' that are crudely painted on the posters carried by those who riot today through Southeast Asia, Latin America, and Africa, do not have their origins in the Communist Manifesto but rather have their inspiration in the American Declaration of Independence."[6] Marsh considered the Bicentennial to be an opportunity to proclaim American ownership over fundamental concepts that were established in the past but upheld in the present.

By the time planning began in earnest three years later, the United States had become involved in the Vietnam conflict, and rhetoric surrounding the approaching celebration reaffirmed America's position in the foreign sphere, asserting a commitment to spreading the ideals of freedom and liberty around the globe.[7] In January of 1966, Congressman Charles Mathis Jr., a Democrat from Maryland, introduced a bill calling for a federally sponsored commission to coordinate national observance of the Bicentennial.[8] President Lyndon Johnson supported the legislation, noting that the purpose of the commission would be to "help state and local groups in their commemoration, encourage school studies of the history of the Revolution and plan national celebrations and recall to America and the world the majestic significance of the Revolution."[9] Emphasizing the international position of the United States, Johnson echoed Marsh in underscoring contemporary American ownership of the concept of "revolution." Significantly, the president consigned the *history* of the Revolution to "school studies"; signaling a desire to move the "majestic significance" of American actions and ideals forward and into the future.

On July 4, 1966, Johnson signed the bill, which called for a thirty-four-member American Revolution Bicentennial Commission (ARBC). The president used the opportunity to once again emphasize the foreign implications of the ideologies supporting the commemoration, particularly given the escalating military action in Vietnam. In the same proclamation that announced the formation of the ARBC, Johnson declared the third week of that month Captive Nations' Week, as per a 1959 congressional resolution giving the chief executive power to declare the week until "such time as freedom and independence have been achieved by nations under Communist domination." Johnson was able to make these connections because mainstream opinion assumed that U.S. actions abroad embodied the legacy of principles established in the past; the "freedom" and "independence" that the "Captive Nations" were fighting for were key tenets of the American Revolution and the Bicentennial celebration.[10]

Johnson named Carlisle Humelsine, the head of the Colonial Williamsburg Foundation and the National Trust for Historic Preservation, to be chair of the ARBC. Humelsine worked with the White House to build a nonpartisan commission made up of equal numbers of public officials and private citizens, and with efforts toward an even distribution of party and regional representation.[11] The final list of commissioners included John O. Marsh, as well as Democratic and Republican senators John Pastore and Edward Brooke, all of whom had been instrumental in the formation of the Bicentennial Commission. Johnson also appointed art critic Aline Saarinen, author Ralph Ellison, historian Richard Morris, and General Lauris Norstad of the U.S. Air Force, among others.[12] The appointees represented a wide variety of perspectives and interests, indicating that, at this stage, Johnson's administration was not concerned about the potential for conflict over either the meaning or the nature of the commemoration. Despite their diverse backgrounds and perspectives, the new commissioners would unite over their interpretations of the ideas and forms underwriting the celebration.

While the discourse surrounding the purpose of the Bicentennial called attention to the place of the United States in the world, proposed programming stressed the Johnson administration's domestic efforts: an unprecedented expansion of rights coupled with economic growth. In early press conferences Humelsine used language that echoed that of Johnson's Great Society, announcing that he wished to use the Bicentennial as a moment to consider not only the United States's position as an international leader, but also to draw attention to and "launch a head on attack" against domestic issues such as the growing urban crisis.[13] Humelsine wanted a strong national commemoration but noted that he wished to avoid the "hackneyed approach of battle reenactments and carnival-like exploitations," a reference, most likely, to the recent Civil War Centennial.[14] Instead, Humelsine avowed, "We ought to think of ways to present to the rest of the world our concepts of the modern relevance of the ideas which made us citizens of the world's first great modern republic."[15] In these early stages, proposals circulating within ARBC and in the public sphere imagined the Bicentennial as an opportunity for domestic funding, social programming, and urban redevelopment.[16] If the American Revolution, founded upon the dual ideals of equality and representation, had improved the lives of its participants, the programming supporting its commemoration would extend those values to contemporary and future Americans.

The actual *history* of the Revolution was not a significant component in early conversations about the Bicentennial. Humelsine and other ARBC members agreed that the Bicentennial would feature social programming, not pageantry.[17] In both public and internal communications, ARBC representatives and employees voiced a desire to move the orientation of the Bicentennial "not toward historical events of the Revolutionary period, but rather toward a time for reappraisal of the principles on which the Country was founded; recommitment by every institution and individual."[18] A few suggestions for historical endeavors, such as publishing a collection of the writings of Loyalists during the Revolution, usually came from specialists like academics and antiquarians and were considered a small part of the anticipated commemoration.[19] For the ARBC at this moment, the American past was relevant only insomuch as it provided the foundations of the American present; the Bicentennial would mark the realization and expansion of these values as opposed to examining their genesis. Humelsine and the ARBC sought to generate patriotic identification with and support for contemporary, not historical, politics.

And so, the first plan seriously considered by the commission was an international exposition that would reflect current accomplishments and provide frameworks for continued growth and improvement.[20] The world's fair was an obvious choice, not only because the 1876 Centennial had been observed with an international exposition in Philadelphia, but also because its model of knowledge production is informed by and in dialogue with many of the same assumptions about material evidence and temporal progression as the traditional commemoration. Robert Rydell has characterized the international exposition as a mode of spectacular pedagogy that teaches subjects about their place in the world through display of artifacts, peoples, and innovations. The accomplishments of the hosting nation are presented in material terms and placed in relation to both its own past and the pasts and presents of other nations, tracing a history that assumes uninterrupted progress and ongoing growth.[21] Especially in the twentieth century, world's fairs, like those held in Chicago in 1933 and in New York in 1939 and 1964, had been used to show off U.S. material abundance and introduce technological innovations that would soon assure more comfortable living.[22] Although a "credibility gap" continued to grow between the people and the government, in 1968 American leaders still remained confident of wide popular support for projects that both expressed and worked toward material and economic advancement. The international exposition, undergirded by the principles of the Great Society, would celebrate the American present as a realization of the ideals of that American past.

Nixon's ARBC and the International Exposition

As Johnson's presidency moved into Nixon's, larger transformations in the American political, economic, social, and cultural landscapes began to shape conversations about the Bicentennial. Historians have described the 1968 election, a close and contested race in which Richard Nixon upset Hubert Humphrey for the first Republican victory in eight years, as a sea change in American party politics, and a spatial restructuring of the United States that realigned both parties and saw the emergence of the Sunbelt region as a new center of political and economic power.[23] By 1968, Americans were divided over both foreign and domestic policy, and the incoming administration faced social unrest at home and an unpopular war abroad. Most importantly, in the late 1960s the Cold War consensus, specifically trust in and support of government actions and unflagging confidence that the future would be an improvement over the past and present, wavered.[24] Under Nixon, planning for the Bicentennial developed in tandem with a growing sense in all parts of American society that the present was out of step with the past.

While party politics had been absent from Johnson's commission, the new administration, likely recognizing the growing polarization in the social and cultural climate of the United States, almost immediately oriented the Bicentennial toward its own political ends. When Nixon was elected president in November of 1968, Humelsine and the rest of the Johnson-appointed members of the ARBC followed customary protocol and dutifully submitted resignations. Because their commission appointments had been made at a moment when commemoration was presumed to exist outside of political partisanship, they assumed that these resignations would not be accepted, and they would be allowed to continue under the new president.[25] But when Nixon finally announced his selections in June of 1969, almost none of the 1967 appointees remained. Nixon named Stanford University chancellor Wallace Sterling as chair of the reformed commission. Other appointees included Dr. Paul Smith, president of Nixon's alma mater, Whittier College; hospitality entrepreneur George Lang; Republican backer Hobart Lewis of *Reader's Digest*; and James Copley, publisher of the *San Diego Union* and the *San Diego Evening Tribune*, news outlets that were most friendly to the new president.[26] All of these commission members were political allies of Nixon, and some, especially Copley and Lewis, had been instrumental in his election. Johnson had sought to create a nonpartisan commission because he felt assured of a commemoration with an uncomplicated and fixed meaning. Nixon's actions suggest that he came into office both believing that there would be contention over the Bicentennial and wishing to use it for his own purposes. As one commentator would write later, "To them, allowing an independent, nonpolitical ARBC to plan freely for the Bicentennial was like fomenting a revolution against the government."[27] From the moment of his close and contested election, Nixon and his administration used the national commemoration to cement his own party's interests.

By late 1968, the projected international exposition was garnering attention in the press, and interested cities began submitting their proposals.[28] Evidence suggests that Nixon waited for the cities to put together their bids so his new appointees would be well positioned to orchestrate a Bicentennial that was concerned less with domestic welfare and more with building political alliances and actively encouraging citizen patriotism.[29] Within the context of the turbulent political and social atmosphere of the late 1960s, the president recognized that the kind of national consensus that would support

The 1969 proposal submitted by the Boston Redevelopment Authority envisioned a futuristic international exposition that celebrated American technological innovation. Courtesy of the Boston Redevelopment Authority.

a centralized Bicentennial was weakening (indeed, his own successful political campaign had been built upon this premise) and acted to rebuild this consensus by shifting the commemoration's meaning to ideological as opposed to material regeneration. For Nixon, an international exposition was imperative for solidifying citizen consent but would need to be engineered by his own allies.

Yet even Nixon's designated commission soon realized that an international exposition celebrating American progress and power might be out of step with an increasingly fragmented society. Internal correspondence through late 1969 and early 1970 shows ARBC personnel beginning to express reservations about the world's fair.[30] The ARBC's doubts stemmed, in part, from the media's questioning the suitability of the international exposition. The press voiced its unease in a language that communicated that the moods of festivity and futurity that underpinned world's fairs might not be in line with the current cultural landscape of the United States.[31] Ada Louise Huxtable of the *New York Times* asked in March of 1970, "Are gaudy, extravagant, technological displays obsolete? Is a World's Fair–type Bicentennial festival appropriate for a country racked with social, racial, and environmental agonies?"[32] Citizens of Boston and Philadelphia, the two leading cities under consideration for hosting the exposition, had begun organizing against the plan as it became evident that rather than bringing

in infrastructure improvements, the influx of visitors the exposition promised would put pressure on the already-fragile resources of each city.[33] In
May of 1970, the Executive Committee of the ARBC met and decided
against recommending an exposition because it would be too expensive;
frontrunner Philadelphia estimated costs that reached $1 billion for the ex-
position itself and up to the same amount for associated projects like highway
expansion and airport renovation.[34] Only a few years earlier, the international exposition had been a popular and uncontested idea, not only because
of the resources that it promised but also because Americans believed in
the superiority of their nation and supported a mode of celebration that
would show this off to the rest of the world. But ambivalence from the cities in question, the press, and the ARBC itself indicated the meaning and
purpose of commemoration were coming into question.

Nixon was ready to overrule the ARBC's hesitations because he remained
committed to the international exposition as a political tool that could be
used to solidify his party's influence and to the Bicentennial as an ideological apparatus that could help the nation regain the confidence that it was
losing.[35] In July, the *Washington Post* reported that, at the behest of two
powerful Republican senators from Pennsylvania—minority leader Hugh
Scott and Richard Schweiker—the commission had reversed its original
decision against an exposition and was now petitioning the international
body for Philadelphia's designation as a "Class II" (that is, somewhat smaller,
but still internationally recognized) world's fair. Alluding to the backroom
politics that had begun to characterize the ARBC, the *Post* described an internal debate over the appropriateness of a fairground exposition.[36] Other
news outlets began hinting at the president's campaign obligations: "the
President has a lot more to take into consideration than the commission
report," one congressional source observed in the *New York Times*, "important people still have to be heard from."[37] Although commemorations, especially those organized on a national level, always have political stakes, Nixon's
direct involvement indicated that because this commemoration's ideological purpose was coming under fire, the president felt it would have to be
closely managed by himself.

The Bicentennial Plan and Introducing Heritage

Faced with mounting controversy and dissent, the ARBC spent 1969 and 1970
working on a document that both reflected and attempted to codify many of
the cultural and political transformations informing ongoing considerations

of the Bicentennial. The Bicentennial Plan, a report to the president outlining the terms of the commemoration, ultimately served as a turning point. A 1969 draft had outlined two major components: "Festival USA" and "USA Redirected." While "Festival USA" referred to the international exposition and other special events, "USA Redirected" was "an opportunity to concern ourselves with the ideas and ideals of the Declaration of Independence, and to consider where we have made progress in meeting those concepts and where we have not."[38] Although the Bicentennial's emphasis on the present and the future remained constant, the wording of this draft, in its acknowledgment of shortcomings, indicates a significant shift and a growing apprehension about both the state of contemporary America and the purpose of the commemoration itself. "Festival USA" continued in a celebratory tone, but "USA Redirected" was not, as the Johnson-era commission had anticipated, about an expansion of ideals, but instead an occasion for reflection. For the first time, the Bicentennial would look back to the past in order to make comparisons with, and assessments of, the present. Significantly, this disjuncture was signaled through a call for the reexamination of the Declaration of Independence, the very document that had previously ensured continuity between the past and the present.

In the months between the 1969 draft and the completion of the document in July of 1970, the ARBC again reorganized the Bicentennial Plan around this new sense of reflection, this time directly addressing the past.[39] The final version of the document introduced three themes: "Heritage '76," "Festival USA," and "Horizons '76."[40] With these categories, ARBC for the first time structured the Bicentennial along a temporal axis: the past, the present, and the future. The "Festival USA" and "Horizons '76" components of the Bicentennial resembled earlier formulations in their attention to, respectively, the present and the future. "Heritage '76," however, was a new element: it called for programming that would "remember our form of government, our Founding Fathers, our forgotten people, the places and things of our past and, most important, our freedoms."[41] The 1970 Bicentennial Plan represented a critical moment in the history of the commission. On one hand, it still envisioned the Bicentennial as a celebration of the contemporary, but on the other, it began to look backward by establishing "Heritage '76" as an equal category. Although in retrospect it seems self-evident that a commemoration should focus on the past, until 1970, planners, the press, and the people did not think of the Bicentennial in this way. It was not until popular opinion came to center on the disjuncture between the ideals of the past and the actions of the present that attention to history became significant. By underscoring the historical aspects of commemoration as a means of identifying and thinking about social and political problems, the 1970 report acknowledged that disjuncture and laid out a framework for addressing it.

While the ARBC was the most visible coordinating body, individual states were also preparing for 1976 and began to use their own regional histories to find relevance in the Bicentennial in ways that often diverged from the federal vision.[42] In 1971, the ARBC's Communications Committee noted that thirty-one states already had commissions working to mount their own Bicentennial festivities. Planners in Yorktown, Virginia, proposed renovating homes and shops to make the town look as it did in 1776, and officials contemplated events to commemorate British general Cornwallis's surrender and the drafting of the Articles of Capitulation. Other state projects looked to more recent history: boosters in Vermont refurbished a nineteenth-century train and readied it to run again.[43] The Texas Technological University Museum in Lubbock built historic ranching structures on a twelve-acre site. The city of Phoenix, Arizona, proposed a 550-acre Pioneer Park with a permanent historical town depicting life in the state's early days.[44] Not only were these ventures more historically oriented than federal planners had originally intended, but they were now coming to encompass *all* of American history, not just the Revolutionary era. These initiatives represented what John Bodnar has called "vernacular celebration," an effort to make the Bicentennial meaningful in a local context.[45] Although this was most prominent in states that had not been directly involved in the Revolution, even the thirteen colonies began envisioning programming that moved forward from the colonial era. ARBC was initially resistant. As late as November of 1972, ARBC's coordinator for Heritage '76 wrote to a correspondent in Illinois who was organizing a lecture on the Lincoln-Douglas debates that programming must be "limited to those events in the era 1776–1789."[46] However, as it became more and more apparent that history was becoming the focus of the commemoration, the commission would come to alter this position.

From International Exposition to Bicentennial Parks

Although Nixon's reversal of the decision on the international exposition resulted in public and media scrutiny of ARBC's operations, this added attention did not stop the president from continuing to exert strong authority over the commission.[47] The White House's management of the commission was similar to other actions that characterized what came to be called an "imperial presidency." But Nixon's investment in this opportunity to both stimulate and shape patriotic sentiment also echoed his larger political initiatives, particularly what Bruce Schulman, Jefferson Cowie, and others have described as an effort to build a new political constituency by invoking nationalistic feelings and appealing to cultural, as opposed to material, issues.[48] Throughout his presidency, Nixon worked to form this new bloc, named first the "Silent Majority" and later the "New Majority," a part of what the president called "the New American Revolution."[49] Reading the commemoration as a small but vital part of Nixon's larger strategy helps explain the extraordinary measures undertaken by the president to maintain control over the ideological imperatives of the Bicentennial, particularly as public opinion about both the commemoration and the support of the American project that underpinned it was becoming more fraught.[50] While commemorations always do the double duty of expressing and reinvigorating nationalistic sentiment, the primary purpose of the Bicentennial was moving from the former to the latter, and this required careful oversight and planning.

After the 1970 resignation of Wallace Sterling, Nixon appointed a new chair, a political ally who would also be able to oversee the complex maneuvers necessary for the international exposition, which continued to be plagued by inefficiency and opposition on both the local and the federal levels.[51] David Mahoney was the protégé and longtime friend of Nixon associates Bob Haldeman and Robert Finch.[52] While previous commissioners Humelsine and Sterling had been scholars, Mahoney was a businessman, a former president of Good Humor and Palmolive, among others.[53] With this appointment and with additional maneuvers that installed members of Nixon's cabinet as voting ex officio members of ARBC subcommittees, the White House secured its hold on the ARBC and assembled a commission that it hoped would be able to gain support for a rapidly deteriorating commemoration and, by extension, Nixon's own administration.[54]

Under Mahoney and his associate Jack LeVant, who was appointed director in November of 1971, the ARBC began to focus on business operations, commissioning efficiency studies by private consulting firms in order to help streamline operations.[55] Mahoney and LeVant wanted to make the Bicentennial a completely privatized celebration. This resembled other initiatives in the Nixon administration, which was restructuring other sectors by decentralizing power and forming semiprivate corporations, a hallmark of the neoliberal economic programs that had begun to take hold

American Revolution Bicentennial Commission chairman David Mahoney (far right) with President Richard Nixon, Speaker of the House Carl Albert, and Chief Justice Warren Burger at the National Archives in 1970. Courtesy of the Richard M. Nixon Presidential Library and Museum (National Archives and Records Administration).

of state policy, replacing older Keynesian models.[56] By the end of 1971, Le-Vant and ARBC leadership had proposed a support corporation that could solicit funding, "without the stigma of requesting the checks be made payable to the Treasurer of the United States." This new venture, echoing Nixon's New Federalism, was to be called Federalism '76 and would comprise current ARBC executives as well as the ex officio subcommittee members from Nixon's cabinet.[57] Looking for other ways to expand ARBC's power and to make it less accountable to representative government (and by extension, American citizens), Mahoney and LeVant also worked to amend the joint resolution that had created the ARBC, giving more power to the chair and director. Interoffice memos on the proposed amendment included a draft of a letter to be sent from Nixon to the commission members, assuring them that the current stage of Bicentennial planning required this new consolidation of authority.[58] The ARBC operated along the trajectory of other Nixon-era initiatives in government, introducing a privatized corporate model that transferred governance and accountability from the representative federal government to states and private corporations.[59]

Despite the Nixon administration's best efforts to build an ARBC that could oversee a national Bicentennial, it had gradually become apparent that the Philadelphia exposition was not going to happen. This was a result of lack of support from not only citizens but also from Congress, which was both unwilling and unable to bankroll such an endeavor. Johnson's original plan for the international exposition had been proposed as a way of revitalizing urban areas. Under Nixon, its function as an ideological tool took precedence, and organizers looked to suburban sites that were poorly suited to any kind of permanent economic or structural regeneration, even as the media continued to raise questions about the appropriateness of a world's fair given the current cultural and political climate.[60] The movement away from urban redevelopment in Philadelphia angered community leaders who had originally backed the city's proposal because of the hundreds of millions of dollars in urban renewal funding promised by the exposition.[61] But residents near the new proposed site, on seven hundred acres of state-owned land in the Byberry area twelve miles northeast of the city, also protested the exposition. Ironically, while residents in the city had come to resent the use of federal money for a fairground instead of as aid for the urban crisis, residents of the area adjacent to the Byberry site feared an expansion of the airport and of public transportation to the area and did not want their neighborhood turned into what they called a "bicentennial slum."[62] The protests of the Byberry residents, white, middle-class suburbanites who were precisely the constituency that Nixon and the G.O.P. were trying to attract, finally put an end to the exposition plan.[63]

By the first months of 1972, the Nixon administration and the ARBC had realized that the international exposition lacked sufficient legislative and public support but were not ready to give up on a unified, national Bicentennial celebration. Instead, the ARBC introduced a hastily produced proposal that acknowledged the changing cultural and political atmosphere that had made the exposition impossible, but expressed a continuing desire to use the Bicentennial as a means to build constituencies and strengthen patriotism. In February of 1972, Mahoney and the ARBC presented a new plan for the national commemoration: a series of fifty Bicentennial Parks, each built on federal land and featuring a pavilion that could contain a traveling

ARBC exhibition sent around the country by caravan. At a press conference, Mahoney dramatically unveiled a three-dimensional model that included a system of plastic domes under which multimedia projections, restaurants, and exhibits could be placed.[64] Each park would be enclosed by an "air-supported membrane" and would contain ponds, bandstands, sports arenas, refreshment kiosks, aquaria, and botanical gardens.[65] Aptly called by one commentator "regional editions of a National Fair," the parks extended the logic of the international exposition, albeit in a decentralized way that echoed the realignment of power in the United States from the "Eastern Establishment" states.[66]

The Bicentennial Parks were never a viable proposal—like the international exposition, they were too costly and would have required massive coordination in locating and appropriating sites and engaging contractors to build the structures.[67] The parks would not be formally voted down until March of 1973, but due to problems with funding, planning, and land procurement, ARBC staff doubted their feasibility even at the outset.[68] The proposal had not been introduced to many ARBC members until the day of the press conference, and some expressed frustration at having been kept in the dark.[69] The Bicentennial Parks proposal was a publicity measure and a last stab at a national commemoration, one that acknowledged and responded to growing interest in natural resources and environmentalism. The unrealistic parks proposal was a turning point in the ARBC's conception of the Bicentennial but also underscored the lengths to which Nixon and the commission would go to mount a centralized, federally organized celebration.

With the demise of the international exposition and the continued failure to settle on a Bicentennial proposal that appealed to a wide public, many critics raised questions about the meaning of the Bicentennial, making connections between the ARBC's inability to plan the commemoration and the larger issues of the Nixon administration.[70] Nixon's politicized appropriation backfired—in making Bicentennial planning an extension of the current administration, and the celebration itself an ideological instrument that did not reflect realities of the contemporary United States, both became available to progressively more frequent public critiques of Nixon and his allies.[71] As one reporter put it, the ARBC at this moment was "a body whose at-large membership was mostly composed of Nixon political payoffs."[72] The contested terrain of the ARBC and the Bicentennial came to be seen as very visible symptoms of a corrupt administration.

By late 1971, Nixon and the ARBC also faced organized opposition from the People's Bicentennial Commission (PBC), a new group that charged the administration and the ARBC with "stealing" the Bicentennial. Jeremy Rifkin, the founder of the PBC, accused the ARBC of "political, ideological, and commercial exploitation of the observance by the White House and commissioners and staff."[73] Rifkin suggested instead that Americans reconsider the radicalism of the American Revolution and find their own meaning in the Bicentennial.[74] Rifkin's ideas quickly gained press and popular attention, supporters of the PBC at this time included chapters of Veterans of Foreign Wars, Rotary Clubs, the YMCA, and the Campfire Girls, all of whom adapted PBC materials in their programming.[75] The PBC found public currency because they were able to articulate what many Americans were beginning to feel about the upcoming Bicentennial.

The Big Birthday Bungle: ARBC under Fire

Although the People's Bicentennial Commission and others had already begun making accusations of partisanship and exploitation, in the summer of 1972 a series of high-profile articles in the *Washington Post* brought new negative attention to the ARBC.[76] In an uncanny echo of the *New York Times* revelation of the Pentagon Papers the previous year, the article series was precipitated by internal documents uncovered by a disgruntled former employee who had made contact with Rifkin and the PBC, who then leaked the papers to the *Post*.[77] Starting in July of 1972, with an article entitled "The Big Birthday Bungle," the *Post* charged Mahoney and the ARBC with corruption, focusing on Nixon and the Republican Party's use of the Bicentennial in support of Nixon's reelection bid.[78] The third article in the series quoted an unsent memo written by Jack LeVant stating that the Bicentennial offered "the greatest opportunity Nixon, the Party, and the government has as a beacon of light for reunification and light within the nation and with the world."[79]

The problems within the ARBC, publicized in the *Post* series and by the PBC, captured the imagination of newspaper readers, who saw ARBC's issues as a sign of larger inefficiencies and misconduct in the government, which were becoming evident with continuing revelations of misdeeds in Vietnam. The *Post* series was extremely popular with the public and was covered in other national newspapers.[80] The public and the press extended the credibility gap that came to define many aspects of the Nixon presidency to both the planning of the commemoration and to the meaning of the Bicentennial itself. While corruption, secrecy, and partisanship at the federal level were issues that were too big to tackle, the ARBC, the organization that was supposed to observe and honor the symbols of the nation, was limited enough to be identified. Condemning the ARBC became a way for citizens and lawmakers to render a critique of a larger, more unwieldy problem onto a smaller, more manageable target.

While the *Post* series mainly attacked ARBC's partisanship, the articles also voiced a new complaint that Nixon and the ARBC were trying to "sell" the Bicentennial.[81] The *Post* reported on backroom deals, including endorsement meetings with Mack Truck, Marriott Hotels, Baskin Robbins, and others. Noting the hypocrisy of Mahoney, who had repeatedly come out against "cheap commercialism" in the press, the articles condemned business relationships that exploited the "meaning" of the Bicentennial. In the coming years, this critique would grow significantly, but at this moment, it was a new development.[82] The charge of commercialization stemmed directly from that of partisanship. It was only when planning for the commemoration was revealed to be a partisan effort that its availability to commerce became particularly noticeable. These two critiques came together because both were connected to the destabilization of the meaning of the Bicentennial. Significantly, at this moment, commercialization was universally considered to be a negative trait—federal commemoration was to be a civic exercise free of corporate influences. By the time of the actual celebration, this position would shift radically.

In the wake of the *Post* exposés and the rising profile of the People's Bicentennial Commission, the ARBC began to garner disapproval from other sectors of government and even from within its own ranks. In late August, Democratic senator John O. Pastore of Rhode Island resigned from his post on the commission, noting that he did not like the "general smell of the thing."[83] Other politicians, including Fred Harris of Oklahoma, Ted Kennedy of Massachusetts, and Democratic presidential candidate George McGovern voiced similar opinions. Perhaps the strongest condemnation came from the Congressional Black Caucus, which called the ARBC "manipulative" and a "fraud on the American people."[84] The Democratic Party newsletter, *FACT*, observed that Nixon was working the language of the Bicentennial into his own reelection campaign, using phrases like "The New American Revolution" and the "Spirit of '76" as political slogans.[85] By the end of the summer of 1972 it was clear that the ARBC had neither concrete plans for the Bicentennial nor the support of the press, the public, or members of government.

Media and popular reactions to the ARBC and its ties to Nixon's troubled presidency now took the form of historical comparisons. The Nixon administration had failed to propose a commemoration that expressed accord between past ideals and present sentiments, so the Bicentennial became instead a symbol of incongruity. As one columnist put it, the Bicentennial needed a "systematic reexamination and reevaluation of the American experiment in order to understand the pluralistic personality of the American people."[86] Other commentators invited readers to consider their own political positions in a historicized perspective, asking, "Would you have joined up in the American Revolution?"[87] Eugene L. Meyer, the *Post* columnist who had written the investigative series on the ARBC, compared the statements of Pastore and others to those of Charles Sumner regarding the Centennial Exposition a century earlier.[88] The People's Bicentennial Commission encouraged Americans to consider the connections between the Nixon administration and the colonial-era British monarchy, pointing out the history of "far out agitators" like Thomas Paine, Benjamin Rush, and Samuel Adams.[89] Americans had begun to look to the past in order to evaluate the present.

The *Post* articles' mobilization of public opinion had direct repercussions for the ARBC, which, by the end of that summer, faced two separate federal investigations, from the General Accounting Office (GAO) and the House Judiciary Committee (HJC). Significantly, reports from both investigations blamed the ARBC's issues not on corruption or a deeper problem with the very nature of the Bicentennial, but on office morale and staff shortages.[90] The reports, themselves generated by bodies that had significant investment in the Bicentennial's potential to encourage citizen support for the government, recast ARBC's partisanship as inefficiency, its power plays as organizational failures. While the GAO issued a gentle rebuke to the ARBC for inefficient staff use and for relying too much on consultants as full-time workers, the HJC, chaired by Massachusetts Democrat and recently resigned ARBC member Harold Donohue, returned much harsher findings, charging the ARBC with a "lack of understanding of purpose and an unworkable structure," paying extremely high salaries to consultants and maintaining a "relaxed attitude towards government economies," among other things.[91] The GAO report cleared the ARBC of commercialism, specifically rebutting the *Washington Post*, but neither it nor the HJC report mentioned the accusations of political partisanship.[92] Instead, both investigations highlighted the shortage of support staff and the lack of adequate planning and speculated that, in its current iteration, the ARBC would not be able to "provide the country with proper commemoration by 1976."[93] With the mounting criticisms that ultimately culminated in these investigations, it was finally apparent that the 1976 Bicentennial would not be a centralized national celebration.

Grass Roots, Grants, and Bicentennial Communities

Responding to the hearings' emphases on the deficiency of Bicentennial activities, ARBC officials finally prioritized programming, moving toward a model of organization that would allow the commission to oversee, rather than to generate, Bicentennial events. ARBC commissioner James Copley wrote, "Our public trouble, in my opinion, traces in part to our lack of coherent and concise presentations of what we stand for and what we are accomplishing. We badly need something to place in people's hands, for the record."[94] In the last months of 1972 and throughout 1973, "grass roots" became the byword of the commission, as the ARBC realized they could solve planning problems by switching their function to identifying and recognizing programs already underway.[95] The movement away from a unified federal celebration toward acknowledgment and coordination of programs introduced from below can be understood in two ways: on the one hand, it took pressure off the ARBC, and, on the other, it protected the agency from censure, as the same public that was both invested in and skeptical of the Bicentennial would now have a stake in it. It was, after all, what Jeremy Rifkin and the PBC had been advocating from the very beginning.[96] More generally, the emergence of "grass roots" revealed a new understanding of the impossibility of a national program. While decentralization resulted in part from widespread denigration of the ARBC and of Nixon, more significantly, Americans lacked popular consensus on the relationship of the national past to the national present. In other words, a traditional centralized commemoration was ill-suited to the contemporary moment.

But this does not mean that government planners gave up on the Bicentennial as an opportunity for the consolidation of patriotic feeling. It does mean that organizers adapted to accommodate cultural and social changes. At that time and afterward, commentary on the Bicentennial framed the shift toward "grass roots" as a response to cultural pluralism—while this is certainly accurate, it elides this shift with downscaled federal investment in the Bicentennial, suggesting that because the Bicentennial ultimately did not resemble a traditional national commemoration, the state was minimally involved.[97] This must not be read as a step back, but as an adjustment in strategy. The ARBC's movement toward coordination indicated a continuing (and perhaps even, in the face of the challenges of consensus, a *mounting*) investment in overseeing the Bicentennial, albeit in a new way that took account of and reacted to the larger political, cultural, and economic developments that had rendered a centralized celebration impossible.

ARBC's new concentration on programming coincided with a profitable new venture that, for the first time, raised funding for the Bicentennial. On July 4, 1972, the ARBC introduced a new line of commemorative medals available for purchase. Over the next two years, the ARBC continued to do brisk business in this enterprise, showing that even if many Americans disapproved of the way that the official Bicentennial was being organized, there was still interest in, and support for, the commemoration at its most symbolic level. By the end of that year, ARBC had earned $6.3 million from selling the commemorative medals and granted over $2 million to state commissions as well as to the National Endowment for the Arts, the National Endowment for the Humanities, the National Science Foundation, and the Smithsonian Folklife Festival.[98] Further earnings allowed the ARBC to reinforce its decentralization process by making fiscal allotments of $40,000 to each state and $25,000 to each territory for the purpose of generating and funding programs.[99]

Alongside direct funding, ARBC program officers also started turning promising proposals over to state Bicentennial Commissions. The extensive network of regional offices, originally put in place to regulate local organizers and to concentrate resources on the national effort, was now used to distribute funding and to coordinate programs. The revenue from the medals would prove to be the turning point of the ARBC and allowed it to transform, in the public eye, from an agency that absorbed resources to one that granted them. While program funding seemed like a form of federal aid akin to something like the National Endowment for the Arts, in reality, it was a way for the ARBC to contract out planning work while still claiming partial credit for the programming. "Grass roots" advanced an impression of the Bicentennial as a publicly generated celebration, but in reality, through its control of channels of funding and by circulating proposals from the national commission to local affiliates, the ARBC still very much dictated the shape and nature of the commemoration.[100]

In order to provide oversight for its new partners in programming, the ARBC introduced an initiative called Bicentennial Communities, which would become the hallmark program of the American Revolution Bicentennial Administration (ARBA), its succeeding organization. Under this program, communities such as townships, neighborhoods, universities, and even army bases could apply to become an official "Bicentennial Community."[101] In order to qualify, a community supported by a local legislature was required to send in an application detailing proposed programming under the Heritage, Horizons, and Festival USA rubrics. Approved Bicentennial Communities were given the opportunity to apply for grant money through ARBC and were designated part of the "official" celebration.[102] The Bicentennial Communities program can be read as a branding move in which the ARBC could put its logo on all kinds of projects that it itself would choose, according to criteria that it would set. If anyone continued to criticize the ARBC for lack of programming, the commission could now point to the Bicentennial Communities and their activities. Bicentennial Communities was an additional way for the federal agency to exercise control over vernacular commemoration, by providing official designation for those communities willing to adhere to its directives.

Many of the programs most heavily supported by ARBC reflected the widespread new interest in history as well as the commission's own growing emphasis on a celebration that looked to the past for answers about the present. ARBC program officer Martha Jane Shay wrote in a briefing memo: "An increasing number of Americans are beginning to realize that the past need not necessarily be past, that the past has not only brought us where we are, but that it can continue to serve our contemporary needs and to enrich our environment."[103] A majority of the sixty-some "national" programs promoted by the ARBC (that is, recognized and supported directly as opposed to through the state commissions) were historical in nature, falling under the Heritage category of programming.[104] These included Above Ground Archaeology, which taught schoolchildren how to investigate the histories of their homes; the Freedom Train, a traveling exhibition of documents and artifacts; and several document-preservation programs through state and local archives.[105] ARBC highlighted Heritage projects because they addressed what the commission saw as a desire by American citizens to reexamine the past.[106] Americans were not only more interested in history as a means of evaluating the present but also engaged the past in new, affective ways, looking for close identification on an emotional level with the people and events of the past. Arguably, ARBC and other state interests found this affective approach appealing because emotional engagement had the potential to regenerate patriotic feeling. If Americans could not necessarily feel patriotic about the *contemporary* United States, they could nonetheless transfer these feelings to the American past.

Accordingly, the *kind* of historical programming that the ARBC sought to support also changed. While the earlier iterations of the commission had bristled against reenactments as an unproductive mode of commemoration, the ARBC now began encouraging these activities. The commission formed a new subgroup to stage reenactments of historic events as an antidote to "today's negative thinking." The National Patriotic-Civic Organizations Co-ordination Committee considered reenactments to be "a positive way of recalling America's heritage and of reestablishing a national pride among young people."[107] Immersive, personalized engagements with the past could move participants to patriotic sentiment, something that was much desired by state interests in that fraught moment. The new attention to reenact-ment programming reversed earlier ARBC policy both in its emphasis on history and in its use of embodied, experiential engagements with the past as opposed to histories formed from or available through historic artifacts.

From ARBC to ARBA

By late 1972, the ARBC was a radically different organization, both in its embrace of the "grass roots" and in its new focus on historical program-ming. In early February of 1973, shortly after his second inauguration, Nixon presented a plan that would abolish the ARBC and replace it with a stream-lined American Revolution Bicentennial Administration (ARBA) com-prising a single administrator, an eleven-member Advisory Board, and a more public Advisory Council. The main task of the ARBA would be to continue to recognize Bicentennial Communities and to create a "Master Calendar" of Bicentennial events.[108] This cemented changes that came from within but provided a legislative directive that would retroactively attribute this to the president's own initiative.[109] What was occurring was a delicate balancing act, precipitated by the realization that a Bicentennial that was unified in focus would not be possible. Following structural changes already implemented within the ARBC, Nixon formally replaced the emphasis on organization with one on coordination, thus shifting the group's adminis-trative influence from power over planning and production to power over designation and management. The new ARBA would still have a say over the nature of the commemoration, but would be presiding over decentral-ized interests. Rather than a national organization that behaved like a cor-poration, the ARBA would remain a federal body, but one that would be free to act in concert with both public and private interests.

At hearings on the new administration, members of Congress worried that the proposed Bicentennial administrator would become a "Bicenten-nial Czar," much in the model of the president himself, but the White

House stood firm, saying that nothing could be done with an unwieldy structure like the previous commission.[110] As the Watergate investigation intensified, a subcommittee added Senate confirmation as a necessity for the appointment of administrator and assistants as a safeguard against the politicization of appointments.[111] The White House's connections to the Watergate burglars had already been revealed, and in two months, Nixon's top aides would be forced to resign. Issues of political appointments, corruption, and secrecy were at the forefront of public opinion.[112] At confirmation hearings for the new agency, ARBC officials began speaking of the coming ARBA as a decentralized, nonauthoritative body, as if to counter the way in which the unilateral actions of the president himself were being interrogated.[113]

As the crisis of the presidency mounted, many continued to look toward the past in order to consider the events of the present. While the ideals of the Revolution had previously been assumed as realized in the present day, Americans now used historical events to understand contemporary shortcomings and to move the meaning of the Bicentennial from celebration to contemplation, turning to the past as a means of making sense of current events. As one commentator put it, "Today the issues that stirred the colonials ring with new timeliness. Should we have a monarch? Should any man be above the law?"[114] In Boston, New England Life Insurance sponsored a series of Bicentennial forums featuring prominent academics and politicians, including John Lindsey, Hannah Arendt, and George McGovern. Nearly all of the speakers compared Nixon to King George, asking audiences to recall the core values of the Revolution in their evaluation of the current crisis.[115] Nixon's problems were likewise often compared to those of another "embattled president" who had presided over a commemoration: the scandal-ridden Ulysses S. Grant.[116] Commentators used these associations to appraise the present situation and to speculate on its likely outcome: the Grant comparison, for example, noted that he had been allowed to stay in office because of strong party support, something that Nixon no longer enjoyed.[117] The Bicentennial had become both a venue and a framework for thinking about the past and relating it to the present.

After Congress approved the ARBA in December of 1973, Nixon signed the bill into law.[118] Two months later, John Warner, the photogenic former secretary of the navy (and future husband of Elizabeth Taylor) was announced as the head of the newly formed administration.[119] On March 11, 1974, in a radio address, Nixon appointed Warner to the position of Bicentennial administrator. Reacting to years of charges that his administration was attempting to "steal" the Bicentennial, and co-opting some of the anti-establishment language of his opposition, Nixon proclaimed, "The Bicentennial is not going to be invented in Washington, printed in triplicate by the Government printing office, mailed to you by the U.S. Postal Service and filed away in your private library. Instead, we shall seek to trigger a chain reaction of tens of thousands of individual celebrations."[120] With this statement, Nixon explicitly reversed the state's position, describing a Bicentennial that was straight out of the pages of a People's Bicentennial Commission publication. Rather than generating an official commemoration from the federal level, the state would now act to motivate and oversee a multitude of "individual celebrations." The mandate for the Bicentennial was now the prerogative and the responsibility of the citizenry. In the same way that the move toward decentralized planning and corporate partnerships echoed a growing impetus toward privatization in government, Nixon's speech responded to and anticipated the antigovernment sentiment that was paradoxically both the hallmark of the principles of the PBC and that would come to characterize the forming New Right.

Nixon also introduced another new supporting agent into the Bicentennial, again contradicting earlier iterations of the commemoration as a federal affair. In the same address, the president declared: "Our Bicentennial observance could not possibly realize its full potential or meet our high expectations without the support of the free enterprise system which has made our country what it is today—the best and strongest nation in history. Interest among private groups and organizations is developing, and we welcome their involvement."[121] The Bicentennial, which had begun as a federal effort to be safeguarded against private interests, was now to be planned by the people and financed by the private sector. This was another subtle maneuver: even though the PBC and other critics had been deriding the Bicentennial's commercialism, here Nixon connected private funding to the twin traditions of democracy and enterprise in America.

The reconstituted ARBA was very different from the ARBC; what had once been a partisan organization became a nonpartisan coordinating body. As administrator, Warner had more executive power than his predecessors, and, instead of working with what had gradually grown to fifty commission members, he answered to an eleven-member American Revolution Bicentennial Board composed of members of the House and Senate, the secretary of the interior, and presidential appointees from state Bicentennial commissions that would oversee ARBA operations, policy, and funding. In addition (and for publicity), Nixon appointed an American Revolution

Advisory Council populated by figures like Lady Bird Johnson, producer David Wolper, writers Alex Haley and James Michener, and poet Maya Angelou, who would meet and "advise" the ARBA as well as make public appearances to foster excitement for the celebration.[122] This most visible component of the ARBA more closely resembled the nonpartisan makeup of the original Johnson-era ARBC. While the old ARBC had been reproached for its closed operations, the ARBA, although an equally powerful federal agency, was to be as transparent as possible—part of the mandate of the council was for the members to act as the public face of the ARBA. Accordingly, the ARBA also would administer BINET, a computer database of Bicentennial activities, and publish the *Bicentennial Times*, described as a widely distributed "tabloid newspaper" that would focus on the two chief concerns of the ARBA: grants and Bicentennial Communities.[123] Considering the ARBC's previous problems with the press, it is not surprising that the ARBA would want its own news outlet. If the ARBC had been attacked for its secrecy, the ARBA would generate a public record of its doings.

A New Light on the Bicentennial

Warner's efforts at publicizing Bicentennial events and funding, named by White House staff assigned as ARBA liaisons "Operation Friendly Persuasion," used the Bicentennial's examination of history as a perspective on the contemporary scene, again building upon a tendency that had originated in wider public opinion.[124] In interviews, Warner stressed that this new approach to the Bicentennial would overcome "residual negativism," creating instead a "groundswell of Bicentennial fervor."[125] At the time, even ARBC's most stringent detractor, the *Washington Post*, seemed placated by this change and proclaimed a "new light on the Bicentennial."[126] At a moment when unimaginable truths were being revealed about Nixon's presidency, perhaps political corruption could be corrected in one area.[127]

The PBC also considered the shift from the ARBC to the ARBA a victory, attributing it to their own activity: "for the first time in anyone's memory, a small band of activists had taken on a multi-million dollar White House agency and stopped it cold in its tracks."[128] The PBC would continue to be active throughout the Bicentennial, changing its target from political to economic corruption, a salient topic given the ARBA's partnerships with commerce, but one less palatable to the American public than the PBC's previous critique.

For his part, Warner did not shy away from the topic of Watergate and instead sought to use the way in which the Bicentennial had become connected with politics to call for a reinvigoration of the commemoration. In this iteration, the Bicentennial would become a celebration of a system that worked under crisis: the Watergate hearings proved that the checks and balances put into place by the founding documents functioned to curb excessive and illegal power.[129] Warner's positive reception illustrates not only the mutable nature of commemoration, but also the complex position of the public with regard to the Bicentennial: it was not a wholesale rejection of the commemoration, instead it was a more nuanced critique of its nature that ultimately resulted in movement away from more traditional forms of centralized commemoration. Even in this contested atmosphere, commemoration remained a key site at which meaning could be made and the current state of the nation could be contemplated.

Nixon had expected to celebrate the Bicentennial as president, but by that time, he was no longer in power, having resigned in August of 1974. Instead, his successor Gerald Ford presided over the Bicentennial, articulating the meaning of the commemoration in ways that reflected the significant transformations that had occurred. While Johnson and Nixon had referred to the participants in the Revolution as instrumental to the present character of the nation, Ford invited contemporary Americans to "emulate the founders in word and deed."[130] In other speeches, he suggested that celebrants "draw strength from the past," "study carefully the character and qualities of the men who founded this nation," and "grasp the stuff that was inside them."[131] Where Johnson's and Nixon's rhetoric had pointed to the continuity between the character of the American past and the American present, in the face of the turmoil of the 1970s, Ford's words emphasized a discontinuity and a desire to realign the "word and deed" of America's great past with its troubled present. Significantly, Ford ended the Bicentennial Era where Richard Nixon had begun it, at the National Archives, where the founding documents in their new display were available to the public for seventy-six consecutive hours, guarded by sentinels in Revolutionary garb. At the July 2, 1976, ceremony that opened this vigil, Ford invited Americans to "join with those brave and farsighted Americans in 1776."[132] Ford, like other Americans, wished to draw upon the past to contemplate and reevaluate the present.

Looking at the trajectory of Bicentennial planning by federal interests shows both how the state remained invested in the commemoration as a way of seeking support from Americans and how its terms changed in tandem with larger political, economic, and cultural developments. Official preparation spanned a decade and was undertaken by representatives from three presidential administrations, all of whom approached the Bicentennial in ways that reflected larger cultural and political contexts, from Johnson's Great Society to Nixon's New Federalism, from the Keynesian to the neoliberal state. While Johnson attempted to use the celebration as a way to bolster the domestic project of the Great Society and the global position of the United States, for Nixon, the Bicentennial and its planning became an apparatus of the "imperial presidency," an effort to manage a rapidly fracturing state from a sovereign position and to consolidate political support through appeals to nationalism via plans for a traditional commemoration that ultimately could not be fulfilled. By 1974, the ongoing Bicentennial seemed greatly different not only from past commemorations, but also from its own earlier iterations. Bicentennial organizers introduced a new mode of commemoration that appeared decentralized yet was still governed by federal standards and oversight, demonstrating the continuing and even growing importance of the historical to hegemonic power. At the same time, the "grass roots" Bicentennial provided a venue for Americans to find their own meaning in the commemoration, to make their own connections between past and present.

And so, the history of the federal planning of the Bicentennial also affords us an opportunity to look at the history of *history itself*. The core argument of this book is that during this period, a significant change occurred in the way that Americans understood and engaged with the past. The early stages of preparation for the Bicentennial were concerned with the abstract principles of revolution as they were used abroad and with using the celebration as an opportunity to address the present and the future. But by 1971 and 1972, both planners and the public were more interested in investigating and reconsidering the whole of the American past. Throughout the Bicentennial Era, the nation was fully engaged in historical activity that was both rooted in larger instabilities *and* fundamentally different in nature. The dissolution of the progressive, linear conception of history, accompanied by the weakening of the archival body of "official history" that shapes commemorative expressions were the results both of social movements that questioned mainstream perception of the past and of larger shifts in historical consciousness precipitated by global economic, political, and cultural transformations. Through all of this, the historical grew more critical as a site at which to contemplate the present through forming identifications with the American past. And because this identification operated on emotional, not informational, registers and led to different possibilities for interpretation, history's potential as an ideological tool remained and even intensified. Looking at how these shifts affected both official and unofficial planning during the Bicentennial illuminates not only the critical relationships between archives, commemoration, and hegemonic power, but also shows how they themselves are mutable.

CHAPTER THREE

Preservation Is People

Saving and Collecting as Democratic Practice

> The events in and around these sites made Boston a leading force
> in bringing thirteen colonies together as a united people. These
> events can become real and meaningful on the Trail. The choices
> made by individual men and women separating Whig from Tory,
> patriot from loyalist, can be understood by the individual citizens
> of our "old" nation, 200 years old, who walk the Trail during the
> Bicentennial.
>
> —Boston 200, Boston Freedom Trail Grant Proposal

In 1972, the American Revolution Bicentennial Commission (ARBC) announced one of its first national programs, a partnership with the National
Trust for Historic Preservation on an initiative called "Meeting House
'76." This project called for the restoration of fifty-five historic sites that
would then become meeting places "for all citizens concerned with the
preservation of our cultural heritage and the quality of our physical environment."[1] Suggestions for historic structures that could be designated Meeting
Houses included theater buildings, frontier hotels, or even remnants of ghost
towns.[2] Potential Meeting Houses were not exemplars of innovative or beau-
tiful construction, nor were they associated with famous people, places, or
events. They were buildings that had been used by everyday people in the
past and were likewise to be used by everyday people in the present and
future. As a representative from the National Trust wrote, "Such a meeting place would intertwine the efforts of citizens concerned with saving
our inherited open spaces, water, air, and other natural resources with the
efforts of citizens preserving our historic man-made features."[3] This language illustrated the way that building preservation initiatives were shifting from a focus on protection to one on use and underscored an emerging
connection between anti-redevelopment, building preservation, and the
environmental movement. But the Meeting House '76 proposal also stressed
that the preserved buildings could help people experience the past firsthand.[4] Put another way, at that moment in time, the primary function of

historical sites like the meeting houses was transitioning from spaces of reflection upon the past to spaces of interaction *with* the past.

The Bicentennial Era saw a heightened interest in history on the part of many Americans, accompanied by new and different possibilities for historical engagement. This was ultimately expressed across many forms and formats, but many early endeavors involved the identification and preservation of historical structures and objects—the visible evidence of the past. Activities like these had long been the preeminent mode of learning about and interacting with the past, but in the late 1960s and early 1970s, the philosophies and processes that undergirded the fundamental principles of object-based historical engagement—what to collect, how to save it, where to house or exhibit it, and how to interpret it—were all in flux. Most critically, the role of historical objects in the formation of historical accounts and experiences was undergoing a significant transformation. I begin with building preservation because of its longer history and because it is one of the most documented and the most visible sites of these early developments, but changes in how Americans were conceiving of and going about identifying and saving historical structures had analogs in many other kinds of preservations.

In thinking through how histories are uncovered and how historical accounts are formed and presented, preservation is particularly important because it is the most traditional activity of historymaking. My definition of "preservation" here is purposefully broad: any form of historical engagement that involves recognizing or fixing an object as evidence of the past or that seeks to gain historical knowledge from something that has been recognized as a historical object. This characterization may seem broader than customary, but, in underscoring its range, I want to emphasize the similar assumptions that inform many seemingly disparate activities that together make up how we learn about and experience the past: building preservation, artifact collection, and oral history practices. The collection and exhibition of certain kinds of historical objects—documents, artifacts, and structures—has also played a major role in shaping historical narratives that legitimate and celebrate dominant ideologies. Recall the twin examples of the Declaration of Independence and the Constitution being housed at the National Archives from the previous chapter. Through the use of preservation to articulate ownership of material resources (both in the preserved object and in its storage and maintenance), the ideological import of the historical becomes evident.[5]

Although preservation has a long history, beginning in the late 1960s, in the context of changing assumptions about the past and the present, the purposes and processes of preservation were redefined as Americans became interested in new facets of the past and wanted to interact with this past in different ways. Meeting House '76 was one of many efforts that, with its emphasis on vernacular building and the importance of use, revealed how the very ideas that underwrote preservation were changing during this period. But endeavors ranging from the Weeksville Project in Brooklyn to Jesse Lemisch's Bicentennial Schlock collection all demonstrated the new ways that Americans were thinking about and engaging with the material evidence of the past.

Preservation Redefined

It is no coincidence that the earliest and most visible developments in the redefinition of preservation writ large occurred in the preservation of historical buildings, because this is one of the most established and recognized forms of public history practice. Many historians trace the impulse to protect individual structures to the 1850s preservation of Mount Vernon, the home of George Washington, by a group of socially prominent women who were dismayed by the deterioration of the first president's home.[6] For many years after, the identification and upkeep of historical buildings was for the most part the provenance of elites and functioned in a manner similar to many archival projects: as a means of demonstrating power by invoking the ownership and display of valuable objects.

Some critics have also argued that early preservation ventures were, like the Colonial Revival movement, a response to the rapid industrialization and immigration that changed life drastically in the late nineteenth and early twentieth centuries. Many, especially the native-born elite, felt that things were changing too quickly, desiring to at once slow these changes and, in the face of the increasing "foreign" influence in arts and culture, to promote native-born aesthetics and architecture.[7] And so, early preservationists selected houses that they felt were representative of patrician ideals of American history and culture.[8] The first criteria for historic preservation, introduced in 1935 by the Historic Sites Act and enforced through the National Park Service and later the National Trust for Historic Preservation, privileged sites that "sketch[ed] the large patterns of the American story" and that were "associated with the life of some great American" or with "some sudden or dramatic incident in American history."[9] Like other archival projects, building preservation helped to create a visible continuity between the nation's past and its present.[10]

But with the exception of some New Deal–era programming in which the Works Progress Administration (WPA) and the Civilian Conservation Corps (CCC) rehabilitated historic sites, the federal government ideologically sanctioned and supported elite endeavors to safeguard the best representations of American life and culture, but did not provide financial support. Most structure and site preservation occurred at the local or state level, despite attempts by the National Park Service to coordinate actions nationwide.[11] In 1949, Congress chartered the National Trust for Historic Preservation, recognizing and formalizing efforts already underway and increasing federal commitment to the preservation of aesthetically or historically significant properties.[12] The new organization would "preserve current examples of art and buildings as they represented each development in the present and future of the country, alongside the great monuments of the past."[13] According to criteria that recalled the standards from twenty years earlier, the National Trust chose buildings that had broad historical import, were identified with historic persons or events, or had architectural or landscape value.[14] Early targets included the Woodrow Wilson House in Washington, DC, and Shadows-on-the-Teche, an antebellum plantation in Louisiana. However, the federal mandate stopped at ownership, as Congress did not allot sufficient funds to the National Trust to rehabilitate these properties. Instead, preservation ventures were funded by wealthy private donors who could be said to have a vested interest in preserving structures that reflected their own class positions.[15]

Throughout the 1950s and 1960s, the National Trust, together with the Park Service, continued to spearhead attempts to centralize and coordinate preservation on the state and local levels. At the same time, massive postwar modernization was rapidly changing the landscape of American cities.[16] In the early days of urban renewal, many preservationists did not see a conflict between the impulse to preserve and the impulse to rebuild. As late as 1963, an issue of *Antiques* magazine had asked members of the preservation community: "Preservation and Urban Renewal: Is Coexistence Possible?" All answered in the affirmative, calling for cooperation between preservationists and urban planners for a "thoughtful transition between the old and new" and stressing the possibilities of adaptive reuse. One commentator went so far as to call urban renewal a "wolf in sheep's clothing," meaning that redevelopment could lead to opportunities for preservation. "Worthy" historic houses could be moved, or modern buildings could be built behind historic facades.[17] What is noteworthy here are the emphases on single structures and exterior forms. Historic houses, for this commentator and others quoted in the article, were meant to serve as visible evidence of material holdings and longevity.

While preservationists reconciled their desire to save historic buildings with support for urban renewal, others worried that preservation was a deterrent to postwar modernization. An editorial published in 1964 in the *Chicago Tribune* warned against preservation, noting that some urban renewal endeavors were already taking historic sites into account: "It is strange that an agency that is supposed to be devoted to slum clearance and better housing for the poor can divert its energies and funds to such matters as historic taverns and gold-rush towns, particularly under an administration as dedicated to warring on poverty as this one professes to be."[18] William Slayton, the commissioner of Urban Renewal under John F. Kennedy and Lyndon B. Johnson, reassured the *Tribune*, "No urban renewal funds are used in the restoration and rehabilitation of any structure. This is prohibited under the urban renewal legislature."[19] Federal funding privileged demolition and modernization, not the preservation of historic buildings.

The impetus for what came to be called "New Preservation" came from the National Trust and its partners, but this was a response to growing popular sentiment against many forms of urban renewal. By the mid-1960s, civic boosters and other local groups charged that redevelopment was obliterating older buildings.[20] A *Washington Post* columnist noted, "There is a revolt against the senseless indignity of urban freeways ruining cities and parks."[21] As activists complained about the lack of federal funding for preservation and rehabilitation, several widely read books further articulated mounting dissatisfaction with urban renewal, lamenting the disappearance of older urban sites essential to the creation and maintenance of communities. Books like Jane Jacobs's 1961 *The Death and Life of Great American Cities* and Martin Anderson's 1964 *The Federal Bulldozer* criticized urban renewal and celebrated older vernacular architecture. Their popularity revealed widespread awareness of history and spurred a concern with the protection of old buildings—specifically, old buildings that were evidence—not of important historical figures—but of communities.

As more Americans were becoming sensitive to the drawbacks of modernization, preservationists found new ways to advocate for historic buildings and places by linking their concerns with the thriving environmental movement, drawing upon connections that had originally been made between preservation and conservation by early Park Service representatives.[22] Stewart Udall, who served as secretary of the interior under John F. Kennedy, administered the National Park Service and helped bring new attention to conservation, blaming modernization and industrial development for the destruction of the natural environment.[23] Preservationists were quick to tie this to the rapid eradication of historic sites and structures. Faced with urban renewal on an immense scale, preservationists also began to look to groups of buildings as opposed to single structures, which made the language of conservation, with its emphasis on "total environments," a good fit. By 1965, Lyndon B. Johnson would include building preservationists in a special task force on "natural beauty."[24] The aesthetic and exterior values of historic buildings remained a central concern, but the new link to conservation was evidence of a changing focus.[25]

The 1966 passage of the National Historic Preservation Act consolidated earlier efforts at organized preservation on the federal level with state and local levels. The Department of the Interior, through the National Park Service, had maintained registers of historically important buildings since the 1930s, but as a result of the new legislation would now administer and grant funds through state liaisons and partnerships with local governments, creating new channels of cooperation and collaboration between the Park Service and other entities.[26] The 1966 act also provided support and transparency, allowing more people to become involved in preservation. With this increase in funding and communication, preservation became an enterprise that included all levels of government alongside nonstate entities such as preservation groups and real estate developers. As more Americans became critical of urban renewal and as preservation and conservation became connected in the popular imagination, the historic preservation community grew.

After the passage of the 1966 legislation, the network of preservation activists grew to include community organizers, environmentalists, and others.[27] By the beginning of the 1970s, even the nation's premier preservation organization, the National Trust, embraced a new vision. In October of 1972, the Trust proclaimed in an editorial in its own *Preservation News*, "Preservation Is People," followed by a catalog of all the different kinds of people (the list included "old people, young people, activists, appreciators, red, brown, yellow, white people, rich people, poor people") who were becoming involved in preservation efforts.[28] Through its newsletter and other publications, the National Trust shared information on obtaining funding, building organizations, and best practices. Throughout the decade, the Trust advocated for new collaborations between the government, cultural organizations, and private interests. This expanded the field of preservation, transferring attention from the object (the historical structure) to the subject—preservation became important not because of the protection of historic places but as a process of community building and historical meaning making.[29] By 1974, Arthur P. Ziegler, an activist in Pittsburgh, would write, in a manual entitled *Historic Preservation in Inner City Areas*, "Preservationists . . . are not fusty antediluvians busily preoccupied with genealogy or misty events of the past; they are committed citizens who want a healthy, interesting, useful and pleasing environment. They are worried about dirty air, befouled waterways, benighted bureaucracies, and the general ugliness and dehumanization of modern life. They will consign many hours of effort to improve the community."[30] Building preservation had once been a way to safeguard the visible evidence of a glorious past. Now it was a way to address contemporary problems.

The National Trust and other federal entities also widened their definitions of preservation-worthy structures. The 1973 version of the Trust's goals enlarged preservation's objects to "sites, buildings, structures, objects, and districts . . . the historic environment comprises areas where significant events have taken place; the cultural environment, areas where distinctive activities and patterns of life have occurred and remain."[31] As James Biddle, the president of the National Trust, wrote in the Bicentennial history of the organization, "Once the term 'preservation' meant saving and restoring buildings of national historical significance, turning them into museums where citizens could come for inspiration."[32] But "historical" buildings were no longer to be held separate from other ones. Biddle continued, "Only recently has the critical need to remember 'where we came from' became obvious to many of us. Only now are we beginning to see how greatly our future depends on our awareness of the past."[33] In the historic preservation community, as in other arenas of American life, the past had become an important part of the present.

From Exemplar to Experience

In a few short years, the organizational structures and the motivations surrounding building preservation changed significantly, in ways that both responded to and helped to further local preservation action. Rhode Island's Providence Preservation Society (PPS) was founded in 1956 in reaction to the deterioration of College Hill, a neighborhood filled with colonial-era residential houses in need of repair.[34] The organization's charter noted that PPS was "dedicated to the principle that the evidence of the past is an asset for the future. We realize that in order to protect our significant architectural legacy we must accept the responsibilities as well as the privileges which come with living in an old city."[35] By 1958, the PPS had been named a leading preservation organization by *Look* magazine and, through private funding and donations, had helped to save or restore several buildings. That same year, the PPS instituted an annual tour of historic houses in College Hill that publicized and raised funding for the society.[36] Echoing preservation criteria at the time, early tours highlighted the architectural details of colonial houses. For example, a house might be described thus: "the lintel-shaped blocks of the downstairs window caps and the upper window caps which are part of the eaves cornice are characteristic detail of eighteenth-century building style."[37] The building preservation community at this time was still rather insular; the audience for public programming was assumed to have prior architectural and historical knowledge.

The PPS continued to have a major impact on the revival of College Hill through the 1960s by working with homeowners and private interests to renovate, rehabilitate, and, in some cases, even relocate houses in the area.[38] A consequence of these ventures was the displacement of older, working-class African American and Cape Verdean communities from the area, as inflating real estate prices made affordable housing more scarce.[39] Preservation in Providence, as elsewhere, gained new prominence at that time, but, for the majority of the 1960s, ventures were spearheaded by local elites and remained fixed upon single homes, exteriors, and—especially in New England—the colonial era.

In the 1970s, the PPS changed along the general trajectory of other efforts, encouraging new ways of thinking about and interacting with historical structures. The PPS discontinued the annual historic house tour in 1971, instead introducing regular tours that emphasized the social and political history of the eighteenth and nineteenth centuries, showcasing groups of buildings to paint a broader picture of life in the past.[40] Between 1974 and 1975, income from the tours increased by 400 percent, indicating wider interest in history in general and in the built environment in particular.[41]

In the first years of the decade, the PPS had also begun to concentrate on Providence's downtown. Alongside the eighteenth-century houses that had been the focus of the previous decade's activities, the organization began to look to nineteenth-century and early twentieth-century department stores, hotels, and the train station, all of which were falling into disrepair. To help people get a sense of their built environment, in 1972 the PPS released a self-guided tour called "City Exploration," which directed tour goers to: "participate in the tensions of the city walls. The interplay of old and new building shapes. Compare old and new. Feel their difference with your hands and eyes. Feel the space, the boundaries of that space and looking up, record the different qualities of the city walls."[42] The guides contained no architectural information and invited visitors to make their own meaning. Preservation in Providence, as elsewhere, was turning toward the environmental and the experiential.

In 1976, to celebrate the Bicentennial, the PPS published two new guides that encouraged self-directed and immersive historical engagement in learning about everyday life in the past.[43] The first of these guides, *Looking Up Downtown*, produced in conjunction with several downtown Providence businesses, painted a vivid picture of the past: "The next five buildings on your left formed the heart of the shopping district at the turn of the century, when countless Gibson-girl Victorian ladies with sweeping skirts and plumed hats filled Westminster Street, shopping and socializing, and meeting at the Shepard's clock for lunch."[44] *Explore Historic Providence!* highlighted buildings and commercial structures in College Hill, with language that again directed tourists not to individual structures, but to the ambiance of the area: "Walk along North Main to Thomas Street, the site of several handsome houses built shortly after the Meeting House. They suggest how a prosperous Rhode Islander lived in the later 18th century. As you continue along North Main, imagine both sides of the street lined with wood frame houses of a plainer sort, as it would have been in 1776 . . . this end bustled with homes and shops."[45] This is a far cry from "the lintel-shaped blocks of the downstairs window" that had described the same structures in 1958. The PPS was only one of countless local organizations that continued to transform throughout the 1960s and 1970s, but it was among the most active and, by the time of the Bicentennial, had embraced new notions of preservation. *Looking Up Downtown* and *Explore Historic Providence!* aimed to create spatial historical ambience in a larger context, pointing out landscape elements as well as the structures they surrounded and inviting audiences to imagine buildings and streetscapes as they had looked in the past.[46]

Ambient and immersive historical space became a focal point of New Preservation, particularly in cities that anticipated significant tourism as part of the upcoming Bicentennial. In Boston, the city government worked with several local historical societies to rebuild prominent buildings along the city's Freedom Trail walking tour, so that visitors could better imagine themselves in the Boston of the Revolutionary era. The Freedom Trail included sites like the location of the Boston Massacre, the Boston Harbor, and Paul Revere's house. Boston 200, the local organization tasked with coordinating Bicentennial programming, saw the importance of historical ambiance: "The sixteen sites [the Freedom Trail] joins together are important not simply because of their age or architectural significance . . . they can call to mind the turmoil and the richness of life in that community of 16,000 at the time of the Revolution." Pitting old against New Preservation, Boston 200 identified outmoded "custodial" preservation principles as a specific barrier to change. The group's proposal for improvements spoke of "making history alive and meaningful" by emphasizing the act of walking through all of these locations and reliving the beginnings of the Revolution from the perspective of Boston's "community of 16,000."[47] The consortium of sites that made up the Freedom Trail moved away from thinking about individual locations that were to be admired and protected, beginning instead to focus upon the interconnectedness of the sites and the experience of moving among and between them. In facilitating this conversion, Boston 200 used language that made evident the transition from old preservation to new.

The Afro-American Bicentennial Corporation

While organizations like the Providence Preservation Society had been active for several years prior to the activity boom that followed the passage of the 1966 National Historic Preservation Act, many groups formed in response to growing popular awareness of preservation and fresh opportunities for funding. Two brothers in Washington, DC, Vincent DeForest and Robert DeForrest (the variance in spelling reflected and symbolized their separate upbringings in foster homes before reuniting as young adults), veterans of the Southern Christian Leadership Conference (SCLC) in Atlanta, created the Afro-American Bicentennial Corporation (ABC) in 1970.[48] Like Jeremy Rifkin's People's Bicentennial Commission, the ABC was modeled upon, and established as a result of deficiencies in, the American Revolution Bicentennial Commission (ARBC), which planned painfully few programs that addressed African American experiences or contributions.[49] DeForest and DeForrest recognized the inadequacies of the Bicentennial celebration, but saw it as an opportunity to encourage African Americans to find relevance in the past. In statements to the press and the public, the brothers underscored this goal: "most blacks probably won't be parading around or singing songs . . . blacks will be asking questions and considering their status in this country since 1776. The Bicentennial must be viewed through the eyes of the beholder. Don't be turned off by it, consider what it means to you."[50] For the brothers, the new sense of history that was beginning to characterize the Bicentennial and American culture at large was an opportunity to highlight the African American experience.

The ABC looked to the entire duration of U.S. history, not just that of the colonial period.[51] The brothers felt strongly that they needed to rebuild a trajectory of African American involvement and achievement to combat the omission and erasure that not only spanned from the founding moment, but also over the last two hundred years. As Vincent DeForest said, "We have to make sure the events commemorated are not just Jamestown, Lexington, and Trenton, but also Nat Turner, the experience and creative expression of the blues, the hopes of Reconstruction and the March on Selma."[52] With these interventions, the ABC enlarged the temporal dimensions of the commemoration, a development that echoed other reinterpretations of the Bicentennial as it moved away from a celebration of a single anniversary to a consideration of all of the American past, both distant and recent.

But in order to create the conditions for realization and contemplation, the ABC first had to find, save, and bring attention to evidence of the rich history of the African American experience. The ABC's earliest initiatives responded to the New Preservation movement and the opportunities accorded by increased federal support for building and site preservation. While some homes of notable African Americans (for example, Frederick Douglass's home, Cedar Hill, in Washington, DC) were maintained and open to the public, DeForest and DeForrest discovered that of three thousand buildings and sites designated as landmarks on the National Register of Historic Places and maintained by the National Park Service, only five of these were associated with African American history.[53] Working with archival records and partnering with historic preservation groups in their hometown of Washington, DC, the brothers searched for sites that could be added to the National Register, addressing the disparity of representation. Although many historical structures, especially those in urban areas, had been demolished during the urban renewal projects of the 1960s, others still remained but had to be located, identified, and researched.[54]

The brothers searched for traces of black work, entrepreneurship, schooling, and bodies themselves in order to reconstruct a more inclusive archive that foregrounded the experience and contribution of African Americans. Unlike earlier African American preservation efforts, which had often focused upon individuals of note, DeForest and DeForrest were looking for documentation of black communities. While some of this information could be uncovered using land records, deeds, and other official forms of documentation, the brothers also sought the help of contemporary communities, requesting "old photos, books, or other materials which will help to illustrate both the work and social life of the early Black inhabitants of our nation's capital."[55]

The ABC's activities fit within and expressed the mandates of New Preservation, but they also functioned to redress previous and ongoing inequalities, particularly those, like segregation and redlining, that continue into the present and operate on a spatial register. If part of the project of segregation had been to render African Americans invisible in the public sphere, the space of political and cultural participation, the search for spaces of black community had an extra resonance. The ABC wanted to show that, in the face of intense legal actions to reduce and narrow the public visibility and activity of African Americans, places like homes, churches, black-owned businesses, and historically black schools and colleges had existed and flourished, helping to build and nurture vibrant communities.[56] By exercising power over their physical movement, segregation had attempted to eradicate African Americans as public actors. The ABC's discoveries would demonstrate that, despite those restrictions, spaces of African American community had always been present.[57] The *act* of preservation, of finding and identifying the places of African American experience, marked out space in ways that were directly oppositional to how segregation had functioned.

The ABC made extensive use of federal granting opportunities to fund their endeavors, securing support from the Departments of Interior and Housing and Urban Development, ARBA, and the Rockefeller Foundation as they worked to recover tangible evidence of African American history. Through a $250,000 contract with the Park Service, DeForest and DeForrest located landmarks significant to black history in the Washington area. This survey would "ensure that we project a truthful interpretation of the American heritage through . . . inclusion of the sizeable, but relatively unknown Afro-American contribution."[58] The brothers uncovered sites that included Civil War–era contraband schools in northern Virginia, sites associated with the life of Sojourner Truth, and traces of Mount Vernon construction and maintenance by African Americans. The ABC did its own archival work in order to counter histories that had rendered historically black spaces, as they had African Americans themselves, invisible.

The ABC had been formed in the context of controversies surrounding another preservation action in Washington, DC, one that illuminates the ongoing relationship between historical preservation and political power. Because the District of Columbia was then (and remains now) a federal city, many decisions about municipal resources were (and continue to be) legislated by the federal government. Even as DeForest and DeForrest researched locations significant to black history, agents from the Nixon administration and the federal government worked to refurbish the section of Pennsylvania Avenue within the federal quarter of Washington while blocking attempts to reconstruct the "riot corridors" of 14th and H Streets, despite objections from local politicians and constituencies.[59] Washington's African American community, which had been disproportionately affected by the uprisings following Martin Luther King Jr.'s death in April 1968, protested the renovation of Pennsylvania Avenue at the expense of 14th Street, as well as other infrastructure projects like the new Metro subway system, scheduled to be completed in time for the influx of tourists expected for the Bicentennial celebrations.[60] This particular conflict shows the continuous connection between preservation and power, and how these impulses are played out on the built environment: the preserved building as a representation of sovereignty, stability, and order. The ABC's efforts to mark out spaces of black community worked in opposition to those of the Nixon administration, but each mobilized preservation's monumental capacities—the ability of visible structures to communicate the significance of the past and its enduring relationship with the present.

The ABC's most significant undertaking involved the restoration of the graveyard of the Female Union Band Cemetery of the Mount Zion United Methodist Church in the Georgetown neighborhood of Washington, DC. Mount Zion was the first African American congregation in the District, having been organized in 1814. The Female Union Band Society, a cooperative benevolent association of free African American women,

Mount Zion in disrepair, 1975. The Afro-American Bicentennial Corporation mobilized to help save this historic cemetery in Washington's Georgetown neighborhood. Courtesy of the Library of Congress, Historical American Landscapes Survey (HALS DC-15).

had purchased a three-acre plot adjacent to the church burial ground in 1842. Over the next century, hundreds of community members were buried there, but by the 1950s, the Union Band Society could no longer afford upkeep of the cemetery, and the DC government prohibited further internment.[61] The land had been bought by a developer and was in the process of being rezoned as a residential area when descendants of the Union Band used deeds to the plots of their ancestors to file paperwork with the District Court to halt development.

The ABC mobilized its media and government contacts to champion this cause, proposing a renovation of the cemetery and the establishment there of a cultural center tracing the history of African Americans in Georgetown. DeForest and DeForrest underscored a visceral interaction with the past, arguing, "Black people need to be able to touch and see their history."[62] The local press followed the court case, which eventually resulted in a ruling in favor of the descendants of the Union Band and an important victory for

DeForest and DeForrest. The legal conflict over the cemetery resembled other urban renewal battles, but this one was fought and won on the register of history. The Mount Zion Cemetery case illustrates how preservation endeavors often came up directly against redevelopment and how they helped to establish a genealogy of black history, in this case, literally with the remains of the former congregants of the Mount Zion United Methodist Church.[63]

By 1975, DeForest and DeForrest had added fourteen sites to the National Register and started searching outside of the boundaries of the Washington area, investigating, among other places, the historically black town of Boley, Oklahoma, which had been incorporated in 1903 as a "haven from oppression."[64] The archival and preservation work of the ABC, supported by substantial funding from the federal government, yielded real results that began to address some of the inequalities inherent in traditional accounts of American history. The ABC persevered beyond the Bicentennial, becoming the Afro-American Institute for Historic Preservation and Community Development.[65] The link between the past and the present and how it coalesced around the physical and spatial is evident in the choice of name for the new organization. The brothers' ongoing project traced a history of black property ownership that, in the context of continued restrictive practices like redlining and busing, had very real effects in the present.

Initiatives in other cities likewise strove to uncover visible evidence of African American life and history. In the Crown Heights neighborhood of Brooklyn, a coalition of preservationists, scholars, and community members launched an undertaking that was emblematic of many of the mandates of New Preservation. In 1968, James Hurley, an instructor of African American history at the Pratt Institute, and Joseph Haynes, a professional pilot who had grown up in Crown Heights, became curious about the location of what had once been Hunterfly Road, the center of a free black community called Weeksville, which had flourished in the mid-to-late nineteenth century, but was, by the 1960s, all but forgotten.[66] By flying over the area, Hurley and Haynes were able to pinpoint four houses that remained from the historic community. When, the following year, the houses were threatened with demolition by the New York Housing Authority, the community sprang into action. Hurley, along with neighborhood activists William Harley, Joan Maynard, and others (including a troop of Boy Scouts, faculty and students from Pratt and Brooklyn Community College, and schoolchildren at P.S. 243, the school that stood adjacent to the property) went looking for artifacts on the property and found, among other things, a pamphlet from a nineteenth-century group called the Abyssinian Daughters of Esther and a tintype photograph of an unidentified African American woman, who they called the "Weeksville Lady."[67] They petitioned the New York City Landmarks Commission and had the structures declared as local landmarks.

In 1971, community members founded the Society for the Preservation of Weeksville and Bedford-Stuyvesant History and concentrated on raising money for the purchase and restoration of the buildings. Students from P.S. 243, which would be renamed the Weeksville School, held a fair that raised nearly a thousand dollars. In years following, the society hosted fundraising dinners featuring guests like Alex Haley, the author of *Roots*.[68] Weeksville's preservation began as, and continued to be, a community enterprise, allowing for many new people to get involved in building and site preservation. The rediscovery of Weeksville was important because it established the history of a thriving black community in Brooklyn, becoming a place of pride for its contemporary residents.[69] By the mid-1970s, building preservation had changed radically: rather than an effort to preserve single structures that had exceptional aesthetic value or that were associated with famous Americans, an increasing and diverse population of activists looked to save groups of buildings that could help uncover new histories, making connections between communities of the past and communities of the present. While established organizations like the National Trust recognized and worked within this change, many new groups, like the ABC and the Weeksville Society, helped propel this shift forward.

Preservation *as* People: New Oral Histories

For the National Trust, the slogan "Preservation Is People" meant the democratization of building preservation, but, in other ways, preservation literally *was* people, as oral history initiatives that documented the lives of everyday people expanded. Historical preservation in Weeksville grew beyond the discovery and safeguarding of structures: these activities were undertaken in tandem with other acts of preservation. As part of the recovery of the lost history of Weeksville in the early 1970s, the Society for the Preservation of Weeksville and Bedford-Stuyvesant History worked with Mary Ann Brown from the neighboring Medgar Evers College to launch an oral history project that would document the lives and experiences of African Americans in central Brooklyn. Between 1970 and 1973, representatives from the Weeksville Society, including Joan Maynard, James Hurley, William Harley, and others, spoke with elderly residents of Crown Heights and Bedford-Stuyvesant. The interviewees included descendants of Weeksville residents from the 1860s, the first black public school teacher in Brooklyn, and a ninety-five-year-old woman who remembered going to see speeches by the African American leader Marcus Garvey.[70] The interviews revealed what maps and documents could not: the experience of living in Weeksville, the timbre of everyday life there, and the complex networks and relationships among Weeksville residents. Along with the houses on Hunterfly Road, and the artifacts that had been found within, these interviews restored an important part of African American history.

Like building preservation, oral history moved notions of historical evidence from the object to the experience, a shift that confirmed an escalating desire on the part of many to understand the feelings, not just the facts, of the past. In the 1970s, oral history was part of a preservation impetus that shared, across myriad forms, many of the same assumptions about the importance of the past to understanding the present. Like some early building preservation, oral history had its roots in the New Deal, but by the 1970s, the practice experienced a resurgence. The Oral History Association reported that between 1965 and 1973, the number of current oral history projects jumped from eighty-nine to over three hundred, as universities, historical societies, and community groups launched new oral history endeavors.[71] Just as sites and structures associated with many different groups and individuals were now being preserved, oral histories became essential to documenting the experience of ordinary people and the everyday past, a development paralleled and informed by shifts in scholarly history.

After the landmark Works Progress Administration (WPA) oral history projects carried out during the New Deal, oral history centers had been established at Columbia University and other institutions throughout the 1940s and 1950s, but these for the most part collected accounts from politicians and other prominent individuals. Oral histories in this context documented well-known historical events, complementing information held in existing political archives. In the 1970s, oral history expanded to include the experience of people from all walks of life. During this decade, oral histories of former slaves collected by the WPA became central to scholarship that examined the experience of the enslaved.[72] Oral historian Studs Terkel's work on the Great Depression and labor in the United States found widespread popularity, indicating the growing currency of first-person experience and testimony.[73] Many of these ventures coincided with and expressed academic efforts to account for the histories and experiences of individuals on the margins of society and resulted in activity that moved these historical imperatives out of the academy and into communities.[74]

Many individuals and organizations undertook oral histories as part of the Bicentennial celebration, as local communities began using the commemoration as an opportunity to consider their own pasts. Boston 200 developed a "Neighborhoods" program, in which local students were hired to interview elderly residents of twenty-seven Boston neighborhoods, collecting oral histories that would be gathered in a series of booklets highlighting each neighborhood as well as presented in modular exhibits in local libraries.[75] In Seattle, the Washington State Division of Archives and Records Management launched the Oral-Aural History Program of Washington State. Led by Esther Hall Mumford, a community activist and local historian, representatives interviewed nearly three hundred respondents from African American and Filipino communities in Washington State, generating three thousand pages of transcripts.[76] For Mumford, this was a transformative experience, and even after the completion of the original program, she continued to work with community members to gather more information, eventually generating several books on black history in Seattle.[77]

As a form of history practice, oral history gained prominence because many of its mandates coincided with scholarly and popular interest in the everyday experience of actors on the periphery of standard accounts. Oral histories brought the past into the present and often resulted in emotional revelations from those interviewed. At the same time, interviewers were also often profoundly affected, as indicated by the extensive body of methodological literature related to this complex relationship and by experiences like Mumford's.[78] For interviewees, participating in oral history programs could be life-affirming and identity-building exercises that, through the process of recognition and testimony, led to concrete activism; there are many examples of community oral history fueling housing protests, labor action, and other kinds of political involvement.[79]

The growth of oral history at that time was part of an intervention in the archive that extended the definition of evidence and artifact while working to increase access. For the community activists in Weeksville, the oral histories they conducted helped to document the experiences of its residents. The four buildings on Hunterfly Road and the artifacts found within were important pieces of evidence about the people who had once lived there, but the accompanying oral histories placed them in the context of a lived experience, making connections between the past and the present. Writing in the preface to *Seven Stars and Orion*, one of the books that

emerged from her work in Seattle, Esther Hall Mumford v
the importance of the accounts that she was collecting: "B
ries are largely unwritten, there is a tendency to view th
Americans and of ordinary people of all races as of n'
She continued, "In my growing-up years, no subject wa₃ .
than history. In the South . . . history was used aggressively. It w₌
important weapon in the campaign to impose white racial superiority."
Mumford's own work added other voices and other experiences to the archive, creating an account that was more inclusive and that countered the
claim that ordinary lives and people were "of no real importance." Oral history practitioners likewise speak about the importance of documentation
and of saving transcripts and recordings for future researchers, for whom
a sense of everyday life in a past historical moment might prove to be in-
valuable. Public use is also a key tenet of oral history; practitioners com-
monly affirm that an oral history does not become an oral history until it is
available to the public in some form.[81] With these frameworks, oral histories in the 1960s and 1970s became a vital means of democratizing the archive, of opening up to new modes and sources of documentation and
evidence, and of expanding the field of who should be part of the record of
history, and how that history might be used.[82]

New Collections

New Preservation and the expansion of oral history were part of larger
changes that were occurring across many fronts of historymaking in the
1970s. In the same way that building preservation began to emphasize more
recent and vernacular structures, institutions and individuals looked to different kinds of artifacts. Many museums broadened their collecting programs to include contemporary and current objects—for example, the
Smithsonian's Division of Political Life sent curators to the Republican and
Democratic National Conventions in order to collect memorabilia, and they
reached out to the Black Panther Party and other contemporary political
groups in an effort to include their stories.[83] Like buildings and memories,
the objects that were now being deemed "worth saving" were increasingly
associated with everyday life and contemporary experience.

While some started collecting evidence of contemporary politics, others
started thinking about the collection as a political process. As part of a course he
was teaching, Jesse Lemisch, a lecturer in American studies at the State University of New York in Buffalo, began gathering Bicentennial memorabilia

a collection he called "Bicentennial Schlock." Lemisch (who inci-
dentally had popularized the phrase "history from the bottom up" in 1967
brochure for Students for a Democratic Society) wanted his students to
consider how Americans were commemorating their history, foregrounding
interactions with consumer culture as a way to make meaning.[84] Lemisch's
collection, eventually exhibited at SUNY-Buffalo and then archived at
Yale's Sterling Library, included commemorative dishes, clothing, posters,
and every other kind of Bicentennial ephemera available, both "official" (i.e.,
sanctioned by ARBA) and not.[85] Lemisch and his students selected objects
(commemorative toilet paper, beer cans, hamburger wrappers) that were
contemporary, ephemeral, and that were uniformly deemed to be in bad
taste, contrary to older practices of archiving only historically and aesthetically significant objects.

The critiques of official commemoration that underpinned this project
were similar to those made by Jeremy Rifkin and the People's Bicentennial
Commission, echoing widespread indignation over the commercialization
of the Bicentennial that was circulating in the press and the public at that
time.[86] By collecting Bicentennial objects and putting them in a new context, Lemisch and his class hoped to underscore the banality of the commemoration and how it had been orchestrated by state and corporate
interests. Writing later for the *New Republic*, Lemisch stated that the souvenirs that made up his collection "floated down from above, and responded
to no popular longing to celebrate the Bicentennial." He continued, "Bicentennial Schlock was, in a sense, the Watergate of patriotism: a healthy de-
mystification which makes us wisely cynical and distrustful of many things
that we should have been distrustful of before."[87] Bicentennial ephemera,
in Lemisch's eyes, represented the government's (i.e., ARBA's) and capitalist
culture's continued ownership and control over the expression of history.
But the Bicentennial Schlock collection also showed that this control
was no longer entirely possible, precisely because the destabilization of
the meanings of the past had made room for critiques like Lemisch's, and
because activities associated with preservation—choosing and saving historical artifacts—had moved outside of institutions and into communities.

Bicentennial Schlock demonstrated the way that collecting was changing at this moment: both how and why objects were acquired, and how they
were used in exhibitions to make meaning. Lemisch used archival practice,
long a way of demonstrating power, as a critique of power—building a collection not to uphold state hegemony, but to question it.[88] The collection
started out in the classroom but soon gained widespread notice. Several

newspapers reported on Lemisch's collection, suggesting the cultural resonance of the venture: Bicentennial Schlock was understood and applauded by an audience far outside the world of universities and museums, who were becoming accustomed to thinking about the past and the production of history in new ways.[89] As Lemisch stated, "After a long year of American history Disneyfied and cartoonified, historians may have a harder time selling an overly deferential view of some of the heroes of our past."[90] In calling attention to what he saw as the dangers of such expressions of history, and arguably by removing the memorabilia from the original context of its use and circulation, Lemisch attempted to create a space for reflection. Bicentennial Schlock signaled the increased availability of preservation activity as a form of politicized intervention.

Preservation projects of different kinds, many undertaken in support of the Bicentennial celebration, revealed larger transformations in how Americans were understanding and interacting with history. While structural preservation initiatives created ambient historical spaces for the immersive experience of the past, oral history emerged as a means of discovering and preserving the history of an enlarged field of subjects and experiences. Projects like Bicentennial Schlock made the politicized potential of collecting explicit. All of these ventures foregrounded not only new forms of evidence (vernacular buildings, oral testimony, souvenir kitsch), but also expressed a new impulse toward immersion, whether it was connecting with and within historic sites and structures, or privileging historic accounts that recalled the past in subjective, personal terms. As the Bicentennial Era continued, the position of the artifact and the purpose of preservation continued to change.

The emphases that undergirded the Meeting House '76 program reveal the developments occurring in preservation writ large at that time: an interest in new kinds of structures, in the role of history in community building, and in personalized encounters with the past. But despite early enthusiasm, Meeting House '76 never came to be, and, within a few short years, the ARBC, its succeeding organization, the ARBA, and other state agencies like the National Park Service had transferred their resources and efforts into projects that indicated the development of an immersive and experiential sense of history as the decade progressed. Although federal groups invested substantial funding in the program in the early years of Bicentennial planning, by 1975, ARBA's promotion of Meeting House '76 had all but disappeared, and its proponents actively sought backing from other public and private sources.[91]

The ARBC's initial support of Meeting House '76 occurred at a transitional moment in the way that state and institutional agents were understanding and responding to heightened public attention to history. In the space of a few short years, focus would swing to endeavors that used preserved artifacts in entirely different ways, or not at all. Historic preservation was one of the first sites at which the transformation in historical consciousness became evident, but ultimately, precisely because forms of engagement were shifting away from preservation of the material and toward the creation of the experiential, state support moved to other kinds of history activity. While building preservation remained a significant mode of popular interaction with the past, by the time of the Bicentennial, it was no longer the primary target of state interests. Instead, ARBA and other agencies were publicizing projects in which historical meaning making occurred through immersion and reenactment.

CHAPTER FOUR

The Spaces of History
Museums, Interactivity, and Immersion

> The National Museum of History and Technology tells the story
> of America and studies the story of America. From household
> goods the colonists brought from their native lands—to weapons,
> military and otherwise that made them free—to technology that
> helped make them wealthy and strong—to memorabilia of men
> and women who led them—the museum's collections comprise a
> tangible biography of the Republic. The depth and scope of these
> collections are unparalleled.

> —SMITHSONIAN INSTITUTION OFFICE OF PUBLIC AFFAIRS,
> *Increase and Diffusion: A Brief Introduction to the Smithsonian
> Institution*, 1970

> The National Museum of History and Technology recaptures and
> interprets the American experience from colonial times to the
> present; from man's basic needs for food, clothing, and shelter, to
> modern social and technological developments. It chronicles the
> lives of the men and women who have contributed to America's
> heritage, and relates two centuries of progress in political, cultural,
> and military history, industries, applied arts, and science and
> technology.

> —SMITHSONIAN INSTITUTION OFFICE OF PUBLIC AFFAIRS,
> *Increase and Diffusion: A Brief Introduction to the Smithsonian
> Institution*, 1975

The quotes above are taken from two editions, published five years apart,
of a pamphlet introducing visitors to the museums of the Smithsonian
Institution.[1] They open the section describing the National Museum of
History and Technology (since 1980, the National Museum of American
History), the nation's primary repository of historical artifacts, and its
most prominent history museum. Both passages convey the same general
information: each outlines the museum's mission and indicates the nature
of its holdings. However, the transformation in language between the two

is striking: while the 1970 edition begins by noting that the museum *tells the story of America and studies the story of America*, by 1975, the museum's activities are explained in radically different terms: the National Museum of History and Technology *recaptures and interprets the American experience*. The earlier account discusses historical knowledge production in terms of narrative information, the second suggests experiential engagement. The remainders of each description likewise diverge: the first focuses on collections, evidence, and artifacts that have been left behind by people of the past, the second centers on those people themselves and their experiences.

During this period, history museums, called by Mike Wallace "the institution perhaps most explicitly devoted to nourishing historic sensibility and acting as trustees of the public memory," were changing their interpretation and representation of history.[2] While some museums began using historical artifacts to create immersive spaces that fostered an experiential perception of history, others worked to elicit in visitors the feeling of "being there" without objects—instead, interactive media and live interpreters helped audiences both see and sense the past. This chapter examines developments at the Smithsonian and other "spaces of history": the museum exhibition, the historic site, and the living history museum. At all of these spaces, curators were both responding to and helping to activate new ways of understanding and using the past.

Feeling the Past at the Smithsonian

Although the Smithsonian had been staging history exhibitions since the 1881 opening of the U.S. National Museum, a new Museum of History and Technology was opened in 1964. During the postwar period, art and culture became important components of American diplomacy, gaining additional financial support from state sources. Alongside the National Historic Preservation Act, this era saw the passage of such legislation as the 1966 National Museum Act and the establishment of the National Endowment for the Humanities and the National Endowment of the Arts. The Smithsonian, as one of the foremost cultural organizations in the country, was a major beneficiary of funding, and as a state-sponsored institution had a special role in the creation and maintenance of an ideology of American exceptionalism.[3] As historian Will Walker notes, the Museum of History and Technology was meant to trace a teleological history perfectly in line with the Cold War atmosphere in which American technological and cultural ad-

Objects on Pedestals: "Growth of the United States," which opened in 1967 at the Smithsonian's Museum of History and Technology. Courtesy of the Smithsonian Institution Archives (image number SIA2010-3463).

vancement was held up as a model to the rest of the world.[4] As Walker details, the Museum of History and Technology was even called a "Palace of Progress" by the *Washington Star*: the purpose of the museum was to show Americans and the rest of the world the extraordinary evolution of the United States.[5]

Inside the museum, exhibitions highlighted objects from the Smithsonian's extensive collections using a variety of display techniques to showcase the artifacts that illustrated the American past. The first and third floors were filled with taxonomical displays of coins, stamps, glassware, and other collections, including the ever-popular gowns of the First Ladies, arranged on mannequins that were grouped in period-appropriate representations of White House rooms. In these exhibits, which had names like "The Vehicle Hall" or "The Hall of Ceramics," visitors could gaze upon progressively more complex rows of combines, automobiles, ceramics, or even locomotives. These artifacts, for the most part, were allowed to "speak for themselves"; they were accompanied by small informational labels and grouped together upon large platforms in the museum's modern interiors.[6]

Two exhibits on the second floor, "Everyday Life in the American Past," and "Growth of the United States, 1640–1851" (both opened in 1967), showed that curators (most notably C. Malcolm Watkins, who had come to the Smithsonian from the living history museum Old Sturbridge Village, and Anthony Garvan, of the University of Pennsylvania's Department of American Civilization) were becoming more interested in social history and new archaeological and anthropological methods in material culture studies.[7] Both of these exhibits made an effort to show collections in relation to their historical environments. While at the entrance to "Growth of the United States," tools and other objects were accompanied by images of them in use, "Everyday Life in the American Past" included a series of period rooms containing furniture, decoration, and even artificial foodstuffs. These rooms showed audience members a sense of the larger context of historical objects as well as an idea of what the past might have looked like. At the same time, audiences were barred from entering, and so the rooms prompted from visitors observation and even a kind of reverence, as opposed to engagement.[8] These exhibits, which reflected, in the words of Smithsonian curator Robert C. Post, the beginnings of an institutional shift from "object" to "concept," were turning points in the way that museums understood the past: although they attempted to tell the stories of ordinary people as opposed to famous Americans, and to display artifacts in context, they still related a history that emphasized progress, growth, and continuous forward development over time.[9]

By 1976, the Bicentennial year, "Growth of the United States" was replaced with a new exhibition called "A Nation of Nations," which began to forge different relationships between audience and artifact. While the earlier exhibition had centered upon the history and experience of European Americans, "A Nation of Nations" highlighted the diverse groups that made up the American past and present, encouraging audience members to look for themselves within these histories. Like previous exhibits at the museum, "A Nation of Nations" used objects to tell the stories of everyday Americans. But, unlike those other exhibits, some portions of "A Nation of Nations" were interactive: rather than looking at period rooms and settings, visitors could sit on a bench from Ellis Island and consider how it might have felt to be an immigrant. In another section, they could use a short-wave radio to listen to transmissions from the past.[10] As a review for the exhibit noted with admiration, "A Nation of Nations is an exhibit that you can see, hear, smell, and play games with."[11] In the space of a few years, the exhibits at the National Museum of History and Technology not only looked very different but also evoked entirely new participation and meaning making from their audiences. These exhibits both modeled and encouraged histories that were personal rather than representative.

"A Nation of Nations" was one component of the Smithsonian's overall Bi-centennial programming, and it was notable because it invited visitor knowledge production through interactivity. But National Museum of History and Technology curators, led by project manager William Miner, also mounted an exhibition entitled "1876" that, by re-creating the look as well as the *feel* of the Philadelphia Centennial World Exposition, went even further in inviting sensory engagement. This exhibition was not at the museum itself, but in the historic Arts and Industries Building across the Mall, the former home of the Smithsonian's nineteenth-century National Museum. Because the Arts and Industries Building was much smaller in scale than the original site of the exposition, curators chose to reproduce just one segment of the 1876 installation: a trade fair portion that displayed new innovations in machinery, farming, and enterprise.[12] The *Centennial Post*, a mock newspaper distributed to exhibition visitors, explained, "The aim throughout has been to return to the Centennial, not to show the Centennial from the perspective of 100 years later."[13] Working from photographic documentation of the original Philadelphia Centennial exhibits, curators packed vitrines and stands with artifacts, creating displays that replicated the overstuffed Victorian aesthetic.

In contrast to the customary museum practice of isolating objects with individual labels, here were groups of objects with minimal identificatory panels of text. The displays at "1876" were more like tableaux, depicting, for example, the agricultural and industrial products of a selection of states, professional tools from dentists and druggists, military ephemera, and farm machinery.[14] As in the original exposition and like the sixties-era exhibits at the Museum of History and Technology, the effect stressed the rapid development of American industry and fostered an understanding of the nineteenth century as an era in which technology improved the quality of life. But here, this display and its aesthetics were consciously of the past, and the message was conveyed not through the arrangement of artifacts, but through the form of the exhibition itself.

The choice of the Centennial Exposition as a subject for a Bicentennial exhibit addressed national celebration in a historical context but, more significantly, that *mode* of celebration itself was, in that moment, being relegated to the past. International expositions had enjoyed immense popularity through the end of the nineteenth century and the first half of the twentieth, a time when the United States was eager to present to the world

Celebrating a century: The Smithsonian's 1976 re-creation of the 1876 Centennial Exposition. Courtesy of the Smithsonian Institution Archives (image number 77-3205).

its astonishing technological and imperial progress. Through highly structured, almost ceremonial display, international expositions placed American innovation and material bounty alongside that of other countries, inviting comparisons about which nations were the most advanced, the most "civilized." Between the 1870s and the 1940s, millions of Americans attended world's fairs in dozens of cities across the United States where they saw new inventions, crafts, traditions, and people from all over the world. As Robert Rydell has argued, the international expositions had expressed and organized American progress for a domestic audience that was proud of their own country and curious about the rest of the world. Through this spectacularization, the world's fairs mirrored ideologies of constant development and improvement associated with Western industrialization and expansion—which were, by the early 1970s, on the wane.[15]

In 1964, it had been possible for critics to call the Museum of History and Technology a "Palace of Progress," because the exhibits within had presented an object-heavy, teleological historical narrative that echoed those of the international expositions. In fact, the same year had seen one of the last world's fairs in New York City. But by the 1970s, America's lead in technological innovation and geopolitical dominance was more tenuous than it had been in previous decades. The international exposition, as an index and celebration of that progress, had become a more questionable form of display, as can be seen from the failure of the 1976 Philadelphia International Exposition originally planned as the central event of the Bicentennial. However, in the new past-attuned cultural milieu, it was now possible to focus on the *history* of this formerly great tradition, to raise questions about the nature of the world's fair mode of organizing information and its brand of nationalist celebration, which institutions like the Smithsonian had adapted. Indeed, Smithsonian curators had taken an active role in the organization of the Centennial Exposition, and the original National Museum had been founded with its artifacts.[16]

The curators of "1876" wanted to replicate the overcrowded visual logic of the Victorian-era world's fairs, and this determined substantial choices made about the treatment of historical objects. Because the original Centennial Exposition had shown functioning machines, conservators restored many technological artifacts to their original condition instead of displaying them with the patina of age, which was then, and remains now, a standard conservation practice.[17] The controversial decision for the "high restoration" of objects inspired debate at the Smithsonian; memos circulating at the time refer to "impassioned opposition" from some curators.[18] Historic artifacts on display are usually allowed to show their age; the material qualities of the worn object underscore the passage of time and past use, emphasizing that the object has been saved and merits saving.[19] To restore an artifact is to create an entirely different understanding of that object's representation of history—it negates the passage of time and purports to show the object as it would have been at the moment of its creation. The artifact, instead of reinforcing the distance between the past and the present, becomes a talisman for acting *within* the past. That for the first time curators at the Smithsonian chose to present historical artifacts in this way, as opposed to in the more traditional manner, shows a shift not only in the principles underlying display of historical objects but also in basic assumptions about how history should be depicted. Seeing and interacting with fully restored and functioning artifacts helped move the viewer into the space of history. The museum became not the repository of the past, but a conduit *to* the past.

At the same time, the artifacts within "1876" performed an important function: because of their status as "museum objects," they acted as links between the past and the present and guarantors of a particular kind of authenticity. Many historians and theorists have written about the importance of artifacts: the unintelligible yet distinctive "sense of the past" that they communicate.[20] The machines and other ephemera inside the displays of "1876," because they were historical, and because they were presented in a museum context, helped make viewers feel that this was a "real" representation of how the original exposition had looked and felt. Ironically, some of the objects within the exhibition were also replicas or restorations, but they were not labeled as such—another deviation from standard museum display.[21] These objects benefited from the legitimacy bestowed upon them by their presence in the museum, but they, like their more "authentic" counterparts, also performed a function of helping audience members feel as if they were communing with history.

Upon entering the Centennial Exposition exhibit, visitors stepped into a total environment, interacting not only with the displays, but also with the decoration, the music, and the people of 1876. Even more than "Nation of Nations," "1876" consciously appealed to all of the senses. To enhance the celebratory ambience of the exhibition, an organ played songs of the era, and museum docents dressed in period costume as tradespeople, describing the machines and other implements, and extolling their innovations and benefits.[22] Much of the information they gave (the names and functions of the machines, their manufacturers and significance) was similar to what would have been printed on labels in a traditional exhibit, but here it was delivered through extemporaneous performance. Adding to the atmosphere, columns, balconies, and display cases were covered in red, white, and blue bunting and festive signage, fostering a feeling of newness, excitement, and celebration.[23]

In "1876," artifacts, decoration, and interpretation together created a living representation of the past, erasing one mode of critical distance for the visitor. While traditional museum displays had figured audiences in the role of something like an amateur curator in their inventory of, and interactions with, a succession of historical objects, "1876" produced emotive as opposed to informational knowledge. Audiences would learn about the feeling of 1876 not by seeing photographs or reading text, but through the sensation of being there. Instead of gazing upon a visual portrayal of the past, visitors were positioned inside of history. They themselves became a part of the display: filling in for and presumably acting like the historical visitors to the original exposition.

In its immersive and affective capacities, "1876" promoted association between contemporary and historical contexts of patriotism and celebration. Conversations around the exhibition's development as well as the eventual critical response connected the political and economic atmospheres of 1876 and 1976.[24] Commentators noted similarities between the economic depressions and political scandals of each era by comparing the troubles of Richard Nixon to those of Ulysses S. Grant, who, as president, had been plagued by the Teapot Dome controversy and allegations about ties to the Tweed political machine in New York.[25] The cover of the *Centennial Times*, the only element of "1876" that provided something like written interpretation, made these links explicit with stories about the political hardships of 1876, featuring items about an insurrection in Cuba, accusations of Grant's corruption, and the contested election between Tilden and Hayes.[26] Despite these difficulties, the original Centennial Exposition had, in the eyes of curators and critics, managed to unite its viewers, resulting in patriotic excitement about American progress and innovation.

The exhibition "1876," then, had several purposes: it functioned not only as a depiction of world's fairs in the nineteenth century and a meditation on exhibition in general, but also as a rallying call and a justification for celebration of the 1976 Bicentennial, the event that marked the occasion for "1876" itself. The exhibition literature noted that, despite its contemporary problems, the Centennial Exposition had successfully celebrated the anniversary of the American Revolution, displaying the progress that the United States had made since that time. The ambience of cheer and optimism created by the music, the bunting, and the sheer volume of machinery on display not only portrayed the past but was also a prescription for the contemporary. "1876" extended its festive air to the contemporary Bicentennial, collapsing the space between the past and the present.

But the exhibition's emotion-based appeal also carried with it the potential for a reevaluation of those positive feelings and recognition of the distinct contexts of the current and past celebrations. The curators of "1876" aimed to inspire in audiences optimism about the nation and about commemoration, but because this was all encouraged through affect, the connection was not guaranteed.[27] Although supporting texts like the *Centennial Times* made it clear that curators intended to stress that political and economic hardship was not unique to the current moment, and thus should not take away from national pride, audiences could just as easily come to understand the celebration of "1876" as distanced from, and in opposition to, the present day. They could read, for example, the disconnect between the gaiety of "1876" and antinuclear protests happening at the White House and elsewhere around Washington, DC, which opposed precisely the kind of technological optimism espoused by the exhibit.[28] Appeals to emotion are wildly unstable and carry with them the potential for many kinds of readings. "1876," because it invited audiences to make personal meaning, and because much of this meaning was made on the level of feeling, relied on an entirely different understanding of history and was more open to interpretation than previous exhibits, in which labels and other text-based interpretive devices combined with a succession of artifacts to present a more concrete and defined narrative.

The exhibits "1876" and "A Nation of Nations" were emblematic of the larger transformations occurring at the Smithsonian and at other museums. Both exhibits presented historical objects, not as evidence of the past but as conduits to a sensory and firsthand experience of history, building identification between past and present and collapsing—as opposed to underscoring—the distance of history. In 1964, just ten years prior, a world's fair, an embodiment of a cultural faith in technological and social advancement, had stood in New York City. That same year, the Museum of History and Technology, the Smithsonian's "Palace of Progress," had opened. But by 1976, new exhibitions at the Smithsonian and elsewhere emphasized not the superiority of the present to the past, but the similarities between and across historical eras, encouraging audiences to form interpretations that were defined by personal experience.

The Revolution in Boston

While the Smithsonian exhibits made new use of that institution's extensive collections, other endeavors attempted to convey the feeling of a specific moment in U.S. history without any historic objects. The shifting trajectory of the planning, execution, and reception of "The Revolution," an exhibit put on in Boston's historic Quincy Market by Boston 200—the city's Bicentennial planning organization—reflects how curators at other institutions were responding to and engaging larger changes in popular history at this critical moment. In 1972, in its earliest stages of development, Boston 200 envisioned "The Revolution" as a compendium of local historical societies' most prized possessions, something like, perhaps, the "block-buster" exhibits that museums like the Metropolitan Museum of Art and the National Gallery had begun mounting.[29] Called in early correspondence a "treasures exhibit," the original plans imagined an object-heavy display of "valuable" eighteenth-century artifacts culled from local and regional history organizations.[30]

By March of 1973, Boston 200 had a new focus: the exhibit would now "show the social and economic conditions surrounding the events leading to the American Revolution of 1776." In a grant application to the National Endowment of the Humanities, Boston 200 provided an extensive list of the kinds of artifacts they would be seeking. No longer organized around treasures, Boston 200 was now looking to showcase objects of everyday life: "weathervanes, tools, utensils, weapons," that would help explain complex themes. Even notable individuals would be presented differently: a famous portrait of Paul Revere to be borrowed from the Boston Museum of Fine Arts would be interpreted with attention to his silversmith's tools.[31] To give the artifacts further context, the proposal detailed the use of enlarged re-productions of images as well as "light and sound presentations" that would help convey a sense of colonial life in Boston. In the space of one year, the proposed exhibition changed from a traditional display privileging aesthetic and historically significant objects to a show that, like the Smithsonian's "Everyday Life in the American Past," used artifacts to relate a larger social and economic history.

But just six months later, by September of 1973, artifacts were no longer a critical component of the planned exhibit, which would now employ in-teractive techniques to make audiences think about the 1770s in relation to the 1970s, and vice versa. Boston 200 hired Michael Sand, an exhibit designer who had worked for Charles and Ray Eames and had been the design di-rector of the Boston Children's Museum, to organize the exhibition. Sand appointed as a consultant Richard Rabinowitz, a Harvard-trained historian and then the director of education at Old Sturbridge Village. Together, Sand and Rabinowitz imagined an exhibit that juxtaposed the political turmoil of the eighteenth century with that of the present. They wrote, "By engaging visitors more actively in the exhibit, we hope to encourage them also to become aware of their own feelings about political power and self-determination, political action and the admissibility of revolutionary violence, the rights of property, and so on."[32] Their proposal explained that viewers were to make connections between then and now, emphasizing identification as a means of understanding and meaning making.

The exhibition planned by Sand invited emotional, as opposed to informational, knowledge production; he designed "The Revolution" to make audiences *sense* the seventeenth century, not see it, explaining, "We want to immerse people in an atmosphere that will act as a time machine in allowing them to drift back two centuries in their thoughts." Sand and Rabinowitz's proposal included a giant mirror maze that would signify the complications of colonial bureaucracy and a speaker system playing "Taxman" by the Beatles. The Boston Massacre would be represented as a life-sized puppet show, with labels that explicitly made connections with the recent events at Kent State University in which the National Guard had shot and killed four unarmed protestors.[33] In every section, the exhibit would evoke affective response from its audience. As Sand noted in a section on the Stamp Act Riots, "The *feeling* of participating in the mob is much of the message."[34] Although Boston 200 eventually parted ways with Sand, the conflation of the eighteenth and twentieth centuries and the appeal to emotive identification in audiences, as well as the reinforcement of emotive identification through physical immersion, remained central to the exhibition.[35]

"The Revolution" finally opened in 1975 and showed eighteenth-century life in Boston, emphasizing the choices made by the city's colonists to support or oppose political actions in the fifteen years leading up to the American Revolution.[36] The actual space of the exhibition was a long, narrow tunnel, described by curators as a symbol of the inevitable road to the Revolution.[37] The finished exhibition contained a combination of physical elements, video projections, and ambient audio tracks that conveyed the look and sound of Boston in the eighteenth century. Publicity material foregrounded these aspects of the exhibition, noting that visitors would be able to "participate emotionally and intellectually in the debates, the incidents, and the political climate that led to the birth of the Revolution in Boston."[38] Each segment directly engaged audiences: in the section about the Boston Massacre, visitors faced life-sized figures of British soldiers with firearms drawn as strobe lights flashed and an audio track played the sounds of a shouting crowd. Outlines of bodies, reminiscent of contemporary crime scenes, were traced on the floor below.[39] Later in the exhibit, audiences walked past a full-scale re-creation of the lynching of a British customs officer.[40] "The Revolution" introduced several different subject positions for audiences to occupy; in some sections, like the Boston Massacre, they were directly involved, while in others, they were bystanders. With this arsenal of interactives, the exhibit presented an environment in which audience members would experience life in colonial Boston from multiple perspectives.

While some exhibit sections portrayed the eighteenth century through diorama, in others, new media helped depict Revolutionary events—again, reinforcing the connection and confusion between past and present. A television report of the trial of the British soldiers involved in the Boston Massacre was set in a contemporary courtroom. It featured a correspondent reporting on developments as they happened as well as man-on-the-street interviews with actors who dressed and spoke in the manner of the present day.[41] A curator wrote of this section: "Our purpose in using a 1976 setting is to bring home to the audience the modern relevance of the principles, prejudices, and concerns that motivated people's reaction to the massacre in 1770."[42] In the display, the trial—a site of contradictory and changing opinions—unfolded as the audience watched. In 1955, the Boston Massacre had been featured on the television program *You Are There*, but while that program emphasized that the incident was long resolved, in this representation, the decision was always in the process of being made. Even though audience members knew that the trial had occurred two centuries prior, they were encouraged to relive it as it happened.[43] Audiences occupied a liminal space, experiencing the emotions of a historical era, yet remaining physically and cognitively anchored in the present day and relating those emotions to a contemporary context. On one hand, this disjuncture favored an interpretation of history from the perspective of current events, reinforcing the continuity of the historical narrative. On the other, it created a space for audiences to relate the difficulties of the present (for example, the developing busing controversy in Boston) to long-past events, placing their present emotions into a historical context.

While the physical and technological aspects of "The Revolution" inspired audiences to envision themselves in the place of colonial-era Bostonians, a computerized component built upon this by inviting audience members to directly measure their own opinions against those of historical figures.[44] As visitors walked through individual sections of the exhibition, they filled out ballots with answers to multiple-choice questions about what they themselves would have done in each circumstance. For example, in a segment describing the Siege of Boston, audiences were asked, "Would you have stayed in Boston and supported the Loyalists, left with your family and joined the patriot militia, or would you have tried to remain neutral?"[45] At the end of the exhibit, visitors entered their answers into a personal computer, were matched with a historical figure whose opinions most closely resembled their own, and then designated either a "Patriot" or a "Tory." There were twelve possible results for the Patriot-Tory test, from Sam Adams, a fervent Patriot, through the indecisive and ambivalent James Otis, to Thomas Hutchinson, a committed Loyalist.[46] The wide range of choices and opinions underscored the difficulty of the decision, as well as the sometimes contradictory opinions held by any given individual.

The sensory environment of "The Revolution" created a historical ambiance, but the Patriot-Tory test forced audiences to become active participants in the exhibit, themselves becoming the subjects of a history that, like the Boston Massacre trial display, was in the process of happening. Rather than weighing the complexities of the events that led up to the Revolution at a distance, visitors *felt* them and were shown that eighteenth-century Bostonians had similar feelings. The exhibit accentuated the difficulty of choice—something that would have resonated with audiences grappling with their own decisions on current events like the war in Vietnam or the Boston busing controversies. "The Revolution" enacted a history that was subjective and emotive, emphasizing commonality between the past and the present.

But, like the festive atmosphere of "1876," the reenactment of colonial indecision in "The Revolution" also contained an ideological charge that reflected the exhibit's status as an official Bicentennial project. "The Revolution" resisted a straightforward and progressive interpretation of the events of eighteenth-century Boston, inviting diverging opinions from audiences. While the stated curatorial objective was to communicate the difficulty of these eighteenth-century decisions by extending them to twentieth-century audiences, the exhibit also functioned as a measure of nationalistic sentiment for visitors for whom, especially in the context of the celebration of the Bicentennial, the unspoken objective was to emerge a Patriot. Exhibit designers, as early as 1974, had considered including a "loyalty oath" or a "citizenship pledge" at the conclusion of the exhibition, and ultimately did produce "Patriot" and "Tory" buttons for visitors to take as souvenirs of the experience.[47]

To gain publicity, Boston 200 arranged for several high-profile figures to visit the exhibit and publicly take the Patriot or Tory test. While Boston mayor Kevin White was designated a Patriot, the British ambassador to the United States tested as a Tory.[48] News coverage and exhibition publicity stressed the desirability of being a Patriot over a Tory—reviewers and visitors interviewed for articles with headlines like "Would You Have Dumped the Tea?," "Boston Separates Patriots, Tories," and "Voting System

Reliving "The Revolution." Visitors were provided with a variety of ways to place themselves physically and emotionally inside colonial Boston: from dioramas to a computerized interactive. Courtesy of the City of Boston Archives.

Tests Revolutionary Fervor" were anxious to testify to their Revolutionary sentiment.[49] Local media kept a running tally of numbers, finding that Patriots outnumbered Tories two to one.[50] Letters that schoolchildren wrote to exhibit curators indicated that they understood the desired outcomes, as several students identified both the character they had been matched with and the character they wished to have been named. "I was James Otis but I wished I could have been John Hancock," explained one student. Another wrote, "I was a Patriot, but my teacher was a Tory."[51] "The Revolution" created a space in which audiences could make their own meaning, but it became clear that some meanings were more appropriate than others. At the same time, the emphasis on ambivalence seemed to suggest to audiences troubled by the incongruity of the celebratory anniversary with recent events like Vietnam and Watergate that one could have mixed or complicated sentiments yet still be a patriot—a particularly appropriate message given the larger questions that were swirling around the meaning of the Bicentennial.

Although critical and popular reception of "The Revolution" was over-whelmingly positive and enthusiastic, its departure from more traditional strategies of exhibition and knowledge production was debated by profes-sional historians. Throughout its development, the exhibition generated controversy and contention among members of Boston 200's Eighteenth Century Task Force, an advisory board culled from local historical socie-ties and high school and college history departments. During the planning of the exhibition, older and more established members of the task force voiced a profound discomfort with what they called the "Disney" qualities of the exhibit, complaining of the irresponsibility of making connections over two hundred years and worrying that history had lost its gravitas. The historians of the task force used words like "manipulative," "condescending," and "carnivalesque," labeling the proposed exhibit as "worse than televi-sion."[52] These conversations provide additional evidence of the substantial transformation taking place, one that was apparent in "The Revolution" as well as in other areas of Bicentennial commemoration, but one that was by no means a smooth and complete transition.

The repeated invocation of "Disney" to describe the exhibit's interpre-tive strategies points to a presentation seen by professional historians as san-itized and accessible but also thoroughly commercial. It also hints at the exhibit's emotional appeal, as the moniker "Disney" implies a specific mode of sentimentality.[53] The debates indicate a divide between the more estab-lished historians and younger practitioners trained in the new social and public history, who, like Sand and Rabinowitz, were committed to making historical analysis accessible to wide audiences and challenging what they considered to be unrepresentative and exclusionary traditional narratives. The changes that were occurring here were twofold: not only did "The Revolution" center upon the feelings and the experiences of everyday Bos-tonians but it also attempted to convey those feelings through identifica-tion, not exposition.

"The Revolution" was dedicated, not to accuracy or authenticity of representation, but to authenticity of affect. The exhibit elements that made historians uneasy—like the contemporary take on the Boston Massacre trial—were precisely those that were meant to help audiences comprehend the emotional charge of the Revolutionary era. That the task force worried over the exhibit in these particular terms, as opposed to, for example, ques-tions of research rigor and accuracy of information—more conventional critiques made of museum exhibition—reveals that the transformation was a structural, rather than simply a narrative, shift. That is, the difference was not only in *what* was being said, but *how*. "The Revolution," by placing audiences in the past and by encouraging association between historical and contemporary issues, invited a very different mode of understanding and engaging with history, one that was, to some professionals, both problematic and unwelcome.

Ghosts of the Past/Ghosts in the Past at the Franklin Exchange

Other institutions created Bicentennial exhibitions that encouraged audience members to inhabit subject positions somewhere between the past and the present. Philadelphia architect Robert Venturi (later the author of the influential study, *Learning from Las Vegas*, taken up by postmodernists in the 1980s) designed a "ghost structure" and underground museum at Franklin Court, where the house of Benjamin Franklin had once stood.[54] The site had long presented a challenge to the National Park Service, which was then in the midst of an extensive renovation of the collection of sites called Independence Park. Historians and archaeologists had begun excavating at Franklin Court in the 1950s and had located ample records pertaining to the design of the house but could not find elevation drawings or exterior images of the building. Scholarly and popular interest in Franklin had begun to surge, and Park Service planners were anxious to open a site that was closely linked to Franklin's life and that, in the words of Park Service officials, focused upon "the man, not the myth."[55] The Park Service had spent the 1950s and 1960s reviewing plans for first, a memorial, and then, a re-creation of the house, but were hampered by the lack of information about its actual appearance. The structure and accompanying museum that opened in 1976 advanced a new model for thinking about and interacting with the past, one that shared many characteristics with other history exhibitions being developed during this time, but that, in other ways, provoked further temporal dislocation. The new Franklin Court stimulated multidirectional historical identification by suggesting not only that audiences could move into the past, but also that the past could move into the present.[56]

Franklin Court was located in the center of historic Philadelphia— within walking distance of other Revolutionary-era sites like Independence Hall as well as Franklin's own gravesite—so, it was likely that visitors would encounter it as part of a larger colonial-era tourism experience like

Boston's Freedom Trail. After walking into a courtyard through a passage-way (a sign noted that Franklin "went to and from his house through this original passage"), visitors encountered Venturi's "ghost house," a steel reconstruction of the outlines of Franklin's home, which was built over a stone floor inlaid with the house's floor plans. Outside of the ghost house, more stone flooring signaled the footprints of such external structures as Franklin's well and privy pit, which did not have their own steel outlines. The effect was of a structure that was both "done" and "undone"—in the process of being built, torn down, or rebuilt. We tend to think of buildings and other historic objects as being finished, solid, permanent (and indeed, historical preservation activity is rooted in some of these assumptions), but Franklin Court was none of those, instead somewhere and something in between.

According to John Cotter, the National Park Service's chief regional archaeologist, the inspiration for the ghost structure came from a drawing that had been made by James Deetz, a pioneer in the field of historical archaeology who was, at that time, working at a site on Cape Cod. Like others involved in social history, Deetz was interested in reconstructing the everyday lives and experiences of people in the past, especially those who had not left behind extensive records or artifacts.[57] In the early 1970s, Deetz had introduced first-person interpretation as the assistant director of the Plimoth Plantation historical site and in 1977 would publish the landmark text *In Small Things Forgotten: An Archaeology of Early American Life*. Deetz sent Cotter a photograph of the foundation and chimney base of a house that he was researching at Cape Cod. In an effort to understand how it might have looked, Deetz had drawn in white ink the outline of the house. This photograph, which Cotter showed to Venturi, served as an inspiration for the design of the Franklin Court ghost structure.[58]

The structure and surrounding elements, including an eighteenth-century garden, placed the visitor within Franklin's physical space, communicating the experience of Franklin's extraordinary but everyday life there. Paradoxically, the spectral elements of the structure, which were concrete, yet to some degree imagined, both rejected and reinforced the distance between past and present, like "The Revolution" had rendered the visitor bodily and emotively stranded between (or over) two historical eras. The effect was a doubling and confusion, placing visitors in a complex position in which they were asked to feel and move as Franklin and his family felt and moved, yet were also reminded of their own contemporary presence by the spectrality of the structure. History, at Franklin Court, was available as a substrate upon which many different meanings could be made.

In the underground museum of Franklin's life and accomplishments, this temporal disjunction persisted in an even more radical way. After entering through a long tunnel, visitors encountered a telephone bank labeled the "Franklin Exchange." An introductory panel told audiences that Franklin was a prolific letter writer but that "today he might well be using the telephone to say many of the same things."[59] Illuminated in large letters on the wall facing the phone bank were two "directories"—alphabetical listings of names and telephone numbers of American and European writers and politicians influenced by Franklin's ideas and accomplishments. While some of the entries (Thomas Jefferson, John Adams) were contemporaries of Franklin, others were individuals who followed him in history, for example, Lord Byron, Ralph Waldo Emerson, and Harry Truman. The listed telephone numbers appeared in correct telephonic form, that is, George Washington's number began with the "703" Virginia exchange and lengthy European numbers contained both international and country codes. This detail—telephone numbers that *could be correct*, assigned to individuals who had lived before the age of modern communication—reinforced the same feelings of temporal confusion as the structure above.

To use the exchange visitors picked out the digits on rotary telephones and, after waiting three or four rings, listened as the individual picked up, delivered a few lines about Franklin, identified themselves ("Franklin was the Prometheus of his time! This is Immanuel Kant!"), and abruptly hung up.[60] In the "Franklin Exchange," historical figures were somehow *physically* present in concrete locations, and thus reachable by telephone. But these historical figures seemed not to know about contemporary telephone etiquette, their voices were rushed and annoyed, and they offered no greetings or salutations. Like the spectral structure of Franklin's former house, these speakers were also ghosts, resurrected for the purpose of this exhibit. The audience was again stranded in between space and time, experiencing "conversation" (albeit one-sided) with a world historical figure *and* the expanse between their time and his, mediated as long-distance telephonic space. The means of communication were commonplace and modern, yet both the interlocutors and the strange experience of "communicating" with them were out of the ordinary. The act of calling or summoning a historical figure, and particularly using a personal technology like the telephone, was another way of creating an illusion of the past as a place with which one could connect and engage.[61]

At Philadelphia's Franklin Court, visitors could walk around the "ghost house" of Benjamin Franklin (photo by Mark Cohn, 1977) or use the "Franklin Exchange" interactive to converse with his interlocutors. Courtesy of the Architectural Archives, University of Pennsylvania, by the gift of Robert Venturi and Denise Scott Brown.

Portrait of a Family, the 1976 film commissioned for the Franklin Court exhibit and shown in a theater in the underground museum, further emphasized the two-sided feeling of bodily and spatial immersion, both on the part of the audience and on the imagined part of Franklin. The film, a biographical sketch of Franklin and his family, begins literally with ghosts, those of Franklin and his wife as they return to Franklin Court to tell viewers their story. Franklin speaks directly to the audience, referring to his life, death, and the time that has passed since. Like the television miniseries that were just then gaining prominence, the film invited audiences to identify directly with the characters by highlighting Franklin's emotions and experiences. *Portrait of a Family* dealt primarily with Franklin's sentiments about aspects of his private life: his diplomatic post in France, his daughter's marriage, and the house he was building. In the story of his life, Franklin moves inside and outside of the narrative, simultaneously acting out scenes from his past and stopping to address viewers and give context to some of the events.[62] Like the Franklin house's ghost structure, like the voices of the Franklin Exchange, and like the audience members themselves, the filmic ghosts of Benjamin and Deborah Franklin straddle the past and the present, enacting a history that is affective and experiential. *Portrait of a Family* posited history as something that one can know through physical and emotional interactions with the sites of the past but, at the same time, as something ghostly that was not quite there. Franklin Court placed audiences and historical subjects within each other's time periods, emphasizing both physical and emotional proximity and, overall, a permeability between past and present.

The surge of new display technology in the 1970s meant that the appearance and experience of history museum exhibition changed dramatically, but it would be an oversimplification to say this resulted merely from the availability of new exhibition media. The new prominence of media in exhibition space can be partly explained by the fact that these instruments were becoming less expensive, but the personalized dimensions of many new technologies of the time, like home computers and personal audio players, evidence an attention to individualized experience that was perfectly in line with the focus on the self that characterized the "Me Decade."[63] Devices such as telephone banks, monitors, and computer systems were used to draw visitors into such exhibitions as Franklin Court or "The Revolution." These media experiences privileged personalized, experiential, and empathetic perception of the historical past over a more informational or factual knowledge based on the artifact as the site of historical meaning.[64]

The Living History Museum

In "The Revolution" and at Franklin Court, spatial ambience combined with new technology to situate audiences in the past, but, in other historical exhibits, living interpreters helped give visitors similar feelings of "being there." Although living history museums—outdoor environments that re-created past structures and peopled them with costumed inhabitants— have a history that starts before and continues after the 1970s, during this decade, exhibition and interpretation at these sites moved from demonstration toward immersion, and the emphasis migrated from the historical structures to the lives of the people within them.[65]

The first living history museums in the United States, modeled on the open air museums of Europe, were founded by elite industrialists and depicted idyllic versions of American life, emphasizing values like industry and independence as instrumental to the development of the United States.[66] They were living demonstrations of American exceptionalism, somewhat akin to the world's fair or preserved sites like Mount Vernon. Automobile manufacturer Henry Ford inaugurated his Greenfield Village in 1929, and John D. Rockefeller's Colonial Williamsburg opened in 1934. While Greenfield Village celebrated the timeless folk values of agrarian America, Williamsburg, founded, appropriately enough, at the tail end of the Colonial Revival, focused on the colonial planter elite and their role in the foundation of the nation. These sites featured restored period homes and businesses and were populated with costumed "guides" and "hostesses" (the distinction was gendered) who could provide directions and general historical information. Inside the buildings, mannequins recycled from local department stores were posed to approximate the activities of the buildings' original inhabitants.[67] The combination of mannequins with costumed personnel underscored the inauthenticity of the scene, pointing to the importance of the structures, as opposed to the people of the past. These sites attempted to visually represent and enliven American history, but the emphasis was on animation as opposed to interaction. Put another way, early living history sites were like giant period rooms, meant to demonstrate how life might have looked in the past, but not how it felt.

Colonial Williamsburg and Greenfield Village were soon joined by Old Sturbridge Village, founded in 1946, and Plimoth Plantation the following year.[68] Not surprisingly, given their ideological imperatives, these living history museums played a significant role in Cold War international politics; foreign dignitaries were often taken to Colonial Williamsburg for official visits.[69] The site, like the federal quarter of Washington, DC, that the Nixon administration was working to refurbish, was imbricated in the dynamics of state power: its space showcased the monumental American past and the influence of that past on the present. Likewise, Sturbridge Village worked with officials from the State Department in the early 1960s to develop tours that illustrated early American craft and industrial traditions to international tourists.[70] Visitors to Colonial Williamsburg, Old Sturbridge Village, and other sites could witness and be inspired by evidence and performance of American ideals like individual freedom, initiative, and industriousness, which had helped make the nation great and stood in direct opposition to values associated with Soviet communism.

The costumed guides and hostesses that populated living history museums were there to lend authenticity to the sites and to demonstrate early American craft traditions, but interpretation at the sites concentrated on the architectural features of the buildings and monumental events in history, as opposed to the experiences of the people who lived through them.[71] Writing in 1981, Cary Carson, director of research at Colonial Williamsburg, reflected on living history in the postwar period, calling interpreters a "supporting cast," and noting, "Small houses, ordinary furnishings and such lesser folk as lived in Williamsburg were part of the picture too, but not in the same way that social historians consider them important today."[72] Historical interpretation before the late 1960s aimed to produce informational knowledge. Demonstrations of household tasks and crafts like candle making or blacksmithing were interactive in that they "showed" as well as "told" history and appealed to audiences by animating the historical and making it interesting, but they did not seek to place audiences in the past.[73]

Living history museums in the 1950s and early 1960s were like pedagogical and demonstrative exhibits, in the words of Colonial Williamsburg's mission, aiming "to stimulate such thinking on the American heritage that will lead to constructive action on the part of our audience."[74] In the same manner, visitors to Old Sturbridge Village could "draw inspiration from the past to give strength and purpose to the present, steadfast assurance for the future."[75] At Plimoth Plantation, the 1948 Articles of Incorporation called the site a "Memorial to the Pilgrim Fathers" (capitalization original), and went on to describe how this would be achieved through the "restoration or reproduction of antiquarian houses and buildings, implements, tools and facilities."[76] The *people* of the past: how they used and interacted with these implements and tools, how they lived in the antiquarian houses and

Costumed "hostesses" at Colonial Williamsburg, 1964. Note the pristine clothing and 1960s hairstyles. Courtesy of the Colonial Williamsburg Foundation.

buildings, were not an essential factor in early conception and planning of these sites.

At sites like Williamsburg and Sturbridge, entire communities were re-created, but smaller living history ventures—often single farms—focused upon historical agriculture. While a few of these had existed in the 1940s and 1950s, living history farm sites, like building preservation, prospered in the 1960s in response to growing urbanization.[77] Farms were among the vernacular architecture that fell under the rubric of new building preservation initiatives and, as a result, agricultural living history projects flourished.[78] The 1970 founding of the Association for Living History, Farm, and Agricultural Museums (ALHFAM) at Old Sturbridge Village recognized and codified this expansion. Through this new organization, member farms shared and exchanged information, cultivated best practices, and established standards for the maturing field.[79] Research and interpretation came to be co-constitutive; with added interest and funding, these farms became important sites of agricultural scholarship where historians and practitioners worked with period tools and researched historic strains of plants and livestock, gaining insight on historical farming by enacting its processes.

As living history farms flourished, living history museums also became a premier site of the new social history in a turn that occurred tandem with related developments in the fields of historic building preservation, oral history practice, museum exhibition, and the academic profession itself. The homes and workplaces of ordinary people of the past could yield critical information about everyday life, social and economic structures, and political beliefs, all areas of inquiry central to social historians. In 1981, Cary Carson recalled how his Harvard colleague Richard Rabinowitz (later of Michael Sand's "Revolution" team) left Cambridge in the late sixties to become the director of education at Old Sturbridge Village in western Massachusetts. Linking the kind of history made possible by living historical sites to the increasingly leftist politics shared by Rabinowitz and other students at the time, Carson remembered, "Like many breakthroughs the connection he made seemed elementary afterwards. Ours were the first crop of American graduate students to get caught up in the enthusiasm for the so-called new social history. We were attracted to its egalitarianism, and to its 'scientific' dedication to finding out how past societies were structured and how their past worked together to form organic communities."[80] Carson would go on to follow his colleague as director of research at Colonial Williamsburg, where he too helped push interpretation toward the new social history, paying attention to the everyday lives of ordinary people.[81] Significantly, Carson noted, this was not merely precipitated by radical academics, it arose in response to a new demand from visitors: "They were a ready audience too, anxious about widespread social change and consequently eager to find out what made human communities tick. From the mid sixties onward, museum interpreters—the listening kind—detected the shift in the tenor of the questions their visitors asked."[82] Living history farms and museums, like other sectors of popular historymaking, both responded to and helped propel more general transformations in how American society thought of and used the past.

Many living history museums began to emphasize social history in the late 1960s and 1970s, but Plimoth Plantation's efforts at authenticity led this site to go further, emphasizing "first-person" interpretation and, consequently, deepening sensory immersion and affective identification for both interpreters and audiences. At most living history farms and museums, interpretation remained in the "third person"—that is, costumed interpreters spoke from the present perspective, using third-person pronouns and the past tense to describe historical persons and activities. This mode of address maintained separation between the past and the present, even as the exhibitions effectively demonstrated some aspects of the past.[83]

In the early 1960s, James Deetz, the historical archaeology practitioner who had inspired the ghost structure at Franklin Court, had become assistant director at Plimoth Plantation. Deetz pushed research and interpretation of the garrison town of Plimoth beyond the sanitized Pilgrim story that the museum had been putting forth.[84] He believed that "to function properly and successfully, a live museum should convey the sense of a different reality—the reality of a different time."[85] The first adjustment that Deetz made was to remove the explanatory signage and mannequins from the Plimoth displays. By the early 1970s, he had auctioned off the ornate seventeenth-century antiques and reproductions that filled some of the houses, replacing them with simpler facsimiles that more closely reflected the real furnishings of the period. The guides and hostesses were given new costumes: instead of pristine (and apparently highly flammable) polyester copies of the kinds of "pilgrim attire" that were popular in nineteenth-century paintings and illustration, they were outfitted in linen and wool clothing that more closely approximated what the original colonists had worn.[86] All of these changes let visitors step into a milieu that *looked* more like the seventeenth century had looked.

But Deetz also wanted his visitors to sense the past and to interact with it. He added live animals, growing crops, and real foodstuffs to the site, and interpreters, mostly college students, attended intensive seminars and workshops. They were taught farming, cooking, and other skills that would have been used by Plimoth's 1627 inhabitants. The trainees also participated in role-playing exercises, which Deetz likened to "group encounter sessions," underscoring the burgeoning connection between historical interpretation and individual self-realization.[87] Rather than lecture to visitors, the Plimoth interpreters went about daily work in the village, stopping to explain their occupations to curious visitors and to answer questions. In contrast to the clean colonial clothing at Williamsburg, Plimoth interpreters were often barefoot, sweaty, and dirty. Deetz also encouraged total visitor immersion— nothing in Plimoth Plantation was kept off limits, visitors could "crawl into bed or sit in a chair. They may chase the chickens or use the implements in the house."[88] The site began to place more emphasis on the experiences of the people who had lived in Plimoth and to put forth a different representation of the past, one that invited visitors directly inside.

Plimoth's new techniques also had a profound impact on its interpreters, who assumed the subject position of their historical counterparts. Writing in 1971, Deetz observed, "Without a word being said, [interpreters] were beginning to shift the whole presentation from third person, past, to first person, present. Guides are frequently saying, *"we do,"* not, *"they did."*[89] Because they were living as seventeenth-century colonists, interpreters at Plimoth consequently began *feeling* like seventeenth-century colonists. Plimoth Plantation presented an interactive environment peopled with living, breathing exemplars of the past. They communicated with audiences in their past personas, for example, feigning incredulity at the sight of cameras and other modern ephemera.[90] Because of their intensive training, they could speak to many kinds of inquiries, from questions about their work to their religious beliefs to their political opinions. Audience experience was self-directed; visitors could feel that they had unrestricted and authentic access to the past.[91] Plimoth became, like Franklin Court, a temporally indeterminate location: its existence could be read as time travel in either direction. It was, and remains, unclear if the conceit of Plimoth, followed to its logical conclusion, is that of a seventeenth-century colony having somehow reappeared in the present day, or of a portal for contemporary audiences to step back into the past. Both sites offered temporal indeterminacy, a collapse between the past and the present.

Many practitioners in the field lauded Plimoth's new approach, but first-person interpretation also provoked debates that echoed and anticipated the ongoing critique of immersive history and reenactment in general. Cary Carson worried that Plimoth left visitors "full, but not nourished": the exciting experience of interacting with seventeenth-century colonists might fail to provide a sense of context and comprehension of larger changes and trends of the seventeenth century.[92] Robert Ronsheim, an education coordinator for Boston 200, was likewise concerned, remarking, "Empathy is not understanding." Writing in the trade publication *Museum News*, Ronsheim stated, "The likelihood of misunderstanding the past is promoted and multiplied by the sense of involvement and approval given by the living history program. The visitors are told that they are reacting to the way it was and thus are assured that they know 'what it was really like.' Responding to costumed individuals carrying out roles from the past, the visitors also gain a sense of knowing how individuals in the culture that has been re-created 'really felt.'"[93]

Like many history professionals at this time, Ronsheim exhibited anxiety about the veracity of the kind of historical knowledge produced from living history.[94] Part of the problem was that meaning made on the affective register was then and remains now very difficult to quantify: we have no way of knowing how exactly visitors to Plimoth came to understand colonial history, or how the knowledge that they gained influenced other arenas of historical perception and identification. The debate surrounding Plimoth Plantation mirrors similar conversations about "1876," "The Revolution," and other innovative history exhibitions. It also prefigures what became a longstanding criticism, perpetuated to the present day, and again, points to anxiety that always accompanies a radical transformation in perception and practice, as well as about modes of knowledge production for which there is no concrete way to measure or gauge understanding.[95]

In spite of these criticisms, others extolled Plimoth's interactivity as an important educational development that would allow new access to the historical, adapting Plimoth's innovations in their own projects.[96] The National Park Service began using living history techniques in many of its sites.[97] The Park Service also launched an initiative called the Environmental Living Program, which, like Plimoth, taught students about the past through experience. This program foregrounded the connection between humans and nature in a specifically historical context. The Park Service described the program as "an actual living, overnight experience for children that takes place at any cultural, historic, or prehistoric site where the interaction and interdependency of man and his environment are presented."[98] Students visited the Tumacacori Mission in Arizona, a nineteenth-century fishing schooner, and a Civil War fort, where they were assigned previously researched historical roles and presented with situations in which to act and react. While students in a pioneer cabin organized provisions for the winter, program participants in the Civil War–era Fort Point were assigned guard duty in shifts and told to keep a diary of what they saw.[99] Across a variety of contexts, learning about the past became connected to acting within the past.

The educational imperative of these kinds of first-person reenactments was taken up in other places as well, especially in the context of the upcoming Bicentennial. Third and fourth graders at an elementary school in Bremerton, Washington, spent every Friday for a semester of the 1975–76 school year in a colonial-era school setting. Students and teachers dressed in colonial clothing and completed lessons commensurate with that era. The school atmosphere changed as well: students wrote in hornbooks, learned by rote memorization, and wore signs and dunce caps when they misbehaved. Both teachers and students enjoyed the experience, reporting that they had learned firsthand about colonial life.[100]

In the 1970s, embodied practices, although hotly contested, began to be adapted across a variety of pedagogical institutions, showing that historical education had come to encompass affective, as well as informational knowledge. The "spaces" of history: the museum, the exhibition, the historical site, became places where one could learn about the past by entering it. Artifacts, media implements, and living people became conduits to direct encounters with history. This development, however, was by no means tidy or complete. Instead, these examples of Bicentennial-Era historical exhibition and the different ways they represented the past and appealed to audiences illustrate that fundamental conceptions of evidence, narrative, and knowledge production were themselves changing. These projects presented the historical as a potential space for consciousness and contemplation of issues of ideology, identity, and, especially in the case of the Bicentennial, nationality and nationalism.

Under what I have called a cultural logic of preservation, the historical was contained within and symbolized by the artifact, while the history-making subject existed and operated within the contemporary moment. Yet, the changes that both expanded and reconfigured preservation activity in the 1970s began to destabilize these temporal and spatial distinctions and to move toward the creation of affective engagements or affinities with the past. The treatment and exhibition of artifacts in museums and other history institutions reflected new perceptions of the past in proximity to, or informing, the present, as curators arranged historical objects to encourage immersive experiences that conveyed the feeling of the historical. Rather than viewing the historical at a distance, Americans increasingly sought to place themselves *within* the past. This shift can be traced through the changing terms and uses of various modes of preservation—from the preserved building to the artifact. More critically, however, the most prevalent site of historical knowledge production ceased to be the preserved artifact, and the historical moved outside of the spaces (the museum, the exhibition, the site of history) it had been proscribed by. This decade saw a proliferation of new, embodied interactions with the past. It is to this cultural logic of reenactment, and the types of activities that it generated, that I now turn.

Cultural Logics of Reenactment
Embodied Engagements with the American Past

> They are a very history minded group of colorful people, not at all
> phony, but genuine pioneer stock. They have no silver trappings on
> their horses or fancy wagons, but are people interested in
> experiencing history and meeting people.
> —*Wagon Train Weekly*, June 11, 1976

By the 1970s, Americans visiting museums and historical sites were regularly encountering immersive history. Among these was the Smithsonian's "1876," in which restored, functioning artifacts and festive decoration reproduced both the look and the feel of the Philadelphia Centennial Exposition. But "1876" also gave audiences the opportunity to encounter the people of the period. Curators instructed docents to dress like tradespeople and mingle with visitors as these historical personas, extolling the virtues of the machines and goods on display and commenting upon the politics and society of the day. The costumed docents served as conduits between 1876 and 1976, their presence helping to transport audiences into the past.[1] This exhibition was only one of many that inspired audiences to learn about history by stepping inside of it. But a great deal of immersive history projects did not include artifacts at all. Instead, visitors to preserved historical structures, museum exhibitions, and living history sites were presented with historical settings and people. Interactions within these spaces of history encouraged a sense of the past that was based on embodied experience and emotional understanding. The site of historical knowledge production had shifted from the artifact to the subject body—from the preservation to the reenactment.

And so, by the time of the Bicentennial, reenactment had emerged as a central strategy of popular historymaking. In my use of this term, I emphasize that reenactive practice depends on an understanding of the past as proximate to the present, positioning subjects not adjacent to but *within* the historical narrative. Rather than learning historical facts, reenactors and audiences want to know and feel the experiences of historical subjects. As a result, this engagement produces a historical consciousness that operates at the level of emotional, not informational, knowledge production. The very ephemerality of the affects that reenactment generates means that, as a practice of history, it yields diverse and often unpredictable interpretations and identifications, ranging from those that reinforce and deepen established or hegemonic accounts of history to others that can lead to reevaluations of both past and present.[2]

Many different individuals and institutions—ranging from state interests to history organizations to community groups—became involved in affective historymaking in the 1970s, staging projects that took varied forms but were nonetheless underwritten by similar imperatives. While some, like Boston 200's "Revolution" exhibition, helped audience members to understand and empathize with the difficult decisions made by colonial-era Bostonians, Philadelphia's Franklin Court allowed visitors to interact via telephone with spectral renditions of Benjamin Franklin and others. Because of the way these two exhibitions used immersive tactics to blur past and present and to encourage audience identification with historical subjects, they can be described as reenactive engagements. But many public history initiatives made use of embodied practice more directly, reflecting both the development and proliferation of reenactment throughout the decade. Living history museums established interpretive techniques in which the majority of historical knowledge production came from encounters with reenactors, not buildings or artifacts. By the mid-1970s, the new emphasis on embodied history was noticeable across a range of public history institutions.[3]

Even more critically, thousands of Americans produced and participated in reenactment as a part of the Bicentennial. While many of these reenactments were organized by state interests in order to elicit patriotic sentiment from citizens, others originated with individuals or small groups and had diverging aims, some of which explicitly countered more mainstream accounts of American history. I am not arguing that reenactment—which can be defined most simply as the embodied experience of historical events—was, in the 1970s, a *new* way of engaging with the past. However, in the 1970s, and particularly through the hundreds of public history projects that were planned as a part of the Bicentennial, the forms and purposes of reenactment did change considerably: the practice became more prevalent and took on new meanings.

New Reenactments

The explosion of embodied history in the 1970s is particularly striking because, only a decade earlier, reenactment as a form of popular historymaking and commemoration had been vigorously dismissed and denigrated. In particular, critics disparaged Civil War Centennial reenactments of the 1950s and early 1960s on the grounds that they were "inauthentic" and did not respect the serious nature of historical reflection. As one media commentator wrote of a reenactment at Manassas, "These sweating charades . . . sham battles threaten to make a farce of the greatest tragedy in American history." The critic continued, "The gaudy show at Bull Run was a noisy piece of amateur theatrics, carried on by overgrown boys who get a thrill out of hearing guns go off."[4] The National Park Service banned the practice in national parks in 1965, and battle reenactment receded into a subculture largely outside of the mainstream.[5] The mistrust of reenactment as a productive mode of historical engagement continued into the last years of that decade, as early Bicentennial planners and commentators likewise derided historical reenactments as an inappropriate form of commemoration, instead looking to more traditional types of celebration.[6] Even Carlisle Humelsine of Colonial Williamsburg, then the head of the American Revolution Bicentennial Commission, did not consider embodied history to be a significant part of the upcoming celebration. In the same way that costumed interpreters were not the focus of Colonial Williamsburg at this moment, so would reenactments be minimized during the Bicentennial.

By the late 1960s, U.S. involvement in the Vietnam War had made battle reenactment even more undesirable—and potentially even traumatic—as it too closely resembled the very real carnage that Americans saw nightly on their television sets. Although battle reenactments continued to attract reproach, the valence of this criticism changed. In the 1950s and 1960s, many considered battle reenactments "inauthentic," but by the 1970s, they were "too real."[7] Alongside other changes, the parameters of the definition of historic value were transforming: realism had previously been judged by authenticity, now it became a question of representation.

Reenactments that took place in the 1970s were distinct from—but a part of—the longer history of embodied performance of the past. The *tableau vivant*, a popular pastime during the nineteenth and early twentieth centuries, involved actors or amateurs dressing up to illustrate a historical occurrence or painting and standing perfectly still to make—as the name suggests—a "living picture."[8] In the first decades of the twentieth century, historical pageantry became extremely popular in the United States. Civic and community groups in towns and cities all over the country staged theatricals that depicted famous events in U.S. history. Pageant topics included battles, incidents in the lives of famous Americans, and the signing of treaties and legislation. In his work on the pageant boom, David Glassberg notes several reasons for this 1920s upsurge, from local boosterism and nationalism to the pageant as a platform for Progressive-era reform measures, but, most significantly, he finds that the sudden rise of the pageant as a public manner of reckoning with history came during a period of rapid upheaval and transformation. The performance of the past, and particularly the spectacularization of historical trajectory, helped make sense of the present and future. Pageantry during this period developed in tandem with larger shifts in beliefs about historical continuity and discontinuity that were challenged after World War I and found expression in antimodernism in general and in specific movements like the Colonial Revival, both of which continued to inspire pageants during this time.[9] The rise of pageants and the way they used the historic to address other societal and cultural ruptures reveals the mutable and symptomatic nature of historical consciousness and prefigures the way that cultural relationships with, and uses of, the past again changed in the 1960s and 1970s.

But 1970s reenactment-based activity differed from these antecedents in both form and content. Earlier *tableaux* and historical pageants centered on famous people and events, recounting stories already well known to most audience members. They were instructional, but, above all, they were celebratory. In the same way that 1950s and 1960s historical television shows like *You Are There* focused on great leaders, early building preservation activists looked to aesthetic or historically significant sites like George Washington's Mount Vernon, postwar oral history projects were concerned with the recollections of prominent politicians, and living history museums in the 1950s and 1960s used costumed guides and hostesses as "supporting acts" for historic structures, earlier performative history took on subjects outside of the purview of everyday life: explorations, founding moments, notable individuals. In addition, real-life historical personages were often distilled into archetypes like "The Pilgrim" or joined by symbolic or allegorical figures like a "Knight of Economy," the "Spirit of the Community," and so forth.[10] This reflected a monumental sense of the past and a general consensus about the important incidents and individuals of history, neither of which were present by the 1970s.

Moreover, performances showcasing these exceptional and well-documented individuals and events did not engender the same kinds of affective identifications as reenactments of more prosaic people and incidents. It is easier to effect an emotive identification with or relate to an ordinary person living in the early republic than, for example, George Washington, especially if you are performing alongside the Spirit of the Community. Tableaux and pageants invited feelings of distance and reverence, memorialization as opposed to historical inquiry. Through framing devices like stages and curtains, earlier performances of the past had accentuated the separation between reenactors and spectators, and thus the difference between the "past" (as represented by the performance and its participants) and the "present" (the space of the audience). Even battle reenactment reinforced this divide through the field of battle as the space of action, as well as the inherent peculiarity of a spectated battle to begin with.

In contrast to earlier modes, the reenactive activity that developed in the 1970s involved reenactors *and* audiences by minimizing the physical and structural divisions between the two. Prior to the 1970s, reenactive exercises were a kind of demonstration; performances were visual, not visceral. Although for the duration of the spectacle, pageant participants might have felt as if they were in or of the past, audiences remained firmly lodged in the present, marveling at the performance as they might gaze upon an object in a museum, or at a costumed and bewigged coachman driving a horse-drawn carriage past re-created buildings in Colonial Williamsburg. In newer reenactments, however, the barrier between actors within the space of the "past" and audiences as spectators began to weaken, creating a variety of subject positions within the space of the reenactment (from the protagonist of a historical event to a witness who was also there, for example). These newer reenactments were immersive experiences that could help *both* reenactors and audiences commune with the past on an emotional or affective level.

Many cultural factors undergirded and contributed to the emergence of new modes of reenactment and their proliferation at this particular moment. The affective identification sought by newer reenactment can be connected to the growth of other types of cultural expression that involved the self, including Transcendental Meditation, with its emphasis on the relationship between environment and human; role playing in personal and group therapy (recall James Deetz's characterization of first-person interpretation at Plimoth Plantation as "group encounter sessions"); the rise of the discourses of the personal as political in social movements like Women's Liberation; and self-help culture at large.[11] These impulses stressed personal discovery through interaction and sensation and have been read by scholars as both symptomatic of and an effort to cope with larger cultural, political, and economic displacements of the time.[12] Aspects of these projects, which foregrounded both self-actualization and empathetic identification between individuals, were characteristic of the larger culture that produced reenactment. This cultural tendency combined with the concurrent transition toward "bottom-up" accounts of the past in academic, public, and popular history to forge a new category of historic consciousness and knowledge production, first seen in the changes in preservation and museum activity and continuing through the rise of reenactive expressions of the past.

The Living Bicentennial

Reenactive forms of historical engagement and meaning making permeated many history-based cultural productions in the 1970s, but the most convincing evidence of this transformation is the sheer number of reenactments that came to be a part of the Bicentennial. As the nature and form of the commemoration moved through several transformations in the early 1970s, federal planners came to reverse its previous position on reenactments and by 1975 even formed a special subcommittee to recognize and support reenactment programming. These projects took on many subjects, from historical occurrences surrounding the American Revolution to concurrent expeditions and initiatives to incidents from the larger American past. Some focused on Revolutionary War conflicts such as the battles of Concord and Lexington, but, rather than the battles themselves, they most often depicted muster or triumph: soldiers preparing to fight or returning from battle.[13] As widespread interest in the feelings and experiences of the past began to inform historical understanding and expression, performative historical practices progressed from battle reenactments to other instances in American history. At the same time, more people were looking for ways to participate in experiential history, either as reenactors or as spectators, and so these projects gained public interest and support.

Most often, Revolutionary War reenactments undertaken by groups and individuals took travel or transportation as their subject, depicting such events as Washington's crossing of the Delaware River or Paul Revere's ride.[14] While some were supported by federal and state Bicentennial organizations, others were outside of the purview of state planning or funding. Sponsored by local 4-H clubs, Jerry Linker, a twenty-two-year-old blacksmith from Charlotte, North Carolina, relived a six-hundred-mile horseback ride between Charlotte and Philadelphia by Captain James Jack, who had carried a declaration of independence by Charlotte militia to the colonial capital.[15] Under the supervision of a professor at Arizona State University, a group of local Boy Scout chapters retraced a historic cavalry trail, hoping to give tourists "an honest opportunity to relive history."[16] Reenacting a once-common trek from Hawaii to Tahiti, a crew of twenty-six, including historians, scientists, and craftspeople, sailed a sixty-five-foot canoe that had been constructed using historic plans and methods. In preparation for the trip, crewmembers learned about traditional means of fishing and distilling water and trained in celestial navigation at a local planetarium.[17] Great effort was put into replicating the original conditions of the past as closely as possible—not only with regard to costume and appearance but also to skills and approaches. It was this sort of accuracy that would lead to authentic emotional understanding: the trip would not only look like the past but would *feel* like it as well.

There are several ways to interpret this emphasis on travel in the context of the socioeconomic and cultural climate of the time: on one hand, mobility had long been a part of the American experience, so these trips might have been building upon this already present inclination.[18] At the same time, interest in nonautomotive transport could have been related to the considerable popularity during this period of commune living and "back to the land" experimentation.[19] Although the majority of Bicentennial transportation projects concerned historical themes, there were other endeavors that made use of unconventional transportation; the largest among them, the "Bikecentennial," featured several hundred bicyclists riding across the United States.[20] The alternative modes of transport (biking, walking, horseback) enacted by Bicentennial reenactments and other trips could also be read as an expression of anxieties about the restrictions to mobility that the gas shortages and the oil crisis of the period presented.[21] Through reenactments of transportation, Americans reasserted the possibility of continued movement in the present by looking to travel in the national past.

The experiential and emotive currency of immersive history was appealing to program coordinators from federal and state Bicentennial initiatives, who encouraged reenactive practice to highlight histories from across the United States. Embodied engagement with the past could underscore commonalities between the personal qualities and experiences of colonial agents in all parts of the nation and extend identification with these qualities into the present. Bicentennial organizers in western states aspired to suture local events into national history through reenactments of Spanish colonial movement westward. Costumed horseback riders retraced the 1776 expedition of Juan Bautista de Anza from Mexico City to San Francisco, using the explorer's diaries to align their activities to the dates and times of two hundred years earlier.[22] A reenactment of the Dominguez-Escalante

Expedition traced the path of the Spanish missionaries across Colorado, Utah, Arizona, and New Mexico.[23]

Ideologically, these reenacted journeys were a way for western states to build themselves into a triumphant narrative of the Revolution: if 1776 had been a critical moment of nation building, then so too were the explorations that would eventually lead to western expansion and "manifest destiny." The Sunbelt region of the United States, the area where the majority of these exploratory reenactments were staged, was growing in wealth, prestige, and—most importantly—political influence in the 1970s.[24] Reenactments that aimed to reassert the importance of the West within the trajectory of American history reflected this new regional prominence. With these projects, Bicentennial organizers in western states stressed their experiences as temporally and thematically correspondent to those of the East. Raul Castro, then the governor of Arizona, made the importance of such activities explicit: "What went on in Philadelphia in 1776 is meaningless here, especially to a guy like me, who came from Mexico. The Anglos are celebrating the Mayflower . . . the Mexican-Americans are looking at the Spanish settlers. But the patriotism and love of country are the same."[25] Castro's statement shows the kind of positive and personalized nationalistic identification that could be facilitated through reenactment.

Other exploratory reenactments used the experiential nature of the practice to question both the history and the legacy of western expansion. In Elgin, Illinois, Reid Lewis, a high school French teacher and Eagle Scout leader who had re-created the Joilet-Marquette Expedition to the Mississippi in 1973, began planning a larger venture for 1976: a reenactment of Robert de La Salle's expedition from Montreal to New Orleans, which took place in 1681 and had opened the way for French colonization in the Mississippi Valley. Lewis saw the exercise as a way to complicate existing knowledge of the settlement of the Mississippi Valley by calling attention to voyages outside of the conventional narrative of westward expansion by wagon.[26]

Lewis, along with five other teachers, a playwright, a priest, and sixteen students, began training in 1974, two years prior to the reenactment. In order to ensure that every aspect of the trip would be as close as possible to the original, Lewis put together an impressive team of experts to conduct new research and to train participants, including specialists in meteorology, physical education, geography, history, French, and environmental studies, and the director of the cartography department at the Newberry Library in Chicago. The group studied and fashioned their own seventeenth-century

Reenacting the 1776 Juan Bautista de Anza Expedition from Mexico City to San Francisco, 1976. From American Revolution Bicentennial Administration, *The Bicentennial of the United States of America: A Final Report to the People.*

clothing and acquired hand-carved replicas of wooden chests of the type used by the original expedition.[27] Throughout the eight-month journey, Lewis and his companions assumed the names of the members of La Salle's group and subsisted on the original expedition members' diet of beans, peas, and fried bread in an effort to approximate the trip as closely as possible.[28] Like other reenactors, the La Salle group placed as much emphasis on the authenticity of experience as on the authenticity of appearance.

Lewis and his companions wanted to use their project to prompt both a deeper understanding and a reevaluation of both past and present. As Lewis said to a reporter from the *Chicago Tribune*, "We'll humanize history for those who see us."[29] In press interviews during the course of the voyage, the La Salle group accented material hardships experienced by the original expedition, hoping that their reenactment of conditions of scarcity could call attention to questions of material inequality and environmental destruction in the contemporary United States. In his original proposal to the American Revolution Bicentennial Administration (ARBA), Lewis had written:

Without this knowledge of our struggling forefathers, we cannot be expected to appreciate the progress which has been made or to understand the errors which have been committed in the development of the Mississippi Valley. People without a sense of history can hardly be blamed for remaining blasé or indifferent in the midst of abundance which, for them has always existed. It is therefore imperative that Americans be imbued with an historical awareness if indeed we are to continue our progress and preserve our environment.[30]

Lewis was addressing environmental imperatives circulating in the present but refracting them through history. For the group, reenactment was a way to contemplate both the progress and the errors of American history as well as to associate the journeys of La Salle and other explorers with contemporary discourses of ecological scarcity. Reenactive historical practices have been critiqued by scholars who worry that they sublimate any sense of historical context, but this is not always true.[31] As Lewis's writings on the La Salle project help demonstrate, reenactment can be more accurately said to allow the emergence of questions and interpretations that connect and compare the past to the present and to transfer historical understanding from the collective to the individual.

For Lewis, another goal of the reenactment was to give his students a new sense of themselves. Reflecting on the experience, he noted, "During the past few years, I've watched my students get more and more cynical about the possibility of individual accomplishment in this society. And I've watched my own generation get more and more contemptuous about youth's ability to respond to challenge."[32] Lewis hoped that his students, in matching the achievements of their historical counterparts, would be moved to reconsider their own roles and actions in contemporary society. And indeed, during the journey and even years later, the students who were a part of the project reported that it had profoundly impacted their lives.[33]

In its attention to historical detail, the La Salle reenactment transported participants and even audiences at least partially into the past. After the reenactment ended, Lewis reported, "so many people told me they looked out on the river . . . and they thought they were back in the seventeenth century."[34] However, because interpretation was self-directed and deeply individualized, audiences and participants made meaning on diverse registers that could not be predicted, or even fully understood. While the La Salle reenactors had carefully considered how the larger history of La Salle and western exploration in general could be used to consider the contemporary scene, the way that the project impacted audiences is more difficult to measure. Even though the La Salle group met with audiences more than five hundred times over the course of the trip, press coverage of the expedition focused on the material and emotional experiences of the reenactors, as opposed to those of audiences.[35] This might have been influenced by the group's own approaches to publicity, but it also points to the difficulty of measuring or even verbalizing affective knowledge, which operates on emotional as opposed to linguistic registers.

The people that Lewis and his party met on their journey were enthusiastic and receptive, coming in crowds to meetings with the reenactors. In some towns, the La Salle group was invited to elaborate dinners prepared using seventeenth-century methods, suggesting that others were interested in participating in the project on the group's own terms.[36] Even though there is no concrete record on how these encounters might have impacted audience knowledge and opinions on the historic La Salle, it is clear that other people were interested and, moreover, that they themselves were open to engaging the past in this manner. The understanding that reenactment forms can be ambiguous and ephemeral, and thus difficult to describe after the moment passed, is a challenging factor for those wishing to study how embodied history generates interpretation. It is evident, however, from Lewis's writings and from the ways in which the expedition was reported upon by the press, that significant historical engagement occurred.

History in Reverse: The Bicentennial Wagon Train

Out of the many reenactments that were part of the Bicentennial, the most prominent was the Bicentennial Wagon Train Pilgrimage. The Wagon Train was organized by the Pennsylvania Bicentennial Commission and featured fifty Conestoga wagons (one from each state) accompanied by trail riders and a coterie of support staff, including chuck wagons and a traveling music review, traveling in reverse from west to east.[37] Project planners were inspired by the heroic histories of westward expansion and Manifest Destiny that had, and continue to have, a lengthy cultural tradition.[38] While some reenactors, like the La Salle group or the Hawaii-Tahiti voyagers, completed original research and saw reenactment as a way to facilitate new historical meaning making, the Wagon Train Pilgrimage was inspired by popular cultural representations of the frontier past and aimed to reinforce an established narrative of westward expansion, one that was at that time losing currency as ongoing social movements and the new social history looked to add more perspectives.

The Wagon Train Pilgrimage, billed by its organizers as "history in reverse," began at five points in the West and, over the course of a year, followed historical wagon trails backward to a July 4, 1976, encampment in Valley Forge, Pennsylvania, where participants celebrated the Bicentennial with thousands of visitors, including President Gerald Ford.[39] Along the way, wagons stopped at numerous communities where locals signed a "pledge of rededication" that the Wagon Train was conveying to Valley Forge.[40] In bringing to life the novels, paintings, and films that informed cultural ideals of American exceptionalism, this state-sponsored project staged a spectacle that attempted to bodily evoke the triumph of the past, bringing it into the present as a renewed patriotism and rededication to civic pride in participants and audiences.

Federal, state, and local Bicentennial organizations across the country supported the endeavor. One of the most heavily funded Bicentennial programs, the Wagon Train Pilgrimage eventually received over $200,000 through the ARBA, as well as additional support from individual states. The Wagon Train had corporate sponsors as well—among them Gulf Oil, Holiday Inn, and the Mayflower moving company, which donated services in kind.[41] Like other programs that celebrated, rather than questioned, American exceptionalism, the Wagon Train was attractive to those seeking to reaffirm traditional American values by invoking a triumphant history of accomplishment that was national in scope. For such sponsors, the pride in the past and belief in national progress that the Wagon Train organizers sought to evoke for spectators would ideally translate to confidence in American business and government, especially in the critical context of the turbulent politics and failing economy of the early to mid-1970s.[42]

Local Bicentennial organizations were involved in the selection of project participants, who included individuals and families chosen from trail-riding and equestrian clubs, the 4-H, and the Boy Scouts of America.[43] In addition to the "official" participants sponsored by their states, independent travelers joined the Wagon Train at every phase of its journey, sometimes with their own horses and wagons, and sometimes on foot. Over the Wagon Train's yearlong trip eastward, the numbers swelled from around three hundred to twelve hundred, demonstrating the widespread appeal of participation in reenactment and the ability of the spectacle to move bystanders to action.[44]

Organizers of the Wagon Train Pilgrimage connected the westward trek that it referenced to the core American ideals that had been established during the Revolution. A widely distributed brochure said of the original pioneers: "the settlers were drawn by a compelling belief in the inalienable rights of man, of liberty, of justice and of freedom—the principles upon which our nation was founded." The Pilgrimage, the brochure continued in civic-religious language, was heading "back to the birthplace of the nation. To rededicate the faith of the nation's citizens to the same principles which inspired their forefathers."[45] The organizers mobilized a familiar monumental history: the image of a mass of wagons moving across the United States. The sight of ordinary Americans reenacting the settlement of the nation was meant to inspire spectators to identify with traditional national values by bringing to life a narrative that they were already familiar with. The trails and wagons that participants used, and the clothing they wore, were characterized as "authentic," not because they were actual historical artifacts, but because they *looked* like historical objects.[46] The emotive response and confusion of temporality created by the spectacle of the Wagon Train would reinforce the values of the triumphant past of the United States and project them onto the more fractured present, ideally resulting in patriotic sentiment among participants and spectators.

If state and corporate endorsement of the Bicentennial Wagon Train resulted from a belief that the enactment of core American values like exploration and industry would motivate viewers to normalize nationalism, the actual participants, or "wagoneers," as they called themselves, were paradoxically both the most critical and the most problematic component of the exercise. The power of reenactment emerges from its volatility: embodied knowledge production can always lead to unexpected forms of consciousness and realization.[47] To planners and sponsors, the wagoneers were necessary to the project but dangerous in that their individual experiences and motivations were complex and unpredictable, often diverging from the "official" discourse of the Wagon Train organizers.

Planners recognized the difficulty of this position and regulated participants in numerous ways. First, they instituted a system that separated groups of wagoneers into elaborate chains of command and asked them to abide by lengthy lists of rules. These measures also separated "official" participants (those who had been chosen and vetted by Bicentennial organizers) from "nonofficial" ones (those who joined the Wagon Train during the trip), ensuring that the former received the most attention from audiences and the media.[48] Organizers also tried to control individual wagoneers through

The Bicentennial Wagon Train rolls through Shippensburg, Pennsylvania.
Courtesy of the Shippensburg Historical Society.

shifting the focus away from them. Publicity material for the Wagon Train omitted participant experience and reflection, in contrast to coverage of other Bicentennial travels like the Bikecentennial, which often included detailed reports on the individuals involved in the trip.[49] Organizers cast individual reenactors as an aggregate: a unified group of bodies with a desire to both commemorate the past and to experience it for themselves. This collective of "authentic" pioneers was meant to stand in for an entire history of American expansion and signal that the ideals associated with that movement continued to exist, even in the embattled present. For audiences, viewing and interacting with participants—but also knowing that they acted on behalf of a state initiative—would ideally help restore positive feeling about and confidence in the United States.

While the official narrative of the Wagon Train stressed pioneer values, looking backward, and patriotism, the wagoneers themselves had many motivations for taking part in the project: some wanted a chance to hone camping, horse training, and survival skills they had previously developed as hobbies, while others wanted to travel the United States in a slow, unhurried fashion.[50] Many were descended from original pioneers and wanted to form a connection with these forbears: as one participant said of her grandmother, who had traveled the Oregon Trail as a child, "I got a wild brainstorm to match her."[51] Cap Galloway, a farmer from Sumas, Washington, rode horseback along the Wagon Train as scout, carrying his grandfather's gun and wearing his Union Army belt buckle.[52] Unlike ARBA, the Pennsylvania Bicentennial Commission, and other official sponsors, the wagoneers were less interested in the grand narrative of westward expansion than in the individual experiences of the pioneers themselves: how they had struggled to survive, how they had felt during their journey—precisely the sort of experiential history that reenactments and reenactment-based projects sought to recover.

It is no surprise, then, that after the journey many wagoneers worked to insert themselves *as individuals* back into the story of the Wagon Train from which they had been excised in promotional and press materials. Following the conclusion of the Wagon Train, the wagoneers built a network that revealed the strong relationships that they had built on the road. The lengthy recollections they circulated in a self-published newsletter called the *WagoNews* affirmed that they did not think of their trip in the context of the traditional sweeping narrative of westward expansion but in terms of daily activities: the monotony of daily travel as well as the camaraderie and community among those sharing the trip.[53] An Iowa couple wrote: "Mostly we remember the days of routine . . . the early morning camp stirrings, the increasing hurrying tempo as departure neared, the hitching and the leaving and the good-byes of the people."[54] Participants were most interested in private, not public, moments. Rather than seeing the original pioneers as heroes, reenactors came to identify with them as regular people like themselves.

In the aftermath of the trip, wagoneers tried to document and make sense of their experience, ultimately coming to reflect upon it in ways that diverged from how Bicentennial organizers and sponsors had conceived of the project. For example, one participant wrote in *WagoNews*, "I have seen the face of America across the country at three and a half miles an hour. It is seeded with pollution and corruption, soiled with personal greeds, and abandoned dreams."[55] His negative appraisal shows why Wagon Train organizers might have been anxious about individual wagoneers. The wagoneers' own accounts of the trip were a direct reaction to their earlier silencing by the Wagon Train organizers. The tension of the reenactment, its unpredictability, and thus its potentiality lay precisely in the multiplicity of meanings made by everyone involved: organizers, reenactors, and audiences. For participants especially, the experience remained an important site of contemplation long after the fact. Emotive knowledge production leaves psychic traces that can be marshaled in the future and applied to different contexts.[56]

For audiences, the Wagon Train also yielded diverse interpretations. Those who witnessed the most public and thus controlled moments of the Wagon Train—the impressive spectacle of westward expansion, the camaraderie and dedication of individual participants—were most likely to feel the pride in both past and present that the organizers intended. In February of 1977, the *WagoNews* published a letter that two wagoneers had received from a woman in Landsdale, Pennsylvania:

> I was in tears and had a lump in my throat when the Wagon Train pulled into Landsdale, your last stop before Valley Forge. I never forgot the thrill and excitement. You brought the 4th of July alive for so many of us. I never dreamed of seeing a wagon train in my life, not a real one. Everyone looked tired, hot, and weary, but Saturday morning it was so exciting seeing you pull out for Valley Forge. I was in tears again. . . . We went to Valley Forge on July 5 and finally found the place you were camped at. The empty wagons look lonely and forgotten sitting there all alone. The effect is lost. I can go to a museum and see empty wagons.[57]

The emotion that this letter writer felt upon seeing the Wagon Train, and the way in which it "brought the 4th of July alive," show how reenactments like the Wagon Train could reinvigorate patriotic feeling. Notably, the letter writer compares seeing the abandoned encampment to "empty wagons" in a museum, suggesting that she found the reenactment to be a much more powerful form of historical engagement. For visitors to the Wagon Train encampments, the encounter highlighted the ability of reenactment to portray the everyday past. In Blair, Washington, wagoneer Francis Parkman told a captive audience about "what the movies skip: biting flies, choking dust, and jarring miles in the saddle or on a spine-whacking wagon seat."[58] Parkman's account, supplemented by his dirty costume, tired horse, and dusty wagon, differed from the more sanitized version of frontier travel to which most audiences were accustomed. At the public intervals of the Wagon Train, when wagoneers in pioneer garb drove dozens of wagons past cheering crowds, when the Scroll of Rededication was produced and signed, the reenactment most often did what planners and sponsors had anticipated:

it evoked for audiences an affirmation of "American" values and accomplishments, albeit with a more nuanced understanding of pioneer life.[59]

But the duration of the reenactment created moments at which the lived present slipped into the performed past: when not participating in civic events along the trail, some wagoneers did not wear their period costumes. They supplemented their pioneer clothing with badges they picked up along the way, and many of the wagons were eventually decorated with bumper stickers.[60] On the road, Wagon Train culture came to resemble contemporary commune culture, an explicitly antistate milieu that also had roots in an interest in historical frontierism and the drive among original pioneers to form communities outside of the government's reach.[61] The meanings reenactors made through this kind of elision diverged from the communal public affect of patriotism sought by Wagon Train organizers. During the liminal moments of the reenactment, when the expectations within which both reenactors and audiences were working broke down, the contingency of affect that always marks reenactment emerged. These are precisely the moments that separate reenactment from other forms of public performance or exhibition. Reenactment moves between the public spectacle and the private introspect.

Similarly, other nonpublic moments during the Wagon Train became sites at which participants and audiences could question the history underwriting the project. Following the most traditional accounts of westward expansion, the narrative put forth in official publicity material ignored the encroachment on native peoples and lands, or cast it in positive light. Wagon Train organizers attempted to publicize a story that wagoneers had "smoked a peace pipe" with representatives from local Native American groups in Washington State. What had actually happened was very different; members of the Stillaguamish tribe in Ferndale, Washington, had threatened to blockade the Wagon Train's route as a part of a demonstration seeking tribal recognition from the government.[62]

While news coverage of unplanned obstacles like the blockade was undesirable and had to be managed and suppressed, organizers felt that spectacular confrontations between native peoples and the Wagon Train, if they could be planned and controlled, could add to the reenactment by bringing it closer to conventional histories of westward expansion. One story that did circulate widely in the media was that organizers had asked tribal representatives in Puyallup, Washington, to "stage an ambush" of the train as it passed through their lands. The tribe balked at this request, and news stories about the event stressed the continued racism inherent in such a demand.[63] This confrontation and the publicity that followed contested the triumphal history promoted by Wagon Train organizers, simultaneously emphasizing wide-ranging experiences of westward expansion *and* the continuity of racism experienced by Native Americans.

In the same way, wagoneers reported that they had been "plenty scared" passing through the Dakotas, where the U.S. military had recently confronted Native American activists at the historical site of Wounded Knee, ostensibly because they recognized that their reenactment might be seen as offensive by Native Americans, but perhaps also in response to historical accounts of frontier travel that foregrounded native violence against pioneers.[64] Again, in this case, the historic and the contemporary came together in interesting ways. The excess of meaning produced by reenactment could lead to multiple and contradictory interpretations and evaluations, particularly with regard to comparison between past and present.

Protesting the Past

The insensitivity displayed by Wagon Train organizers in their dealings with tribal representatives was typical of more widespread attitudes among commemoration planners. Native Americans arguably had the most fraught relationship with the Bicentennial, since it celebrated a milestone in the consolidation of a colonization effort that had resulted in countless displacements and deaths of native peoples.[65] Native Americans were wary of the Bicentennial, calling attention to continued oppression and the incongruity of the celebration, a contradiction that continued to be ignored by many white Americans.[66] Charles Johnson, director of the Portland Urban Indian Program, reported that organizers had asked his group to join the Bicentennial Wagon Train as it made its way through Oregon. Echoing the feelings of many Native Americans, Johnson commented, "We felt the invitation was like the Germans inviting the Jews to celebrate Hitler's rise to power."[67] This lack of consideration for the perspective of Native Americans is illustrative of the majority of the mainstream Bicentennial and symptomatic of the marginalization experienced by many Native Americans.

As a result, many Native American activists—like the group who had blockaded the Wagon Train—situated themselves in direct opposition to the Bicentennial, on the grounds that it symbolized a history that not only ignored the Native American experience but also celebrated its suppression. Among the most prominent groups was the American Indian Movement (AIM), which was just one of several groups that had been inspired by the

African American freedom struggle and that had been building momentum since the late 1960s.[68] AIM leaders Dennis Banks and Clyde Bellecourt made several statements to the press about the inappropriateness of the celebration, calling upon Native Americans to protest the Bicentennial and telling journalists, "If they're going to have a party, we're going to be there to blow out their birthday candles."[69] For Banks, Bellecourt, and others, the commemoration was an opportunity to question the assumptions that many held about Native Americans, and about the longer history of colonization and conquest. AIM saw the Bicentennial, and the type of normative patriotic sentiment that groups like the Wagon Train organizers encouraged, as an occasion to underscore ongoing problems.

Apart from the Bicentennial, American history, especially the history of American brutality toward Native Americans, figured prominently in AIM movement discourse and actions. The group staged several interventions in mainstream commemorations, calling attention to the erasures evident in dominant narratives of the American past. One of AIM's early actions had been a 1970 Thanksgiving Day occupation of Plymouth, Massachusetts, where the 1620 *Mayflower* landing had brought early white settlers to the American continent. In later memoirs, AIM's Russell Means and Dennis Banks both recalled that a local tribe, the Wampanoag, had invited AIM to Plimoth Plantation. The museum and the nearby town of Plymouth had long celebrated the first Thanksgiving with parades and other festivities. That year, the Wampanoag wanted to commemorate Thanksgiving as a "day of mourning" to call attention to the theft of land and violence perpetrated by the original colonists and to continuing problems for contemporary Native Americans. Also marking the 350th anniversary of the settling of the colony, the 1970 celebration was to be especially significant for both native and white residents of Plymouth and its surroundings.[70]

A delegation of AIM activists, accompanied by the Wampanoag and tribal activists from all over the country, met at Plimoth Plantation, disrupting a reenactment of the first Thanksgiving dinner already underway. The reenactors, assuming that contemporary Indians had come to celebrate the occasion, invited the activists to join. In the middle of a welcoming speech, Banks upended one of the tables, yelling "We won't eat this crap!," which in turn provoked the other tribal representatives to do the same before making a hasty exit.[71] This incident brings to the foreground the complexities and potentials of embodied history. The myth of Thanksgiving as a shared meal between colonists and Indians being re-created at Plimoth erased the history of conflict between the groups and propagated a narrative of a peaceful and consensual settlement rather than a violent imperial action. Like the Bicentennial Wagon Train, it took for source material a commonplace American myth that downplayed the brutality of colonization.

For planners at Plimoth Plantation, the Thanksgiving reenactment functioned as a spectacular reconstruction of the two groups meeting and sharing food and as a means of channeling affective identifications in reenactors and spectators that recast native-colonist relations as friendly and mutually constituted. The confusion that followed the entry of the AIM and Wampanoag groups, and the invitation that stemmed from the assumption by the Plimoth reenactors that they would want to join in the reenactment as representatives of Indians simultaneously past and present, speaks to the complex way that affective states generated in reenactment are articulated. Banks's own gesture, the overturning of the table and the disavowal of participation, may also be interpreted as temporally indeterminate—he was refusing on his behalf and on the part of the historic Native Americans who had participated in the first Thanksgiving, as well as disrupting the "script" of the reenactment—that is, the assumed outcome of community that the exercise attempted to build, and was not achieved.

AIM's next move reflected their historical perspective on links between the occupation of land and the erosion of rights. From Plimoth Plantation, the delegation headed to the town of Plymouth, where Plymouth Rock stood alongside a new replica of the ship *Mayflower*. By midmorning, nearly two hundred demonstrators had assembled under a nearby statue of Massasoit, who had been chief of the Wampanoag in 1620. There, Means made an impromptu speech, saying "Today you will see the Indian reclaim the *Mayflower* in a symbolic gesture to reclaim our rights in this country."[72] Next, twenty-five activists boarded the *Mayflower* replica, removed the British and American flags from on board, and threw a mannequin of the ship captain overboard.[73] Again, this was a temporally indeterminate act: AIM activists were operating in the present by protesting the *Mayflower* replica's commemoration of the original landing but also performing the past: both presenting and experiencing an empowering counterfactual history in which *historical* Indians resisted the initial landing. The speech and the action illustrate how Means and AIM mobilized history in order to redress present wrongs, and how they did this in opposition to mainstream commemoration.

AIM was not alone in this perception of embodied history as a site at which to contest mainstream historical narratives and to forge and explore comparisons between the injustices of the past and present. Several other groups staged Bicentennial reenactments to call for a reevaluation of the

American political project. The Boston Tea Party, one of the best-known incidents leading up to the Revolution, was reenacted on its own bicentennial in December of 1973, not only in Boston but in cities all over the United States.[74] In these reenactments, the events of the Revolution and the political and economic grievances they articulated were connected to a variety of contemporary concerns. The stagnant economy of the 1970s led many actors on the political spectrum to find meaning in the historical Tea Party's economic protest. Reenactors channeled the frustration and anger felt by the original colonists into their own projects, making the historical Tea Party stand for a range of contemporary interests, including government taxing, anticorporatism, the ratification of the Equal Rights Amendment, and continued racism toward Native Americans.[75] Protesters viewed the American past as a storehouse of empirical and affective information for framing their own contemporary social movements. A feeling of empathy drove them to make identifications that in turn reinterpreted Revolutionary history. These histories were both contested as narratives and deployed as strategies by activists.

By the early to mid-1970s, the impulse to learn about the past by feeling it was consolidated and extended with the emergence of embodied engagement with the past as the predominant mode of thinking about and interacting with history. This can be seen in the reenactive practices that began to characterize history exhibition, but the preponderance of reenactment activity surrounding the Bicentennial demonstrates the magnitude of this transformation. Projects that produced historical knowledge at the level of emotional understanding and identification relied on embodied, not textual, interpretation, building upon a permeable sense of temporality created by bodily immersion into aspects of the past. While some used reenactment to engender sentimentality and pride in the American past and motivate nationalist support of the ongoing U.S. political project, others—both participants and spectators—found reenactments to be productive sites at which to reevaluate their own ideas about the American past and present. These historical cultural productions thus made and circulated more ambiguous meanings. A comparative view of the past and the present, particularly filtered through emotion as well as information, could bring about raised consciousness about individual and national identity and past and present inequality. Embodied, immersive history, by the 1970s, led to a number of different interpretations.

CHAPTER SIX

History Comes Alive

Activism, Identification, and the American Archive

> These are not done just as play acting. They are done symbolically,
> for their profound meaning to this generation. We respect, we
> recall, we reenact historic events because they clarify and emphasize
> for us that we today face issues from which we cannot shrink.
>
> —"The Boston Tea Party . . . and This Generation," *Boston Globe*
>   editorial, December 10, 1973

> If history were past, history wouldn't matter. History is the
> present. . . . You and I are history. We carry our history. We act
> our history.
>
> —JAMES BALDWIN, *A Rap on Race*, 1971

On December 16, 1973, the city of Boston kicked off its Bicentennial celebration with a widely publicized commemoration of the 1773 Boston Tea
Party. The official planning body, Boston 200, worked with carefully chosen corporate sponsors like John Hancock Insurance and the Salada Tea
Company to schedule several programs: a lecture series on colonial history,
an exhibition on teas of China, an eighteenth-century music concert, a lun-
cheon, and a parade. But the central event of the day was a reenactment. At
the Boston Harbor, a crowd of over twenty thousand watched as professional
actors dressed as Native Americans boarded the brig *Beaver II*, an exact replica of one of the original British merchant ships, and dumped tea crates
over the railing, just as colonialists dissatisfied with high taxes on teas had
done two hundred years earlier.[1]

But alongside the official events planned by Boston 200, others were also
making their voices heard, using the commemoration and the contemplation of history that it inspired to promote contemporary issues. While a local
chapter of the National Organization for Women marched in the parade,
accompanied by a fife rendition of "Yankee Doodle," the conservative Committee for Individual Liberty held a rally. Delegates from the Disabled
American Veterans, who had long been reenacting the Tea Party, were dis-
placed by the official celebrants and instead threw chests of maple leaves

The National Organization for Women was one of many groups that used Boston 200's 1973 official commemoration of the Boston Tea Party to bring attention to their own issues. Courtesy of the City of Boston Archives.

into Boston Harbor. On the other end of the harbor, the Boston Indian Council protested the Native American costumes worn by both the veterans and the Boston 200 group.[2] It was evident that the history of the Boston Tea Party, one of the first acts of revolution on the part of American colonists, was a source of inspiration for many who connected that historical protest with their own contemporary ones.

Although many groups capitalized upon the official reenactment to bring attention to their own concerns, it was the People's Bicentennial Commission (PBC), the largest and most visible oppositional group in dialogue with official Bicentennial planners, that made the biggest impression. PBC members from local chapters all over New England and from the national office in Washington traveled to Boston for the occasion, which they renamed the "Oil Party" as a response to the recent embargo on oil by the Organization of Petroleum Exporting Countries (OPEC). Carrying signs that read "The

Spirit of '76 Lives On," "John Hancock Didn't Sell Insurance," and "Impeach Richard I," protestors hurled empty oil drums into the Charles River. One PBC delegate, wearing an oversized papier-mâché head of Richard Nixon and dressed in a royal robe and a crown covered with the logos of Exxon, Texaco, and other major oil companies, boarded a small boat and was rowed around the replica ship.[3]

For Boston 200, the Tea Party was meant to commemorate an incident at the foundation of contemporary democratic practice, but one marking a grievance that had been resolved long ago. In contrast, the PBC wanted to use the event not as a remembrance, but to protest against persistent problems that threatened the body politic. Spectators, the PBC hoped, would identify with their colonial predecessors in their outrage at the contemporary status quo, linking current political and economic complaints to prior ones. Through this association of shared emotions, the revolution of the past would help ignite action in the present.

Media coverage of the Tea Party focused overwhelmingly upon the PBC's efforts; newspapers across the nation reprinted photographs of the crowd of protestors and the Nixon head circling the *Beaver II*.[4] Instead of the patriotic support that official planners had expected to instill in Boston residents, many critics and spectators made exactly the connections between the past and the present that the PBC had hoped to encourage. At one point, a reporter from the Associated Press recounted, a PBC member had shouted over a loudspeaker, "How many think he [the Nixon effigy] should be taken to the boat and hung?" The crowd had responded with loud cheers. Stephen Isaacs, writing for the *Washington Post* the next day, noted that the PBC's actions responded to a "quiet desperation," calling Boston 200's celebration "artificial" and "contrived" in comparison to the PBC's more authentic protest.[5] It was evident that, for many participants and spectators, the day's events had not, as had been intended, marked a commemoration of an inspirational moment from the past but had instead sparked an appraisal of the present.

By this time, for many Americans, the past had come to be a space in which to explore and build individual and community identities. But for those who wanted to bring about political, social, or cultural change, history became both a language with which to express contemporary problems and itself a site to be examined. Many different activists organized around new historical inquiries and interpretations, making the past central to their discourses. During the Bicentennial Era, agents working for change across a variety of fronts engaged with and used accounts of the American past in order to form politicized subjectivities, to create constituencies, and to demand rights and equality in the present. While museums and other history institutions staged historical encounters that helped audiences understand the past by thinking about it in terms of present-day experiences, for many activists during this era, this relationship was reversed: learning about, rethinking, and finally identifying with the past, at a moment during which the entire nation was newly interested in American history, was a way to build politicized consciousness and encourage change in the present.

Activists working from many perspectives held differing views on the Bicentennial's relationship with American history. While the PBC saw widespread ambivalence as an occasion to review the state's management and articulation of history and to advance its own affective reinterpretation of the connection of the past to the present, many African American cultural workers, building upon an ongoing project that had begun much earlier, used interest and funding created by the federal Bicentennial to introduce documentation and accounts of the African American experience into mainstream representations of history. Others disavowed the state-sponsored Bicentennial as a celebration of continued exploitation but still emphasized that a sense of history—a usable past—was critical to movement building. The Black Panther Party and other members of the Fourth of July Coalition questioned the Bicentennial, instead calling attention to the long history of inequality that standard accounts ignored. These activities represent very different understandings and uses of American history, yet all were in close relation with the more general reformulation of historical consciousness that was occurring at the time. The different ways that activists engaged the past during this period illustrates how a sense of history based on emotional identification informed, and sometimes even defined, politicized consciousness and action.

Activists' interactions with and expressions of history in the service of inclusion, equality, and change testify to the different ways in which the past can be mobilized toward explicitly political ends. Looking at these efforts, I return to the politicized context of chapter 2, not from the perspective of state articulation of history and commemoration in the interest of maintaining hegemonic power, but from that of opposition, resistance, and refusal from individuals and groups outside of the mainstream. For a range of interests, the historical became the terrain upon which to marshal political positions.

Modern-Day Tom Paines: The People's Bicentennial Commission

The events of the 1973 Boston Tea Party made national headlines, but it was not the first time that many Americans had heard of the People's Bicentennial Commission, which, by that time, had become a prominent part of public discourse around the Bicentennial. The PBC had first appeared two years earlier, amid a larger destabilization and reorganization of progressive activism. Throughout its five-year existence, the PBC criticized the U.S. government's and other dominant interests' investment in and uses of American history in the expression and maintenance of hegemonic power, encouraging, instead, widespread reevaluation of and identification with the principles of the American Revolution.[6]

While the 1960s had seen significant organization and mobilization by progressives, by the early 1970s, activists on what had become the mainstream Left were divided over ideology and strategy, searching for fresh perspectives on both. A broad coalition had supported the effort to end the Vietnam War at the beginning of the decade, and individual movements like women's, gay, and Chicano liberation, and antinuclear organization continued to flourish throughout the 1970s.[7] But New Left groups like the Students for a Democratic Society (SDS) floundered, as factions debated forming alliances with American workers on one hand, and Third World revolutionaries on the other.[8] Disagreements led to divisions within the movement, as progressives struggled to plan their programs of action. Older Communist and Socialist organizations also split over issues of constituencies, labor, politics, and, above all, foreign policy.[9] For many activists affiliated with the now-splintering student and antiwar movements of the previous decade, the 1970s were characterized by contention, confusion, and disunion.

In the midst of these splits and reorientations, many progressives began reconsidering the American past as part of their evaluation of the American present. In the early 1970s, John Rossen, a Chicago-based veteran of the U.S. branch of the Communist Party who had traveled with the Lincoln Brigade to Spain and had been active in Chicago's SDS, began writing pamphlets that combined Marxist principles with a concept he called "revolutionary nationalism." Rossen argued that American progressives, in their emphasis on struggles in the Third World, had forgotten their own revolutionary tradition.[10] Reacting to what he considered to be the failures of sixties-era activism, Rossen wrote, "This weakness, this shortcoming of the

American Left, Old and New, has played right into the hands of the American imperialists . . . who find it easier to keep hidden from the American people their own revolutionary roots and traditions, and are able with greater ease to smear revolution and revolutionaries as foreign-inspired and alien to America and Americanism."[11] For Rossen, American progressives' neglect of American history not only led to a misunderstanding of American character, but also left them vulnerable to attacks from the Right. Rossen called for renewed awareness and consideration of the American past that would realign nationalism with a heritage of revolution. Rossen's concepts proved attractive to many progressives who, in the wake of the dissolution of unified movements, were searching for ways to move forward.[12]

In the fall of 1971, around the time that official Bicentennial planning was gaining its first critiques from commentators, Jeremy Rifkin, a business student and activist who had worked with some of Rossen's groups in Chicago, embraced the idea of a homegrown revolutionary tradition and formed the People's Bicentennial Commission, a new group that planned to use the upcoming celebration of the Bicentennial to criticize U.S. state and corporate interests and to call attention to what they saw as a forgotten history of revolution. In an article for the leftist journal the *Progressive*, Rifkin wrote: "For the American Left to develop a strategy that can win popular support for programs that answer present grievances, it must first gain a clear understanding of the role which the American heritage plays in the formation of the American people's political attitudes and behavior."[13] In Rifkin's eyes, the Right—symbolized by Richard Nixon and the American Revolution Bicentennial Commission (ARBC)—was co-opting the American past in order to legitimize its own position. A reevaluation of this past and its legacies in the present could inspire activists and reorient citizen support toward more progressive causes. The Bicentennial presented an opportunity to gather wide support for a movement that would build its ideas on a reflection of American history and its resonance in the contemporary.

The PBC's earliest media statements and publications attacked the official Bicentennial as an assault on the very terms of the past.[14] The PBC was founded precisely at the moment that the ARBC's original plans to stage an international exposition to celebrate the Bicentennial began to lose popular support. The delegitimization of the state's automatic ownership over national narratives and the terms of commemorations opened up space for the PBC to make its intervention. Seizing upon allegations of mismanagement by the ARBC that had begun to surface in the press and with the American public, Rifkin wrote that the Nixon administration, the commission, and their corporate partners were undertaking "psychological warfare, of a scope and magnitude unparalleled in American history. . . . Their objective is to maintain and expand the power they already enjoy by neutralizing the discontent and by mobilizing millions of Americans into enthusiastic support of the very institutions, values, and power relationships that are the source of the present social crisis."[15] By focusing upon state manipulation, the PBC aimed to "redirect" the Bicentennial campaign "to build a mass-based social movement for a just and humane society for us all to live in."[16] Rifkin recast the state's use of the commemoration in alarmist rhetoric, using language that recalled the terms of the Vietnam conflict and placing them within a domestic context. His antigovernment discourse pointed to corruption and ideological manipulation and was consistent with a long-standing leftist critique of state action, but its transposition onto the meaning of American history was new. The historical and, particularly, collective memory had become contested ground.[17] For the PBC, the Bicentennial represented a struggle to redefine ideas of national heritage and of patriotism, to be fought on the symbolic terrain of the American past.[18]

From the beginning of its existence, the PBC positioned itself as a direct alternative to the ARBC, dedicated to exposing the corruptions and manipulations of the state agency and searching for more meaningful ways to celebrate the Bicentennial. In this first goal, the PBC was almost immediately successful. In one of their first initiatives, the PBC leaked documents to the press that exposed the Nixon White House's control over the supposedly nonpartisan planning of the Bicentennial. As detailed in chapter 2, the leak led to the resignation of ARBC chair David Mahoney and subsequent General Accounting Office and House Judiciary Committee investigations that resulted in the dissolution and reconfiguration of the ARBC into the American Revolution Bicentennial Administration (ARBA). The media, especially the *Washington Post*, covered the PBC and Rifkin favorably, publishing a series of articles praising the PBC's watchdog activities.[19] Rifkin and the PBC proved adept at garnering media coverage and accumulating support from a range of interests, including the Eagle Scouts, the American Legion, and the congressional Black Caucus.[20] Early enthusiasts, including conservative columnist James J. Kilpatrick, praised the PBC's "healthy questioning" of the Bicentennial, reflecting wide resistance to a top-down celebration and growing unease with the Nixon White House on the part of many Americans.[21] The PBC's accusations of corruption and partisanship came as the Nixon administration was increasingly under fire for the cover-ups surrounding the Watergate scandals; it was easy for the press and the public to believe that this kind of maneuvering had extended to the Bicentennial itself and to support activists who advocated a more relevant and nonpartisan observance of the history and ideals of the Revolution.

As the PBC worked to discredit official Bicentennial planning, the group also invited Americans to learn about the Revolutionary past for themselves.[22] In *America's Birthday*, a planning and activity guide published in 1973 by Simon & Schuster, the PBC again accused federal interests of "a bicentennial plan to manipulate the mass psychology of an entire nation" and appealed to readers to look to "the real importance of historical figures" by applying the past to the present.[23] *America's Birthday* featured capsule histories and reading lists but also called for local TEA (Tax Equity for Americans) parties and the introduction of Student Bills of Rights in high schools and colleges.[24] These projects capitalized upon popular interest in the past, comparing the present social, political, and economic conditions with those of two hundred years prior. With these publications, the PBC provided a framework by which readers could apply Revolutionary principles to their own lives.

The PBC's historical revisionism identified exemplars of Revolutionary thought and action spanning the previous two centuries but carefully omitted the most recent New Left from this history, on the grounds that those movements did not represent a nationalistic patriotic heritage. Their list of progressive American "patriots" included the Grange movements, Mother Jones and the Industrial Workers of the World, W. E. B. Du Bois, and Eugene Debs.[25] From the beginning, the PBC in their publicity materials distanced themselves from the internationalism of the New Left and other radical movements of the 1960s and 1970s, denouncing their adherence to the rhetoric of Lenin, Mao, and Castro. Instead, Rifkin and the PBC called for a return to the homegrown values of Revolutionary America, those that had been passed along in the Declaration of Independence and the writings of Thomas Paine and Samuel Adams, among others.[26]

Although the PBC had grown out of Rossen's Marxist framework, the group worked to obfuscate these associations. This was partly because Rifkin and others, disillusioned with the splintering of the New Left, felt that it had strayed from the nationalistic patriotic tradition, but, more specifically, it was because, at this point, identification with the New Left, and especially radical factions like the Weather Underground, was a liability for the broad consensus that the PBC was attempting to form. As Sheila Rollins, a staff member in the PBC's national office, noted in a press interview, "It's a populist movement. Democratic with a small 'd.' We are not really a liberal plant."[27] The PBC worked to create a movement ideology supported by a new conception of U.S. history that would appeal to many different Americans.

In its reconsideration of Revolutionary history, the PBC underscored persistent parallels between the past and the present, calling for a social activism legitimated through the history of the American Revolution. The PBC's intervention was not in adding new information to accounts of the American Revolution, but in challenging the state's avowals of a direct correlation between historical revolutionaries and the political leaders of the present. PBC publications emphasized comparisons across the two eras, making statements like, "This is America in the '70s. The 1770s and the 1970s."[28] The preconditions for revolution that existed in the 1770s were, for the PBC, also present in the 1970s. Contemporary leaders were not, as Nixon and the ARBC were implying, the heirs of the patriots, but instead more akin to the British Parliament, invested in a conservative account of the Revolution in order to quell revolutionary sentiment in contemporary citizens.[29] The PBC advocated for a second American Revolution that would stem from a reassessment of and a new empathetic identification with the past: "the Bicentennial can provide a common language and psychology that can unite individuals and groups into a force for real change during the Bicentennial decade."[30] Movement discourse took up figures like Tom Paine and actions like the Boston Massacre and reoriented them to the present day, forming connections with disaffection in the contemporary.

PBC publications highlighted the links between the 1770s and 1970s using a rhetorical strategy that posited that historical figures, returning to the present in the manner of the *Meeting of Minds* television program or the Franklin Exchange telephone bank, would be disappointed when faced with the America of contemporary times. For example, in support of an upcoming demonstration, the PBC published a pamphlet that read as follows:

If the patriots of the 1770s could take a look at the economy of the 1970s, they'd be staggered by our silence. The burning issues of 200 years ago read like the front page of today's newspapers. High prices, shortages of vital goods, new taxes, growing unemployment, gross discrepancies in wealth. Back then, a handful of troublemakers we now call the patriots pointed an accusing finger at rich merchants and the monarchy. In fact, economics were behind many of the protests that led to the American Revolution. Take the Boston Tea Party for example. The East Indian Company was a multinational tea monopoly of its day. With stockholders and friends sitting in Parliament. When the King tried to help the company corner the American market, the patriots tossed the idea over the side. Two hundred years late, PBC is rocking the boat again. In the tradition of Paine, Adams, and Franklin.[31]

On one hand, the patriots of the past were depicted as somehow reanimated into the present. On the other, the past is described using contemporary terms: the East India Company is a "multinational monopoly," and the king is seen as helping them "corner the American market." The language used by the PBC here and in other publications deliberately fashioned a stronger link across time by bringing both the people and the circumstances of the past and present into direct conversation.

Other PBC materials emulated the visual style of broadsides of the 1770s or included historical writings by Thomas Paine, Sam Adams, and others as "guest opinions" in the PBC newsletter, *Common Sense*.[32] History museum exhibitions like Boston 200's "Revolution" and the Smithsonian's "1876" engendered a temporal indeterminacy that inspired audiences to learn about and contemplate the past by comparing it to the present, but the PBC actively invited these associations, orienting them to a specific politicized context. The PBC worked to legitimize the idea of patriotic revolt, moving away from the correlation that the state had established between patriotism and consent to stimulate indignation, identification, and finally action in those who would recognize that the current trajectory of American history was off course.

To call attention to this discrepancy, the PBC staged events that reinterpreted the relationship between past and present, challenging the state's own program of reenactments of the same material. The PBC recognized the significance of sponsored reenactment as an important site of discovery and meaning making and attempted to disrupt these events by contesting the terms of identification. In the case of the December 1973 Boston Tea Party, this tactic had worked very well, gaining even wider notice and approval for the PBC's cause.

In the months following the Tea Party, the PBC received letters of support from people all over the country. One woman wrote, "I am past forty and have two grandchildren—but a patriot through and through. America needs all ages to WAKE UP!" A correspondent from Cocoa, Florida, said,

"There are three of us here—middle aged, disgusted Republicans—and very concerned Americans." Significantly, many of these letters took on the language of historical identification of the PBC, for example, a man writing from Minneapolis: "if you can put me in contact with any backwoods Sam or Abigail Adams out this way, I'll see what we can carry on."[33] The Tea Party protests occurred at a moment during which parallels across history were clear: the president was being investigated for abuse of executive power, and the continuing oil embargo and economic depression threatened the material abundance that Americans had enjoyed since the end of World War II. More importantly, federal Bicentennial planning had not captured the public imagination, leaving the terms of the commemoration open to public interpretation. The PBC's success in changing the meaning of the Tea Party reenactment testifies not only to the organization's effective co-optation and reorientation of the past toward protest, but also the presence of a willing audience for this mode of consciousness building.[34] The identifications the PBC fostered appealed to many kinds of supporters who were ready to engage with them using the PBC's own language of identification.

But by the next time the PBC organized against another state-sponsored reenactment, both the official Bicentennial and the political climate had undergone significant developments. On April 19, 1975, the PBC called for a rally at the official observance of the skirmishes at Lexington and Concord, the first shots fired in the American Revolution. The PBC began the rally at midnight in the town of Concord and claimed to have amassed 45,000 "new patriots." Promotional materials stressed links to the past: posters and leaflets illustrated with the original image of the "shot heard round the world" resembled eighteenth-century handbills, declaring "Sons and Daughters of Liberty Take Notice."[35] The event included dramatic readings of Revolutionary-era writings by Abigail Adams, Thomas Jefferson, and others, as well as speakers from a selection of labor groups, including Richard Chavez of the United Farm Workers, Don Tormey of the United Electrical Workers, and Aileen Gorman of the National Consumer Congress. Although billed explicitly as a reenactment, the rally also featured contemporary music, speakers, and entertainment, including musical performances by Arlo Guthrie, Pete Seeger, Phil Ochs, and others.[36] The site of reenactment, thus, was not visual or spectacular, but emotive: it was not the *sight* of revolution that would be re-created, but the *feeling*. The political speeches and folk music, although contemporary, would help create an atmosphere of protest and solidarity, encouraging affective identification with patriots of the past and conveying a sense that, in 1975 as in 1775, the United States was on the verge of a revolution.

Once again, the PBC's activities aligned directly against those of the state-sponsored celebration and helped to form a discursive space that questioned the meaning and motives of commemoration. The official program began in the morning, with a speech by President Gerald Ford at the North Bridge of the Concord River, ironically where the British had stood two centuries prior. The PBC protestors across the river loudly booed Ford's speech, and some attempted to approach him by wading into the water and moving to his side. An uneasy Ford rushed through his speech, ultimately leaving Concord earlier than had been planned. The PBC and its supporters celebrated and felt that, in standing down Ford and other state representatives, they had replicated the conditions of the first battle of the Revolution, in which Revolutionary soldiers had similarly stood down British troops.[37]

While the PBC counted this disruption as a success, the media and the public likened the PBC not to the Revolutionary colonists, but instead to the much-denigrated counterculture. Overwhelmingly, the press depicted this effort not as an inspirational political action, but as a troublesome reverie.[38] Perhaps because of the rural location and the relative youth of the protestors, the rally was too reminiscent of Woodstock and other occurrences associated with the counterculture. The media language echoed descriptions of countercultural activity, with one commentator calling the protesters "bearded beer drinkers."[39] The slippage of reenactment, which is never quite predictable and never quite works the way in which one intends, moved in both directions. The state commemoration was ineffective, but while the PBC intended to forge a connection between the protests of the 1970s and the 1770s, the Concord event ended up being read in terms of a more recent, and lately pathologized, history—that of 1960s political activism and counterculture, which were themselves often conflated in the public's mind and memory.

The PBC's commemoration also might have been less potent because it was no longer the only alternative to state-sponsored celebration. By the time of the Concord incident, the ARBC had transitioned into the ARBA and, rather than attempting to mount a centralized commemoration, had adopted the Bicentennial Communities model, encouraging all interested celebrants to plan their own programming.[40] This meant that, just as Rifkin and the PBC had been suggesting, the ARBA invited Americans to make

Protestors from the People's Bicentennial Commission (across the river in the background) disrupt President Gerald Ford's 1975 commemoration of the skirmishes at Lexington and Concord. When PBC representatives started wading in the water to cross the river toward the official event, Ford and his party ended the commemoration early. Courtesy of the Gerald R. Ford Presidential Library and Museum (National Archives and Records Administration).

their own meanings, celebrating whichever aspects of the Bicentennial they found personally significant. In a March 1975 interview with *U.S. News & World Report*, recently appointed Bicentennial administrator John Warner used language that could have come out of a PBC publication: "the word 'bicentennial' is in the public domain. I have no control over it, nor should I have any control. It belongs to the people."[41] The PBC's strongest argument against the state's politicization of the Bicentennial was no longer viable, and the press and the public did not greet its newer critiques, now of economic inequality and corruption, with the same strong popular support.[42]

The new negative reaction against the People's Bicentennial Commission culminated in an investigation by a subcommittee of the Senate Judiciary Committee and a report entitled "The Attempt to Steal the Bicentennial."

The investigation gathered information and evidence from the long history of the People's Bicentennial Commission—including its ties to Rossen, described as a longtime member of the Communist Party and a leader in the Fair Play for Cuba Committee—to characterize the PBC as a subversive, terroristic organization with links to the Weather Underground and socialist parties backed by Fidel Castro.[43] Although there had always been confusion in the media over the PBC's political orientation, after the terms of its protest changed from political to economic, and as a result of the events at the Concord reenactment, it became easier to paint the PBC as a socialistic organization with radical and countercultural affiliations.

The investigation, report, and subsequent media reactions reflected the persistent specter of the 1960s that haunted leftist organizations in the following decade, but, more significantly, they underscored the unpredictability of reenactive practice. While the PBC treated the investigation and subsequent report as a joke, even selling copies of the report signed by PBC leadership, the damage had been done, and the PBC, despite its earlier efforts at distancing itself from radical organizations, became identified with the extremist Left in the media, even by the formerly supportive *Washington Post*.[44] The culmination of the PBC's protest against the Bicentennial, a Washington, DC, rally on July 4, 1976, was poorly attended.[45] Yet the investigations into the group can also be read as a testament to at least the partial success of the PBC's overall project, as a recognition that they had managed to alter press and public opinions about national observance of the Bicentennial and caused many to cast a new and critical eye on American history. The PBC's adoption of history demonstrates that affective historical practice can be used to question dominant perceptions of historical significance and to generate identificatory forms of meaning making that lead to political consciousness.

However, it also shows the ways in which reenactive history is both contingent and often limited to accounts that are already present in the archive, that is, familiar narratives. The PBC's greatest success came from its ability to animate and question already well-known Revolutionary history, in which patriotic colonists staged a political rebellion against an unjust tyrant. When the movement shifted to emphasis on the American Revolution as a form of economic—not political—protest, the press and the public quickly aligned the PBC with leftist extremism because that is what the movement then, on a surface level, resembled. Even so, the PBC played a significant role in unfolding developments within mainstream conceptions and planning for the Bicentennial.

The Black Panther Party and the Bicentennial without Colonies

While the PBC's affective identification was built upon and stemmed from standard and accepted histories, other activists did not work from this template, instead questioning and rejecting established historical narratives. Rather than reorienting the past in the service of change in the present, they looked to deepen and alter popular knowledge of history. Put another way, for the PBC, widespread politicized realization would ideally come from reevaluation of and new associations between past and present. For groups that were further marginalized from the mainstream, a "usable past," that is, a history that could be mobilized to stress ongoing inequalities and encourage change through new identification, would first have to be uncovered. This usable past would need to be simultaneously freed from and added to the archive, our shared storehouse of historical information.[46]

The Fourth of July Coalition, a loose confederation that included the Black Panther Party, the American Indian Movement, the Weather Underground, and activists for the independence of Puerto Rico, called for a "Bicentennial without Colonies," invoking historical comparisons that were quite different from those of the People's Bicentennial Commission.[47] The coalition planned rallies for July 4, 1976, in San Francisco and Philadelphia, designed as an alternative to the celebratory observation of the Bicentennial. In its publicity material, the Fourth of July Coalition called itself the "People's Bicentennial," deliberately appropriating the name from the PBC because the coalition felt that the PBC, in its erasure of race and class from its critique of political and economic power, did not truly represent "the people." While the PBC's movement ideology was built around support and avowal of the original principles of the Revolution, the coalition focused upon inequalities that had been reinforced throughout the two-hundred-year history of the United States.[48] The member organizations of the Fourth of July Coalition considered the settlement of America to be an imperial act and the Revolution to be not a triumph of the disenfranchised but a struggle that ultimately expanded the rights of those already in power.[49]

Some of the most vocal support for the Fourth of July Coalition came from the Bay Area Black Panther Party, which covered planning for the rally in the weeks leading up to Independence Day in its weekly newspaper, the *Black Panther*. Echoing other members of the coalition, the Black Panthers contended that, for the past two hundred years, a liberal democracy purporting to stand for liberty and equality had perpetrated extraordinary oppression. As Ericka Huggins, a leading member of the party, said in her speech at the Fourth of July rally, "Two hundred years ago, a country was born on the sweat, blood and tears of slaves. This country was taken from the Indian by savage adventurers. When the U.S. was founded, its flowery principles of democracy and freedom never included Black people."[50] Huggins was also the director of the Oakland Community School, which emphasized African American history in education programs for local students. Studying history, for the Black Panther Party, was an important part of the longer struggle for self-determination and representation.[51]

The Black Panther Party's Ten Point Platform and Program, instituted in 1966 and revised in 1972, again stressed the importance of the past to the present, echoing calls by James Baldwin, Stokely Carmichael, and others and continuing history education projects begun by efforts like the Freedom Schools of the civil rights movement.[52] The platform stated, "We want education for our people that exposes the true nature of this decadent American society. We want education that teaches us our true history and our role in the present-day society. We believe in an educational system that will give to our people a knowledge of self. If a man does not have knowledge of himself and his position in society and the world, then he has little chance to relate to anything else."[53] The platform linked historical knowledge directly to political identity and consciousness, and so made intervention into mainstream historical narratives both a demand and a plan of action for the Panthers. The Ten Point Platform ended by quoting the preamble to the Declaration of Independence, reappropriating one of the archival cornerstones of the American political project. This adaptation shows the way that meaning could be challenged: in the context of the platform, the use of the Declaration's avowals made connections between the Black Panthers and the historical Revolutionaries but also put pressure on the disjunction between the founding premises of the United States and the lived experience of African Americans. It at once created an affective identification across time and questioned the Declaration's contemporary relevance.

Reflecting the importance of knowing and understanding the past, the *Black Panther* contained a long-running weekly column, "This Week in Black History." Entries included the Denmark Vesey Rebellion in 1822, the removal of antislavery pamphlets from the U.S. mail in 1835, the birth of W. E. B. Du Bois in 1868, and occurrences from the party's own history, such as the 1969 police attack on its Chicago headquarters and the 1970 release of Huey Newton from prison. By aligning these more recent events with those of the past, the Panthers worked to articulate the party's own central position within this trajectory and, like the PBC, placed themselves within the history of revolution.[54] "This Week in Black History" traced a history of continued black presence and activity in the United States, emphasizing that this history was an essential part of African American identity and consciousness. By simultaneously highlighting the history of African American achievement and exposing continued oppression, the Black Panthers articulated a shared identity that would ideally help their constituents come to consciousness in the present.

Building the Archive of African American History

Through initiatives like "This Week in Black History," the Black Panther Party built upon and continued a project that had been started many years before. Material evidence of the African American experience had been omitted from the historical record, and so, a great deal of politicized African American historical activity before and during the Bicentennial often took the form of uncovering histories and adding to the archive. The opportunities and the resources provided by the commemoration allowed African American cultural workers to find and call attention to evidence of contributions, using them as a way to generate and solidify collective African American identities. At that point in time, disparate activities were united by efforts to bring the African American experience to the foreground and to link this history to politicized transformation.

The Black Panther Party shared an ethos and concerns with the Black Arts Movement, which was likewise informed by both cultural nationalism and a desire to effect change. Beginning in the mid-1960s and continuing into the mid-1970s, African American artists, writers, poets, musicians, and dramatists explored African and African American identity and experience through their creative efforts, also building institutional structures like artist collectives and performance spaces to publicize this work and to bring it into communities. Mike Sell, James Smethurst, and other scholars have noted that Black Arts cultural production invoked a complicated set of engagements with the past, often generating work that accentuated continuities between different epochs of African and African American history and culture, and revisited and built upon African and African American traditions of performance and ritual. Black Arts cultural production like that of Sonia Sanchez, Larry Neal, and Sam Cornish often articulated a politicized Pan-African identity, finding, referencing, and recombining cultural and aesthetic forms to underscore the rich heritage of contemporary African Americans.[55]

The LeRoi Jones (Amiri Baraka) play *Slave Ship*, written in 1967 and staged several times in the following years, was somewhat unique in its references to both specific and recent historical incidents, but resembled other Black Arts works in its politicization of the African American experience and its complex representation of the historical. The plot of *Slave Ship* spanned from the Middle Passage to contemporary times and involved both performers and audiences. The same actors played multiple parts across the play's historical progression, and ghostly voices from the slave ship were heard during the play's restaging of contemporary events.[56] Harry Elam Jr. has described the work of Baraka during this period as "social protest performances," that is, theater that was meant to inspire performers and audiences to action.[57] Baraka himself foregrounded affective immersion, writing in his stage directions that the performance should include the sounds and scents of the ocean, as well as the smells of incense and "dirt/filth." For Baraka, this would create a "total atmos-feeling."[58]

In a 1969 production of the play staged at Brooklyn's Chelsea Theater Center, director Gilbert Moses (who would go on to direct an episode of *Roots*) and set designer Eugene Lee envisioned a performance space that situated both performers and audience members directly within the slave ship. Walls were covered in wood planks, and audience members were squeezed together on narrow wooden benches and invited to interact with actors during the course of the play.[59] *Slave Ship* emphasized the importance of history (Baraka even called the play a "historical pageant") and presented an immersive milieu, and encouraged affective, visceral knowledge of and engagement with the past, one that would ideally move audiences to form a new awareness of both the historical and contemporary African American experience.[60] *Slave Ship* was singular in the way that it interrogated the very *form*—the pageant—of the presentation of the past but was also an expression of larger questions of history that were underwriting African American political activity and cultural production at this time.[61]

While Baraka and others were exploring and even foregrounding embodied, affective history, activists affiliated with or working on behalf of public history institutions concentrated on uncovering, as opposed to animating, the past. Given the sheer number of reenactments that took place during the Bicentennial Era, very few of these concerned African American history.[62] Reenactment, as an embodied performance of established archival knowledge, most often requires a material documentary foundation and was thus less available as a strategy of historical activity to a population that had been excluded from the archive in conscious and unconscious ways. Reenactments such as the Bicentennial Wagon Train, the Boston 200 "Revolution" exhibit, and the development of first-person interpretation at Plimoth Plantation were embodied realizations of already-accepted histories of occurrences that had been documented and preserved as evidence. Even the PBC's oppositional reenactments, which attempted to advance new identifications with the Revolution, were grounded in and depended upon public knowledge of a familiar past. The occasion of the Bicentennial underscored the still-prevalent absence of black history in standard accounts and afforded an opportunity for activists and cultural workers to address this problem. The majority of projects with which cultural workers sought to recover and highlight African American history, including the Afro-American Bicentennial Corporation, the Weeksville Society, and Esther Hall Mumford's oral histories in Seattle, concerned the discovery and preservation of materials, stories, and the built environment that demonstrated the existence and contribution of African American individuals and communities throughout the entire existence of the United States.[63] These projects had an affective valence: cultural workers were invested in bringing to light histories that could help form and strengthen collective African American identities.

African American public history in the 1960s and 1970s developed along a trajectory that reflected larger shifts during this period. Although black historians like Carter G. Woodson, Arthur Schomburg, and W. E. B. Du Bois had long argued for the importance of the African American experience in the history of the United States, only a few exceptional individuals like Booker T. Washington or George Washington Carver had been included in conventional accounts like those found in textbooks or in many museum exhibits. The majority of the black experience, including slavery and emancipation, social movements, and cultural activity, was relegated to the periphery of mainstream history. Even African American historians working in earlier decades of the twentieth century had, like others at the time, focused on the legacies of individuals who had managed to achieve success within the racist culture of the United States, as opposed to the everyday experience of African American communities. Part of the challenge was the paucity of preserved material having to do with the everyday African American experience. The archival evidence that informed the formation and dissemination of historical accounts was overwhelmingly associated with those who had had the resources to produce and save materials like publications, diaries, and heirlooms. This lack of sanctioned documentation, combined with enduring structural racism that minimized the role of African Americans in the past and the present, made the legitimization and popularization of African American history an ongoing struggle, and one that was both informed by and embedded within politicized action.[64]

The civil rights movement's emphases on representation and equality and the concurrent rise of social history in museums and the academy led to a radically expanded perspective. In this institutional context, African American scholars and curators in the 1960s and through the 1970s worked to show not only the participation and accomplishment of an enlarged field of individuals, but also to trace daily life in the context of the systematic oppression and brutality that African Americans had suffered. New Black Studies departments were being founded all over the country. Likewise, the opening and expansion of several museums of African American history and culture, including the DuSable Museum in Chicago, the International Afro-American Museum in Detroit, the Smithsonian's Anacostia Neighborhood Museum, and the African American Museum of Philadelphia, were steps in this direction.[65] These projects and others emphasized that African Americans had always been a vital and central part of the American experience, and that it was time that this be acknowledged and celebrated.

Despite these initiatives (and in some cases because of the backlash against them), scholars and cultural workers noted that black history was still being left out of standard accounts, most notably by Bicentennial programs that downplayed or completely omitted African Americans. Except for some recognition of Crispus Attucks, who had been among the casualties of the Boston Massacre, both national and local accounts of the Revolution omitted African Americans and enslaved Africans.[66] Worse still, many Bicentennial commemorations, especially those planned in the early 1970s, tended to elide the time between 1776 and the present as an era of progress, during which the principles of the Revolution had been upheld and broadened. African Americans appeared in more comprehensive narratives as occasional beneficiaries of expanded rights rather than as important contributors to American innovation, politics, and culture. The Bicentennial's representation of the American past, like many accounts of American history, treated African Americans as objects rather than subjects, and often removed altogether their presence from narratives of the Revolution and subsequent events.

In response to these silences and erasures, many African Americans expressed a reluctance to take part in the Bicentennial's celebration of the

American past, which they saw as an affirmation of a political system that had been used to legitimize inequality, brutality, and exclusion. Many African Americans felt that these contradictions needed to be acknowledged and addressed as part of America's self-evaluation. A poem entitled "Bicentennial Blues" that was published in *Ebony* magazine in June of 1976 underscored this disparity: "Got the Bicentennial Blues, blue as I can be / Men and women marching from sea to shining sea / And after 200 years, there ain't no freedom for me."[67]

The tension between the promises and the achievements of the Revolution was not lost on media commentators, who regularly reported on black ambivalence toward the Bicentennial even after figures like Alex Haley, Maya Angelou, and Betty Shabazz were named to the ARBA Advisory Council. In a 1975 survey, the *Washington Post* queried black Washingtonians on their attitudes about the Bicentennial. A typical answer came from a local pharmacist who remarked, "I've never been too keen about celebrating the Bicentennial—we're too far away from realizing the idea of the American Dream."[68] Other observers charged that the Bicentennial, like history itself, ignored African Americans.[69] Black refusal to participate was grounded in a dual understanding of the American past as problematic and of the Bicentennial celebration as a disavowal of those problems.[70]

Some saw the absence of African Americans from Bicentennial histories as an opportunity to address and amend these omissions, advocating for a "Black Bicentennial" as a way of both affirming black achievements and examining the ongoing struggle. The Black Bicentennial would highlight the experience of African Americans in the United States to demand equal representation in history. Margaret Burroughs, the director of the Du Sable Museum of African American History in Chicago noted, "Blacks have been here longer than 200 years, and we'll be right there celebrating with everybody else. But the way we do it may be a little different. It doesn't necessarily mean standing up and yelling, hip, hip hurrah. It should also be used to point up the inequalities of this system."[71] Shirley Graham Du Bois, writer, internationalist activist, and widow of W. E. B. Du Bois, echoed these statements: "It is up to us to refute the lie that the only American history or the only American experience is white."[72] With these goals in mind, Burroughs and Du Bois pointed to the achievements of African Americans as well as their exclusions. Ultimately, because ARBA moved away from a central script and a national observance for the Bicentennial, the commemoration provided both opportunities and resources for many to make their own meaning by challenging or enlarging existing interpretations of U.S.

history and by connecting these realignments to questions of identity, representation, and citizenship.[73]

Local African American history initiatives thrived in the context of the Bicentennial. As described in chapter 3, Washington, DC–based brothers Vincent DeForest and Robert DeForrest of the Afro-American Bicentennial Corporation (ABC) worked to find and safeguard landmarks significant to black history, and in Brooklyn, the Weeksville Society did the same. In Baltimore, the Citizens for Black History Exhibits received an $18,000 grant from the National Endowment for the Arts to hire a researcher for the mounting of an exhibition of black Baltimore history from 1720 to 1870.[74] In Rhode Island, Rowena Stewart founded the Rhode Island Black Heritage Society and began to collect artifacts and documents from locals, saying, "The Bicentennial is the time to write Black history, I feel it in my bones." For Stewart and others engaged in collection projects, the redefined archive made it possible to include objects that would tell new kinds of stories. Ephemera of everyday life—letters, sentimental heirlooms, and craft objects—had been overlooked by previous generations of collectors and preservationists; the Bicentennial provided an opportunity and resources for the documentation of the day-to-day experience of the past. The integration of this new history into already-present accounts was equally important for Stewart: "as long as you teach black history separately, you will keep blacks separate."[75] For these activists, studying and emphasizing the experiences and accomplishments of African Americans over the past two hundred years provided a way to begin redressing current inequalities.[76]

At the same time, cultural workers who wanted to use the Bicentennial to underscore African American roles in history continued to face challenges from official planning bodies. One of the more ambitious projects that requested recognition and funding from the ARBC, and later the ARBA, was the National Black American Museum and Cultural Center, to be built in Niagara Falls, New York. Like many other museum exhibitions during this period, the proposed center took a "multi-media, multi-sensory approach" and had worked with effects teams at Disneyland, the Ontario Science Center, and others, "hoping to produce a 'real life experience' for the viewer."[77] The museum was the idea of Frank Mesiah, a community leader and local historian in Buffalo, and had backing from the National Endowment for the Arts, the New York State Regents, and the New York State Educational Department, but could not win the support of Bicentennial planners.[78]

From 1973 onward, the Museum and Cultural Center attempted to gain recognition from the federal planning body but consistently met with roadblocks. In December of 1973, a feasibility study and proposal submitted by Mesiah and his associates was sent out to a scholar specializing in African American history who wrote back that he was "quite disappointed" in the proposal. An ARBA program officer in charge of "Ethnic and Minority Heritage" passed the comments along to the Cultural Center with a patronizing tone: "To be quite frank, it's one thing to have public relations expertise and the ability to raise funds. It is quite another to be a Black historian or a curator of a Black Museum. . . . I would hope that you and your colleagues would address yourselves to these very real questions as it is our view that such questions must be answered before the new ARBA can begin the process of official recognition."[79]

It is easy to see how the historical emphases of the Black American Museum and Cultural Center made the ARBA, a nominally bipartisan but ideologically conservative organization, uneasy. The first page of the illustrated booklet on the museum stated "In the sixties, we saw a polarization of the races as this country moved towards two nations—one black, one white—separate and unequal." The museum planned to trace African American history up through the present and hoped to achieve "a demonstrable attitudinal change experienced by those who visit the museum."[80] If ARBA was looking to sponsor proposals for projects that engendered positive feelings about the American past and present, the difficult issues that the museum was raising did not fit this dynamic, and so ARBA officials found other reasons to deny the application.

In other cities, African American history endeavors also faced challenges from local planners. The Afro-American Bicentennial Corporation was often frustrated by their dealings with the ARBC and later ARBA. While the ABC worked closely with ARBC in order to publicize their programming and to gain funding, the two organizations had a troubled affiliation, which can be read alongside the larger issue of African American participation in the Bicentennial.[81] ABC founder Vincent DeForest met with an ARBC program officer in August of 1973 and criticized the "paternalistic attitude" of the commission. At its inception, the ABC had looked to the ARBC for cues and guidance, but as time wore on, DeForest and ABC co-founder Robert DeForrest became frustrated with the ARBC's unwillingness to introduce programming that investigated and celebrated the black experience in America, instead depending on the ABC and others to develop their own initiatives, which official planners could then choose to sponsor or publicize.[82] Historian Andrea Burns has likewise documented the ongoing problems of the African American Museum of Philadelphia to find support from city Bicentennial planners.[83] In these instances and others, the ARBA and other official planners maintained firm control over Bicentennial celebration, continuing to exclude some groups and instead channeling its resources into endeavors that embraced a more traditional narrative of U.S. history. While African American cultural workers made many gains before and during the Bicentennial Era, important work remained, and still remains, to be done.

Reframing the Archive

Ultimately, conversation and participation in the Bicentennial, and around the American history it enacted and celebrated, took many forms, from efforts to use the commemoration to demand reappraisal of and inclusion in the national narrative to skepticism and protest calling attention to the failure of political projects in the United States and abroad. Some activists read into the already existing archive the absences and erasures that continued to define the experience of marginalized groups in contemporary times. Others worked to find material evidence of African American life and accomplishments to expand the archive. These activists strengthened the connection between the historical and the political, but instead of looking to reenactive activity as a means to forge identification between the past and the present, they focused on new possibilities for inclusion allowed by the destabilization of consensus history. They felt that an affirmation of equality of representation of experience would lead to equality of rights. These new preservations instilled pride in achievements that then served as the foundation for appeals for inclusion, again capitalizing on the potential of the past to create politicized feeling in the present.

In all of these cases, activist engagement with the past continued to be underwritten by the archive. Reenactive practice needs source material; that is, the majority of reenactments during this period—whether orchestrated by official Bicentennial planners or by those outside or in opposition—animated histories that had already been uncovered, circulated, and sanctioned in the public sphere. Whether the subject matter was westward expansion, as in the Bicentennial Wagon Train, or the confrontation at Lexington and Concord, these were familiar histories. What reenactment did was allow participants and audiences to form closer or different understandings of these histories.

But the way that activists interacted with the archive was informed by their own relationships with both the past and the present and how they could and did locate themselves in already-established histories. The People's Bicentennial Commission, with its critique of the state-sponsored Bicentennial's use of history, had as members mostly white, middle-class activists who enjoyed enfranchisement in American political, economic, and cultural life. Members based their interaction with, and uses of, the past on an ingrained belief in a historical right to representation. The PBC believed strongly that some iteration of the American political system *had* worked and *could* work. This protest, grounded in a reinterpretation of and empathetic affinity with American history (and one that centered upon the Revolutionary activity of another set of white males) ultimately took the form of constitutional activism as they began calling for congressional legislation to check political corruption and to safeguard the economic rights of Americans. The PBC's investment in the American political project was supported by their reverence for the founding documents already within the canon of the archive and their belief that the ideals in those documents should be applied to present political and economic failures.

Others had a more fraught relationship with the Bicentennial and the archive-grounded political history that it commemorated: both African Americans and Native Americans voiced cynicism about the celebration, as it represented two hundred years of systematic oppression and erosion of rights. Paradoxically, these rights had been both granted and limited by the founding documents, often touted as the most tangible legacy of the Revolution. For groups whose history had not been previously documented, historymaking took the form of new preservations—adding to an archive that had, because of the weakening of consensus history, become more inclusive.

If the 1960s activist imagination was preoccupied with the present and the future, it can be said that in the 1970s, individuals and groups looking to enact significant social and political change turned a new eye toward the past. Historical activity, as realized through cultural productions, research initiatives, and public projects, often helped to form, interrogate, and reconstruct individual and collective identities. At the same time, individual and group historical consciousness took on an explicitly politicized valence. The People's Bicentennial Commission looked to affective identification with history and reenactments of the American Revolution to address contemporary problems and turned patriotism into protest. Likewise, African American history groups worked to build black accomplishment into dominant accounts of U.S. history, looking to the achievements of the past to stimulate pride in the present. Like the actions of the PBC, this intervention illustrated the fading dominance of traditional, top-down, consensus history. The concurrent destabilization of the archive, the storehouse of this history, allowed new opportunities for interventions into retellings of the past.

But through this destabilization, the archive still persisted. All of these actions were animated by the centrality of the archive as the source material of understandings and reconceptualizations of the past. Whether the aim was, like that of the PBC, to repurpose the already-present figures populating the archive, or to add new histories to the repository of evidence, like the ABC and other black history initiatives, or to challenge dominant articulations of archival material, like the Black Panther Party and the Fourth of July Coalition, the connection between historical consciousness and evidence was not lost, only reconfigured. I end with these examples not only because they illustrate the ongoing importance of the archive and the ways in which, in the context of wider transformations in historical consciousness, it continues to function as the foundation of historical engagement and knowledge production, but also because they demonstrate the sites at which political interventions can be made.

The transition from a form of historymaking that was organized around preservation to one that foregrounded reenactment was in some ways about animating the archive—recognizing and building upon the emotional import of the historical and making central the relationships between the past and the present, not as foundational, but as co-constitutive. This historical consciousness, one that is built upon an affective understanding of the past, remains with us today. Understanding it on its own terms—how it emerged from a specific cultural context, how it was sanctioned and extended for different reasons by a variety of agents, and how it informed historical meaning making and identification—can help us be better historians in both senses of the word: in how we read, *and* how we produce, accounts of the past.

Conclusion
Making History

When you walk through this door, you will no longer be students, you will make history. Lives are at stake! Adult staff members are not here to answer questions or to help you—the responsibility is entirely yours!

—Staff docent at Air Force One Discovery Center to fifth-grade school group

On January 14, 2011, during a broadcast entitled "Kid Politics," the weekly radio program *This American Life* aired a segment recorded at the Air Force One Discovery Center, part of the Ronald Reagan Presidential Library and Museum in Simi Valley, California. A group of fifth-graders posing as the Reagan Cabinet, the White House press corps, and members of the military, participated in a reenactment of the events of "Operation Urgent Fury," the 1983 U.S. military action in Grenada. After students were assigned roles such as President Reagan, Vice President George H. W. Bush, and General John Vesey, they were separated and put in three rooms: scaled replicas of a battleship command center, the Oval Office (precise even to the jar of jelly beans sitting on Reagan's desk), and the White House Press Room (with video cameras and microphones). Starlee Kine, *This American Life*'s reporter, observed the students playing Reagan and his advisors as they planned the invasion of Grenada. First, students had to choose whether the action was to be a full-scale military offensive or a smaller mission to rescue some eight hundred medical students stranded in the country, the ostensible reason for the intervention. Then, after the role players were told that the press had leaked critical information about the stealth mission, they had to decide whether to continue as planned. The class was prepared to weigh these choices; they had spent several weeks studying Reagan and the Grenada invasion before the trip to the Air Force One Discovery Center.

Although the students profiled by Kine had been told before the reenactment began that there were no right or wrong answers, when they input their choices into the red phone on the replica Oval Office desk, a loud buzzer sounded, indicating whether their decisions aligned with that of

Reagan in 1983. Kine observed, "The whole thing is rigged to make what Ronald Reagan did in 1983 look like the most appealing option." The students took their choices seriously and, as Kine reported, at various moments throughout the reenactment appeared genuinely worried, angry, or celebratory.[1] Their engagement with the past was affective as well as reenactive; the class learned about Operation Urgent Fury from the perspective of those who had been there and clearly felt some of the stress that accompanied such planning. But at the same time, they were guided through the choices *as the Reagan Cabinet had made them*; their affective identification was to be with those in power. The scaled nature of the replica environments also helped school-aged children move bodily into their roles: the majority of fifth-graders were not yet big enough to feel at home in places like offices, press rooms, or military control centers, yet at the Air Force One Discovery Center, their grown-up decisions took place in grown-up settings. This account of the Reagan interactive illustrates the contemporary relationship of reenactment to archives like those of the Reagan Presidential Library and Museum and how the practice continues to be used to generate hegemonic interpretations of history. The exercise at the Air Force One Discovery Center trained a new generation not only to revere Reagan but also to act like him; by reenacting critical moments in the Reagan presidency, the students featured in the segment inhabited the president's mind-set, feeling as if his choices were also their choices.

Presidential libraries are crucial examples of archives as I have been discussing them; they collect and preserve documents and artifacts related to particular presidents, seeking to glorify their actions. Although the presidential libraries are part of the National Archives system, they are paid for and planned by each president.[2] But, as we can see from the Reagan example, presidential libraries are not only repositories of documents, they are archives in action—using and interpreting their contents to generate a celebratory and reverent depiction of that president's life and career. At the John F. Kennedy Library in Boston, one can visit a mock television studio featuring the control panel and camera used in the famous Kennedy-Nixon television debate. The audience vantage point is from behind the control panel; as they watch the debate on the screen, they become firsthand witnesses of telegenic Kennedy's triumph over the haggard, sweating Nixon.[3] At the Abraham Lincoln Presidential Library and Museum in Springfield, Illinois, visitors file past an exhibit of Lincoln's flag-draped coffin lying in state at the U.S. Capitol. As solemn music plays and lights dim, audiences mourn the assassinated president as if the event has just occurred.[4]

I have argued that reenactive engagement with history emerged in the 1970s as a primary mode of historymaking: the result of a complex mix of political, economic, and cultural changes that led to reconsiderations of the past, the present, and the future, as well as the relationship among all three. I suggested—especially in my accounts of televised history programming and on the use of computers, telephone banks, audio tours, video and sound projection, and other technological implements in museum exhibition—that new developments in technology, particularly personal technology, while not directly responsible for this transformation, helped to create and communicate immersive and reenactive situations. The high-tech environments at the Presidential Libraries and other contemporary history exhibitions show how, with additional advances in media technology, the complex relationship between reenactive historymaking and new media has flourished and developed.[5]

As personal technology advanced rapidly between the 1970s and now, it is easy to see how reenactive engagements with the historical have extended and even taken on new forms in the present moment. The Internet and other digital technologies afford ample opportunity to place oneself in the past. Role-playing video games like *Call of Duty* allow players to participate in immersive renditions of the Civil War, World War II, and other conflicts. Players join historic military formations and simulate usage of appropriate weapons. Other games, like *Bioshock* and *Fallout*, present interactive "alternate histories," that are nonetheless rooted in extensive historical research and represent historical ephemera, motifs, and backgrounds. Aside from simulating war, these games create complex narratives that lend users backstories, experiences, and emotions, allowing players to move outside of themselves while gaming. In recent years, scholars have turned a critical eye on these engagements, asking questions about how game playing influences the formation and maintenance of identities and ideologies.[6]

The digital has also expanded the possibilities of preservation—digitization, tagging, and advanced searches make archives more accessible and more knowable. All of the presidential libraries have extensive digital holdings. The National Archives' Digital Vaults project, billed as the "National Archives Experience," allows users access to a variety of documents on such subjects as the Declaration of Independence, the Supreme Court, and Albert Einstein.[7] This site is pedagogical and has already done the work of research, whereas the Archives' search engine gives researchers remote access to a great number of texts and images.[8] Finally, user-driven online archiving on sites like Flickr and YouTube as well as community collecting initiatives like the Roy Rosenzweig Center for History and New Media's September 11th digital archive again signify an expansion and democratization of preservation activity.[9] It might be fitting to note here the degree to which my own project has relied on such access; most of the television programs I discuss are available online through YouTube, Netflix, and other platforms; many individuals have posted personal photographs and recollections from the Wagon Train, the Freedom Trail, and other Bicentennial activities on dedicated Web sites. For researchers like me and for individuals curious about their family, their neighborhood, or anything else, the Internet provides incomparable resources.

More museums now have living history programs, including highly controversial reenactments of slave auctions, the experience of the Holocaust, and other traumatic events.[10] Reenactment has also thrived on television: historical reality television programs like *Frontier House* and *Colonial House* likewise place "regular people" in the past. Participants are taught about dress, cooking, and everyday rituals from the corresponding time period and are outfitted with replica clothing, tools, and leisure items.[11] Significantly, and in a departure from the "authentic" experience the project strives to create, they are also given hand-held "diary cameras," which they can use to record their own thoughts and perspectives, an aspect that reinforces the centrality of connecting the experience of reenacting the past to the present and testifies to the complex relationship between embodiment and mediation.

While it is undeniable that reenactment and emotional knowledge production have become more prominent in both public and popular history efforts, older models of historical meaning making have likewise endured, or even returned in new forms. At "Our Peoples and Our Lives," a permanent exhibit within the National Museum of the American Indian, visitors encounter an enormous case of firearms, which, at first, resembles the taxonomical displays of museums past. But the collection of guns also makes evident the long history of violence against native populations: it makes its meaning both by referencing the epistemological tradition of western exhibition (in which native peoples were often objectified) and by subverting it: an important aspect that is central to the museum's mission of shared authority. Accompanying text describes not the physical or technical features of the guns, but how, when, and where they were used.[12] Robert Post, who spent many years working at the National Museum of American History, has observed that object-based and informational exhibitions there have survived and thrived into the present. One needs only to think about the recent renovation of the "Star Spangled Banner" exhibit at the National

Museum of American History, which now focuses on the materiality of the giant flag, using new media techniques to reveal and highlight conservation efforts.[13] But this exhibit is accompanied by "Broad Stripes and Bright Stars," a regular performance developed as part of the museum's new History Alive! programming: an interpreter portraying Mary Young Pickersgill, who helped make the original flag, interacts with curious visitors.[14] Clearly, embodied and affective history remains central in the present day, with commentators like public historians Cathy Stanton and Benjamin Filene likewise arguing that it needs to be an even more significant part of public history practice.[15]

Accordingly, critiques of reenactive or empathetic history also endure. Vanessa Agnew has written extensively about reenactive practice, echoing previous critics in her concern about the way that its affective dimensions lead to inaccuracy and misunderstanding. Agnew sees potential in reenactment, but notes that it must be "rescued" and participants must regain a critical distance in order to renew history's ethical and political responsibilities.[16] In 2010, the historian Jill Lepore published a study detailing the Tea Party movement's engagement with the past. Lepore notes that the Tea Party both identifies with and misunderstands Revolutionary history, seeing a causal relationship between the two. Fittingly, she traces this tendency back to the Bicentennial, which she calls a "carnival of presentism."[17] I would add another key observation: it's not that the Tea Party's reenactment generated bad history and, thus, bad politics, rather, their politics have generated reenactment precisely *because* of history's availability as a way of thinking about politics. Another example in Lepore's book helps make this point: she ends the book describing a scene from a history lesson in which elementary schoolchildren, echoing both the original *You Are There* and the way the program was adapted in Boston's "The Revolution" exhibit, simulate a television broadcast from the American Revolution. For Lepore, this is a constructive engagement with the past, because it allows the children to explore and contemplate historical issues in a nuanced way. But the impetus that underlies both of Lepore's examples is the same.[18] While I believe that reenactment has both positive and negative aspects and that it must be examined critically, I resist positioning reenactive and affective engagement in contrast to some other, more objective, practice of history. As I hope to have shown, in contemporary American culture, reenactment *is* history, for better or for worse.

The potential—the unpredictability of reenactment—is evident even in the Reagan example. In the *This American Life* segment, Starlee Kine follows two groups of fifth-graders through their reenactments of Reagan's Cabinet during Operation Urgent Fury. While one group makes the "right" choices, behaving as Reagan and his cabinet did in 1983, later that day, a second group makes the "wrong" ones. Instead of choosing to send a large force to Grenada, this Reagan cabinet does not invade, instead moving to evacuate the stranded medical students. In 1983, after the press leak ruined the "element of surprise" the Reagan cabinet had been relying on, the president continued with the attack. But again, this second group of students reenacting Reagan differed from the script—they decided to call off the action.[19] Their assessment of the Grenada invasion was derived from firsthand experience; their divergence and disagreement with the president's action came on emotional, not informational terms. Instead of making students feel closer to Reagan, this episode made them more critical of the president. Reenactive practice now, as during the Bicentennial, can make multiple meanings.

In these chapters, I have traced large-scale shifts in the understanding and practice of popular and public history to argue that affective understanding of the past was central to the creation of identity and political consciousness in the 1970s and remains critical even now. Looking closely at the continuum of production and reception of various kinds of history projects, I have shown the beginning of transformations that extend into the present. It is only by looking at this development and consolidation of reenactive practices that today seem like second nature in their pervasiveness that we can take the next step and begin to see how the past is deployed in contemporary cultural and political discourse.

Notes

Introduction

1. Randal Kleiser, *Grease*, Paramount Pictures, 1978; George Lucas, *American Graffiti*, Universal Pictures, 1973; Garry Marshall, *Happy Days*, ABC, 1974–84; Earl Hamner Jr., *The Waltons*, CBS, 1972–81; Garry Marshall, *Laverne and Shirley*, ABC, 1976–83; Jean Murphy, "70s Audience Hails Musicals of the 30s," *Los Angeles Times*, February 20, 1970; John Peacock, *Fashion Sourcebooks*.

2. Doctorow, *Ragtime*.

3. Henry Allen, "Yesteryear Shock," *Washington Post*, March 7, 1971; Lawrence Van Gelder, "Nightshirts, for Fashionably Cozy Sleepwalkers," *New York Times*, February 24, 1976.

4. Paul Showers, "Up-to-date, Out-of-date," *New York Times*, December 5, 1972; Frederick M. Winship, "Nostalgia Business in Full Bloom," *Los Angeles Times*, November 22, 1970; John Bartlow Martin, "One Nation, Indomitable," *Chicago Tribune*, April 28, 1975.

5. Skinner, *Fashionable Clothing from the Sears Catalogs*.

6. See also Marcus, *Happy Days and Wonder Years*.

7. See Rydell, Findling, and Pelle, *Fair America*; Zukin, *Landscapes of Power*. See also Spigel, *Welcome to the Dreamhouse*.

8. Gerald Clarke, "The Meaning of Nostalgia," *Time*, May 3, 1971; Jonathan Rodgers, "Back to the '50s," *Newsweek*, October 16, 1972; "The Nifty Fifties," *Life*, June 16, 1972; Barbara Klaw, "The New Nostalgia . . . Many Happy Returns," *American Heritage*, June 1970. Historians have also connected this nostalgia boom to the upheavals of the 1960s: see Kammen, *Mystic Chords of Memory*; Lowenthal, *The Heritage Crusade and the Spoils of History*; Glassberg, *Sense of History*.

9. Donal Henahan, "What Has the Hunt for Novelty Brought Us?" *New York Times*, August 15, 1971.

10. Whyte, *Organization Man*; Friedan, *The Feminine Mystique*; Ehrlich, *The Population Bomb*; Bellah, *Beyond Belief*; Reich, *The Greening of America*. For an analysis of social critique in the postwar period, see Daniel Horowitz, *The Anxieties of Affluence*.

11. Art Seidenbaum, "No More Nostalgia," *Los Angeles Times*, May 10, 1971.

12. Martin E. Marty, "Looking Backward into the Future," *New York Times*, February 6, 1975.

13. Wolfe, "The Me Decade and the Third Great Awakening."

14. Lasch, *The Culture of Narcissism*, xiv, 5. See also Toffler, *Future Shock*, 17.

15. The characterization of the 1970s as a moment during which American culture lost a "real" relationship with history has pervaded cultural critique, beginning with postmodernists like David Harvey and Fredric Jameson, and continuing with work by cultural historians like David Lowenthal and Michael Kammen. See Harvey, *The Condition of Postmodernity*; Jameson, *Postmodernism, or the Cultural Logic of Late Capitalism*.

For similar accounts, see Lyotard, *The Postmodern Condition*; Baudrillard, *Selected Writings*. See also Lowenthal, *The Past Is a Foreign Country* and *The Heritage Crusade and the Spoils of History*; Kammen, *Mystic Chords of Memory*; Huyssen, *Twilight Memories*.

16. Marling, *George Washington Slept Here*, 192.

17. For more, see Marling, *George Washington Slept Here*; Glassberg, *American Historical Pageantry*; Lears, *No Place of Grace*; Wallace, *Mickey Mouse History and Other Essays on American Memory*.

18. Here, Robin Bernstein's work on "scriptive objects," or how material artifacts help form and reform subjects through interaction, is particularly useful. Bernstein, "Dances with Things."

19. Landsberg, *Prosthetic Memory* and *Engaging the Past*; Taylor, *The Archive and the Repertoire*; Magelssen, *Living History Museums* and *Simming*; Schneider, *Performing Remains*; Kirshenblatt-Gimblett, *Destination Culture*; DeGroot, *Remaking History*; Dean, Meerzon, and Prince, *History, Memory, Performance*. See also Agnew, "History's Affective Turn"; and Alexander Cook, "The Use and Abuse of Historical Reenactment."

20. For other accounts that complicate postmodern engagements with nostalgia, see Hutcheon, *A Poetics of Postmodernism*; Felski, *Doing Time*; Radstone, *The Sexual Politics of Time*; Freeman, *Time Binds*.

21. Rosenzweig and Thelen, *The Presence of the Past*.

22. Novick, *That Noble Dream*; Fitzpatrick, *History's Memory*; Foner, *The New American History*; Kammen, *The Past Before Us*.

23. Glassie, "Meaningful Things and Appropriate Myths"; Levine, "The Unpredictable Past"; Wise, "'Paradigm Dramas' in American Studies"; May, "The Radical Roots of American Studies—Presidential Address"; Meringolo, *Museums, Monuments, and National Parks*.

24. For accounts of political, economic, and social transformations of the decade, see Carroll, *It Seemed Like Nothing Happened*; Schulman, *The Seventies*; Killen, *1973 Nervous Breakdown*; Perlstein, *Nixonland*; Rodgers, *Age of Fracture*; Stein, *Pivotal Decade*; Borstelmann, *The 1970s*; Cowie, *Stayin' Alive*; Self, *All in the Family*.

25. Friedman, "Muscle Memory"; hooks, "Performance Practice as a Site of Opposition."

26. Examples of preservations and reenactments in support of civic identity include the monumentalization of such landmarks as Independence Hall in Philadelphia and Plymouth Rock, as well as Wild West shows of the late nineteenth century and the increase in historical pageantry of the early twentieth century. See Glassberg, *American Historical Pageantry*; Seelye, *Memory's Nation*; Mires, *Independence Hall in American Memory*.

Chapter One

1. Cecil Smith, "CBS Will Air 731 Bicentennial Spots," *Los Angeles Times*, May 29, 1974; John J. O'Connor, "TV: CBS Begins Variety and Mini-History Shows," *New York Times*, July 3, 1974.

2. Not many examples of the *Bicentennial Minutes* have survived for public viewing, but a few are available on YouTube: *Bicentennial Minute*, August 31, 1975, www

.youtube.com/watch?v=UUoto1lsX50, accessed November 8, 2008; *Bicentennial Minute*, December 31, 1976, www.youtube.com/watch?v=M101Mc6Yujw, accessed May 5, 2011. Additionally, see *Bicentennial Minute*, November, 30, 1974, December 22, 1974, March 31, 1975, Television Archive, CBS June Regional Meeting: Bicentennial Minutes & Sports (Reel 2) B:50048, Paley Center for Media.

3. See, for example, "Pepper . . . and Salt," *Wall Street Journal*, February 14, 1977.

4. For discussions of "modernist" conceptions of time, see Huyssen, *Twilight Memories*; Whitrow, *Time in History*, 1–17, 177–86; Berman, *All That Is Solid Melts into Air*.

5. For an industrial history of U.S. commercial television, especially the way that the medium has capitalized upon concurrent cultural developments, see Barnouw, *Tube of Plenty*; MacDonald, *One Nation under Television*.

6. "Minute Man to the Bicentennial," *Los Angeles Times*, July 2, 1974; Mary Knoblauch, "Bicentennial Minute Is 12 Hours Long," *Chicago Tribune*, January 22, 1976.

7. Williams, *Television*; Feuer, "The Concept of Live Television"; Doane, "Information, Crisis, Catastrophe."

8. For discussions of television and history, see White, "Television"; Edgerton, "Television as Historian"; Sobchack, *The Persistence of History*. Television's unique relationship with history is further expounded by the observations of theorists of the postmodern regarding a transformation in cultural understandings of temporality in the 1970s, a development precipitated by and extended through mass media, most explicitly television. Fredric Jameson, Jean Baudrillard, and Jean-Francois Lyotard have all argued that, as a result of changes in global capitalism, most notably in mass mediation, "modernist" cultural perception of the passage of time as progressive and linear was at this moment replaced by a temporality described, like television itself, as presentist and schizophrenic. This postmodern sense of temporality is marked by a highlighted awareness of experience in the present, a quality that television both shares and exacerbates. For Baudrillard and for Andreas Huyssen, the medium of television in particular both impels and illustrates this shift. Television's relationship with the historical is thus always seen as intimate, complex, and co-constitutive. See Jameson, *Postmodernism* and *The Seeds of Time*; Baudrillard, *Simulacra and Simulation*; Harvey, *The Condition of Postmodernity*; Huyssen, *Twilight Memories*; Lyotard, *The Postmodern Condition*.

9. *The Carol Burnett Show*, Episode 9.4, writer Ed Simmons, director Dave Powers. Originally aired October 4, 1975, on CBS.

10. As Richard Slotkin, Fred MacDonald, and others have noted, the American Western genre has long been deployed to mediate issues of the American experience, but these engagements more often than not minimize the historical. For example, while the television program *Gunsmoke* was set in the 1870s, it rarely referenced any historical moments outside of its immediate surroundings. Other shows took this confusion further. MacDonald has described the historical ambiguity of *The Roy Rogers Show*: Rogers rode a horse but his partner drove a Jeep. On the same program, Dale Evans worked as a waitress in a modern café but was also a sharpshooter on the model of Annie Oakley. This tendency has been present since the origins of the genre: frontier characters like Buffalo Bill Cody and Wild Bill Hickock appeared as showmen in

Wild West revues and were the stars of fictional dime novels while still working as U.S. agents in the "real" West. The Western operates as a parable, an aesthetic, and a genre—it cannot be considered a historical program in the same vein as others that attend to the past in more significant ways rather than introducing some elements as part of a motif. The Western demonstrates the importance of the past in U.S. culture, but does so in a completely different way—by taking events *out* of, as opposed to placing them within, a historical trajectory. The tendencies of the Western, from its beginning, toward temporal confusion do, however, serve as an early portent of what later became a dominant logic of history programming across many mediums. See Slotkin, *Gunfighter Nation*; MacDonald, *Who Shot the Sherriff?*; Newcombe, "From Old Frontier to New Frontier."

11. See Gabler, *Walt Disney*.

12. For more on 1960s documentary, see Curtin, *Redeeming the Wasteland*.

13. *You Are There*, dir. John Frankenheimer, CBS, 1953–57.

14. Steve Anderson, "Loafing in the Garden of Knowledge."

15. *Profiles in Courage*, dir. Sherman Marks, NBC, 1964–65. For discussions of *Profiles in Courage*, see Curtin, *Redeeming the Wasteland*; Marcus, "Profiles in Courage." For more general discussions of television in the 1950s, see Spigel and Curtin, *The Revolution Wasn't Televised*; Boddy, *Fifties Television*; Watson, *The Expanding Vista*.

16. For the relationship between narration and documentary, see Nichols, *Representing Reality*, 32–75.

17. *I Remember Mama* (also called *Mama*), dir. Ralph Nelson, CBS, 1949–57.

18. See also Lipsitz, "The Meaning of Memory."

19. "Walking Distance," wr. Rod Sterling, dir. Robert Stevens, *The Twilight Zone*, CBS, October 30, 1959.

20. For more on familial models in the 1950s, see May, *Homeward Bound*; Spigel, *Make Room for TV*.

21. "A Stop at Willoughby," wr. Rod Sterling, dir. Robert Parrish, *The Twilight Zone*, CBS, May 6, 1960.

22. This latter reading is particularly intriguing as it posits that historical thinking is, in actuality, future-oriented thinking. Both modes, however, rely on a progressive, or linear, sense of temporality.

23. For discussions of television's representation of midcentury anxiety about modernity, see Spigel, "From Domestic Space to Outer Space"; Sconce, "The 'Outer Limits' of Oblivion." For a discussion of fiction concerning the advertising profession, see Smulyan, *Popular Ideologies*, 116–55.

24. For more about how the logics of containment operate within the domestic sphere, see May, *Homeward Bound*.

25. "Back There," wr. Rod Sterling, dir. David Orrick McDearmon, *The Twilight Zone*, CBS, January 13, 1961.

26. "No Time Like the Past," wr. Rod Sterling, dir. Justus Addiss, *The Twilight Zone*, CBS, March 7, 1963.

27. "City on the Edge of Forever," wr. Harlan Ellison, dir. Joseph Pevney, *Star Trek*, NBC, April 6, 1967.

28. For more on the "fantastic" sitcom, see Spigel, "From Domestic Space to Outer Space," 204–29.

29. The most prominent of these is the "Salem Saga," several episodes filmed in Salem in 1969 and aired during the 1970 season. See Peter Alachi, "The Salem Saga, 1970," www.harpiesbizarre.com/salemsaga.htm, accessed July 13, 2011.

30. "Eye of the Beholder," wr. Sol Saks, dir. William Asher, ABC, February 25, 1965.

31. For ratings, see Brooks and Marsh, *The Complete Directory to Prime Time Network and Cable TV Shows, 1946–Present*, 1679–99.

32. "Ghost Town, U.S.A.," wr. Sherwood Schwartz, dir. Oscar Rudolph, *The Brady Bunch*, ABC, September 17, 1971.

33. On sitcom repetition, see Mittell, *Television and American Culture*, 213–68.

34. Steve Allen, *Meeting of Minds*, PBS, 1977–81. See also Ginny Weissman, "He Belongs in the Yellow Pages; Steve Allen Does It All," *Chicago Tribune*, February 6, 1977.

35. For full scripts, see Allen, *Meeting of Minds*, 69–122.

36. Wilder, *Little House on the Prairie*; Michael Landon, *Little House on the Prairie*, NBC, 1974–83.

37. "Little House on Prairie 'Reel' Authentic Prairie Town," *Los Angeles Times*, December 15, 1974; Jake Newman, "Little House Divided," *Washington Post*, October 12, 1980.

38. See Lentz, "Quality vs. Relevance." For more on how fictional texts appeal to "the real" in ways that are themselves informed by cultural contexts, see Kaplan, *The Social Construction of American Realism*, 1–14. Although Kaplan writes about literature at the turn of the twentieth century, her association between fictional realism and historical context is valuable here.

39. For more on emotional realism, see Ang, *Watching Dallas*, 1–85; Creeber, *Serial Television*, 19–29.

40. Jake Newman, "Little House Divided," *Washington Post*, October 12, 1980.

41. See Wilder, *Little House on the Prairie*, for comparison. For media commentary on disparity between the books and the television series, see Anita Gold, "Michael Landon Defends His Little House on the Prairie," *Chicago Tribune*, April 27, 1975; "Too Many Egos in a Little House," *Chicago Tribune*, November 19, 1974.

42. Jerry Buck, "Landon Proves His 'House' Not Made of Cards," *Chicago Tribune*, June 7, 1978.

43. "Soldier's Return," wr. Blanche Hanalis, dir. William Claxton, *Little House on the Prairie*, NBC, March 24, 1976.

44. Television addressed issues of Vietnam through another show that purported to be about a different era: *MASH*, a program that was ostensibly about medics in the Korean War, but which audiences and critics assumed to be about Vietnam. See Himmelstein, *Television Myth and the American Mind*, 163–95. For more on the experience of Vietnam veterans in the postwar United States, see Lembcke, *The Spitting Image*; Lifton, *Home from the War*.

45. Joel Swerdlow, "'Little House' Has Big Ideas about the Value of Family Life," *Chicago Tribune*, March 31, 1980.

46. Jake Newman, "Little House Divided," *Washington Post*, October 12, 1980.

47. Feldman, *Little House, Long Shadow.*

48. Andee Beck, "'Little House' Star Karen Grassle Defends Role of the House-wife," *Chicago Tribune,* August 14, 1977.

49. "Times of Change," wr. Blanche Hanalis, dir. William Claxton, *Little House on the Prairie,* NBC, September 19, 1977.

50. "Little House Divided."

51. Robert Berkvist, "Some People We Can Care About," *New York Times,* October 8, 1972.

52. Aljean Harmetz, "Why My Sons Watch 'The Waltons,'" *New York Times,* February 25, 1973.

53. John J. O'Connor, "TV's Miniseries—Refreshing Change or Just Less of the Same?" *New York Times,* March 27, 1977.

54. Les Brown, "ABC-TV Plans to Stress Serialization of Novels," *New York Times,* December 14, 1974.

55. "ABC to Develop 'Roots,' 'U.S.A.' as TV Novels," *Los Angeles Times,* January 24, 1975; Les Brown, "TV Is Again Looking to Books for New Specials," *New York Times,* March 17, 1975.

56. David Susskind, *Eleanor and Franklin,* ABC, January 11, 1976; David L. Wolper, *Sandburg's Lincoln,* NBC, May 1, 1974.

57. For more on similarities between the soap opera and the miniseries, see Rapping, *The Movie of the Week,* 118–46. For more on characterization and serial form, see Feuer, Kerr, and Vahimagi, *MTM,* 4.

58. On the soap opera, see Ang, *Watching Dallas*; Modeleski, "The Search for To-morrow in Today's Soap Operas"; Kuhn, "Women's Genres."

59. *Rich Man, Poor Man,* wr. Dean Riesner, dir. Bill Bixby, ABC, September 1976–March 1977; David L. Wolper, Stan Margulies, *Roots,* ABC, January 23–30, 1977.

60. *Lincoln,* NBC, 1974.

61. Joyce Haber, "Bringing Books to the Small Screen," *Los Angeles Times,* March 13, 1975; Dick Adler, "The Book-to-Movie Trend: TV Starts to Roll Its Own," *Los Angeles Times,* May 25, 1975; Cecil Smith, "More about Mrs. Roosevelt," *Los Angeles Times,* February 13, 1976; Percy Shain, "*Rich Man, Poor Man* Tops Emmy List," *Boston Globe,* April 16, 1976.

62. Sander Vanocur, "Filling America's Need for the Continuity of 'Storytelling,'" *Washington Post,* March 28, 1976.

63. Jacqueline Trescott, "An Emotional Preview of Haley's *Roots*—It All Came Alive," *Washington Post,* January 13, 1977; "Deep Are the Roots in Television's Finest Hour," *New York Amsterdam News,* January 29, 1977; Vernon Jarrett, "An Epic TV Tale of Our Heritage," *Chicago Tribune,* January 30, 1977; "Roots Finale Most Watched Show in History," *Los Angeles Times,* February 2, 1977.

64. Mary Knoblauch, "From Africa to America—One Man's Search for his Roots," *Chicago Tribune,* June 14, 1976; Jacqueline Trescott, "The Guest," *Washington Post,* February 22, 1977.

65. Described in McCauley, "Alex Haley, A Southern Griot." See also Delmont, *Making Roots.*

66. See Smethurst, *The Black Arts Movement*; Woodard, *A Nation Within a Nation.*

67. Alex Haley, "My Search for Roots: A Black American's Story," *Reader's Digest*, May 1974, 78.

68. "The Black Scholar Interviews: Alex Haley," *Black Scholar* 8, no. 1 (September 1976): 39.

69. Dorothy Gilliam, "*Roots*: History off Balance," *Washington Post*, January 28, 1977; Ellen Goodman, "Haley Never Insisted He Wrote Pure History," *Los Angeles Times*, June 24, 1977.

70. For critical and audience responses to *Roots*, see Fishbein, "*Roots*: Docudrama and the Interpretation of History"; Rapping, *The Movie of the Week*, 118–46; Murray, "Black Crisis Shuffle."

71. Marty Bell, "Debts, Stubborn Faith Drive Alex Haley to write 'Roots,'" *Chicago Tribune*, February 27, 1977; Alex Haley, "Roots: Memo detailing particular arrangements of contract," [n.d., ca. 1967], folder 51: "Haley Correspondence, 1966–69," Fulton Oursler Jr. Papers, Georgetown University, Washington, DC (hereafter cited as FOJ).

72. By 1970, *Reader's Digest* had forwarded Haley over $25,000 in expenses and had not seen any progress on *Roots*. Two years later, Haley had run out of money again and was engaging in extensive college lecture tours as a means to raise more. *Reader's Digest* executives speculated that Haley did not intend on committing anything to paper, instead preferring the lecture circuit. Michael Blow to Tony Oursler, May 30, 1972; Tony Oursler to DeWitt Wallace, May 31, 1972, folder 52: "Haley Correspondence, 1970–74," FOJ.

73. Les Brown, "ABC-TV Plans to Stress Serializations of Novels," *New York Times*, December 14, 1974; "ABC to Develop 'Roots,' 'U.S.A.' as TV Novels," *Los Angeles Times*, January 24, 1975.

74. John Camper, "Lots of Firsts for Haley Film," *Los Angeles Times*, July 6, 1976.

75. Haley to Stan Margulies [n.d., ca. 1975], box 106, folder 1: "Alex Haley-Outlines," David J. Wolper Collection, University of Southern California (hereafter cited as DJW).

76. Kay Gardella, "TV Networks Give Up on Documentary," *Chicago Tribune*, July 21, 1976.

77. David Wolper, "Roots: Suggested Viewer Advisory," October 6, 1976, box 282, folder 9: "Letters from Public: Criticism," DJW.

78. "3 Universities to Offer Classes on TV's 'Roots,'" *Los Angeles Times*, January 22, 1977.

79. Teacher's Guide, box 304, folder 4: "Roots: The Next Generation," DJW.

80. Gregg Kilday, "Sprouts a Film Sequel, *Los Angeles Times*, July 27, 1977; Lee Margulies, "Haley Ascribes Success to God," *Los Angeles Times*, February 22, 1977.

81. Colin B. Campbell to David Wolper, September 17, 1978, box 288, folder 1: "Letters from Public: Praise," DJW.

82. Stacie Gerken to David Wolper, February 16, 1977, box 288, folder 1: "Letters from Public: Praise," DJW.

83. See Dayan and Katz, *Media Events*.

84. Jacqueline Trescott, "Alex Haley: The Author Astride Fame's Moment," *Washington Post*, January 28, 1977; Cecil Smith, "*Roots* Reaps Vast Harvest," *Los Angeles Times*, February 2, 1977.

85. Charlayne Hunter Gault, "'Roots' Getting a Grip on People Everywhere," *New York Times*, January 28, 1977; Jerry Buck, "Viewers Pulled In by 'Roots,'" *Los Angeles Times*, January 28, 1977; Larry Lane, "'Roots' Sparks Race Conflict in Lynwood; Police, School Officials Working to Avert Black-White Confrontations," *Los Angeles Times*, February 3, 1977; "Coulter says 'Roots' Was His 'Spiritual Awakening,'" *Cincinnati Post*, undated (February 1977) clipping found in box 288, folder 3: "Letters from Public: Criticism," DJW.

86. Bob Wiedrich, "Roots Deserves a Page in History," *Chicago Tribune*, February 3, 1977. The long and complex relationship between television and the representation of race and racial difference is worth noting here, as both the production and reception of *Roots* was informed by this history. While civil rights activists used television to bring attention to their struggle, representation of African American life continued to be absent from commercial television through the postwar period. Because of television's central role in depicting and helping to inform American culture, this absence was noticed by both black and white audiences. Given this complicated relationship, it is no surprise that *Roots* made the impact that it did, not only because it featured some of the most prominent African American actors on television, but also because it stood alone as a primetime broadcast that took African American culture seriously and featured a mostly black cast. For more on representations of race on American television, see Torres, *Black, White, and In Color*; Bodroghkozy, "Is This What You Mean by Color TV?"; Gray, *Watching Race*; Riggs, *Color Adjustment*.

87. This was echoed in media accounts. See Sander Vanocur, "Roots: A New Reality," *Washington Post*, January 19, 1977.

88. "Concerned Public," to VP-Programming, ABC, February 2, 1977, box 288, folder 3: "Letters from Public: Criticism," DJW.

89. Anonymous to ABC, February 21, 1977, box 288, folder 3: "Letters from Public: Criticism," DJW.

90. E. C. M., to David Wolper, February 8, 1977, box 288, folder 3: "Letters from Public: Criticism," DJW.

91. L. H. W. to David Wolper, January 31, 1977, box 288, folder 1: "Letters from Public: Praise," DJW.

92. Mrs. H. E. P. to ABC, January 31, 1977, box 288, folder 1: "Letters from Public: Praise," DJW.

93. I. C. to KABC, January 27, 1977, box 288, folder 1: "Letters from Public: Praise," DJW.

94. Mrs. M. E. B. to David Wolper, February 28, 1979, box 288, folder 1: "Letters from Public: Praise," DJW.

95. Michael Kirkhorn, "A Saga of Slavery That Made the Actors Weep," *New York Times*, June 27, 1976.

96. LeVar Burton, *Roots: The Complete Collection*, DVD Commentary, Episode 2. Warner Home Video, 2007.

97. Thomas Johnson, "Roots Has Widespread and Inspiring Influence," *New York Times*, March 19, 1977.

98. See Jacobson, *Roots Too*.

99. Phillip E. Lothyan, "In the Aftermath of Roots: The Experience of the Seattle Archives Branch," [of the National Archives]; Jim Gordon Manchester, "The Genealogical Gold Rush . . . It All Started with TV's Roots," October 6, 1977, Society of American Archivists Salt Lake City, session: Reference Services for Genealogists, both found in box 304, folder 37, DJW; Thomas Grubisich, "Register of Freed Slaves Bares Fairfax 'Roots,'" *Washington Post*, February 1, 1977.

Chapter Two

1. Eugene L. Meyer, "Proclaiming a 'Bicentennial Era,' Nixon Urges Leadership and Peace," *Washington Post*, July 4, 1971.

2. Critics writing across a broad range of scholarly fields have commented on the relationship between archives, knowledge, and power. See Benjamin, "Theses On the Concept of History"; Foucault, *The Archaeology of Knowledge*; Nora, "Between Memory and History"; Taylor, *The Archive and the Repertoire*; Trouillot, *Silencing the Past*.

3. Critical work on memorials and monuments underscores the way that memorial activity addresses the present through invoking the past. This is especially evident because memorials are permanent structures yet their meanings and interpretations change with each new generation. For examples, see Levinson, *Written in Stone*; Savage, *Standing Soldiers, Kneeling Slaves*; Doss, *Memorial Mania*. At the same time, when a monument addresses a history that is contested, the monument itself will also be contested. See Sturken, *Tangled Memories*.

4. See Bodnar, *Remaking America*, 13–20, 206–44; Glassberg, *American Historical Pageantry*; Benedict Anderson, *Imagined Communities*. See also Christiansen, *Channeling the Past*.

5. Rep. John O. Marsh Jr., "A Proposal for the Current Establishment of a Federal Commission in Connection with Appropriate Observance of the Bicentennial of the Period of the American Revolution," [n.d., ca. 1963], RG 452-A1-O1, ARBC Central Classified Records, 1965–73, box 1, folder: "Organization & Management," Records of the American Revolution Bicentennial Administration, National Archives and Records Administration II, College Park, MD (hereafter cited as ARBA).

6. Ibid.

7. This impulse can be seen alongside other Cold War cultural projects designed to reaffirm America's position both domestically and abroad. See, for example, Von Eschen, *Satchmo Blows Up the World*; Dudziak, *Cold War Civil Rights*, 203–49.

8. "Coordinators for Revolution Event Sought," *Washington Post*, January 31, 1966.

9. "Revolution Anniversary Commission Requested; House Chairmen Asked to Talk with President," *Washington Post*, March 11, 1966.

10. Don Irwin, "President Signs Plans on July 4 Bicentennial," *Los Angeles Times*, July 9, 1966; Carroll Kilpatrick, "President Looks Ahead to Our 200th Birthday," *Washington Post*, July 9, 1966; Robert Young, "Lyndon Signs Order to Mark Bicentennial," *Chicago Tribune*, July 9, 1966. For more on Johnson and Vietnam, see Kaiser, *American Tragedy*; Logevall, *Choosing War*.

11. Carlisle Humelsine to Special Advisor to the President John Roche, November 21, 1966, RG 452-A1-O1, ARBC Central Classified Records, 1965–73, box 1, folder: "Organization & Management, Commission Members," ARBA.

12. "Unit Named to Plan 200th Anniversary of U.S. Revolution," *New York Times*, January 19, 1967; American Revolution Bicentennial Administration, *The Bicentennial of the United States of America*, 2: 10–12.

13. For more on Great Society programming, see Farber, *The Age of Great Dreams*; Schulman, *Lyndon B. Johnson and American Liberalism*; McKenzie and Westbrot, *The Liberal Hour*.

14. Robert J. Cook, *Troubled Commemoration*.

15. "Goals Cited for Bicentennial of Revolution," *Los Angeles Times*, April 4, 1968.

16. See, for example, "Cities Salvaging Proposed by HHH," *Washington Post*, February 24, 1969; Wolf Von Eckardt, "Mission '76: A Spanking New Capital; Goal for Bicentennial Sense of Belonging," *Washington Post*, April 14, 1968; Proposal for Polis '76, undated, RG 452-A1-O1, ARBC Central Classified Records, 1965–73, box 9, folder: Polis '76, ARBA.

17. In part because the visibility of the Vietnam conflict through television and other media coverage, "sham battles," the reenactments that had been the bulk of popular engagement with the history of the Civil War, suddenly had a new and more problematic context. In a letter to Humelsine, Republican senator and ARBC appointee Edward Brooke wrote, "in view of the world situation, I would prefer fewer reenactments of battles than occurred during the Civil War Centennial." Edward Brooke to Carlisle Humelsine, March 31, 1967, RG 452-A1-O1, ARBC Central Classified Records, 1965–1973, box 1, folder: "Meeting: Theme Committee, 1967," ARBA. For more on commemorations and battle reenactment, see Cook, *Troubled Commemoration*.

18. Lauris Norsted, cited in Wolf Von Eckardt, "Mission '76: An Idea vs. Frameworks," *Washington Post*, April 20, 1969; ARBC timeline, 1970, RG 452-A1-O1, ARBC Central Classified Records, 1965–73, box 7, folder: "Organization & Management," ARBA.

19. Harry Gilroy, "Scholars Plan to Publish Papers of Loyalists to 1776 Revolution," *New York Times*, November 16, 1968.

20. "International Exhibitions," *Washington Post*, May 17, 1968.

21. Rydell, *All the World's a Fair*, 1–8; Rydell, *World of Fairs*, 61–217; Rydell, Findling, and Pelle, *Fair America*, 100–131; Samuel, *The End of the Innocence*.

22. Smith, "Making Time: Representations of Technology at the 1964 World's Fair."

23. For more on the realignment of American politics at this moment, see McGirr, *Suburban Warriors*; and Lassiter, *The Silent Majority*.

24. Isserman and Kazin, *America Divided*; Lytle, *America's Uncivil Wars*; and Matusow, *The Unraveling of America*.

25. In December of 1968, Humelsine wrote S. Dillon Ripley, the secretary of the Smithsonian Institution, "I have just succeeded in making a good contact with the incoming Administration and have every reason to believe the Commission will soon be in a position to move ahead," and suggested that the two "discuss the Bicentennial in the near future." In April, historian Richard Morris wrote to Humelsine, asking, "Are we still on the Commission and do you know what the President's intentions are in that respect?" Humelsine responded that he himself had not been able to make satisfactory contact with the White House. Carlisle Humelsine to S. Dil-

lon Ripley, December 12, 1968, RG 452-A1-O1, ARBC Central Classified Records, 1965–73, box 6, folder "Dillon Ripley," ARBA; Richard Morris to Carlisle Humelsine, April 22, 1969, Humelsine to Morris, April 30, 1968, RG 452-A1-O1, ARBC Central Classified Records, 1965–73, box 23, folder "Richard Morris," ARBA.

26. "Nixon Appoints 17 to Plan Activities for Bicentennial," *New York Times*, July 4, 1969.

27. Susan Dworkin, "The Bicentennial: Is It Slowly Sinking into the Potomac?" *Ms.*, June 1974, 46–51.

28. John Fenton, "Two Cities Seeking '76 Bicentennial," *New York Times*, March 16, 1969; "2 G.O.P. Governors Back Philadelphia for Bicentennial," *New York Times*, March 1, 1969.

29. Memo from Wallace Sterling to all governors, October 17, 1969, RG 452-A1-O1, ARBC Central Classified Records, 1965–73, box 1, folder "International Exposition 1969," ARBA; Richard Powers, "Boston Opens Drive for '76 World's Fair," *Boston Globe*, January 16, 1969; Robert M. Smith, "Boston, Philadelphia and Washington Put in Bids for Site of American Expo in 1976," *New York Times*, September 25, 1969; William Ecenbarger, "Boston, Philadelphia Vie for Bicentennial," *Washington Post*, April 3, 1969.

30. "Lead-In for a discussion of the whole matter of an international exposition as an activity associated with the Bicentennial," draft, July 26, 1969, RG 452-A1-O1, ARBC Central Classified Records, 1965–73, box 1, folder "International Exposition, 1969," ARBA.

31. Paul J. C. Friedlander, "The Spirit of 1976 May Mix Fusillade on Pollution with Colonial Hoopla," *New York Times*, April 5, 1970; Wolf Von Eckard, "After 200 Years, Is There Still a Spirit of '76?" *Washington Post*, June 14, 1970; Eric F. Goldman, "Topics: The Real Revolution—Or Doodle Dandy?" *New York Times*, September 27, 1969.

32. Ada Louise Huxtable, "Whither World's Fairs?" *New York Times*, March 29, 1970.

33. Richard Grayson (Boston) "Give 1976 to Philadelphia," letter to the editor, *New York Times*, July 6, 1969; Mrs. John A. Salkowski, "To Save Boston Harbor," letter to the editor, *New York Times*, August 10, 1969.

34. Jeremiah Murphy, "Is Expo 76 to Be Scratched? Panels Reported Ready to Recommend No Single Celebration," *Boston Globe*, May 26, 1970.

35. Donald Janson, "Bicentennial Decision May Be Revised," *New York Times*, June 13, 1970.

36. William L. Claiborne, "D.C. Loses Bid for Bicentennial; Document Obtained Philadelphia Awarded Bicentennial Program," *Washington Post*, July 2, 1970.

37. "'76 Backing Goes to Philadelphia; Bicentennial Panel Said to Urge Exposition There," *New York Times*, July 3, 1970; Donald Janson, "Senator Scott Appears Far Ahead in 3rd Term Bid; Lack of Identity and Lack of Funds Hurt Democrat in Pennsylvania Campaign," *New York Times*, October 9, 1970.

38. "Outline for the National Bicentennial Plan," November 4, 1969, RG 452-A1-O1, ARBC Central Classified Records, 1965–73, box 3, folder: "Organization & Management," ARBA.

39. "Bicentennial Report Handed to President," *Los Angeles Times*, July 4, 1970; "And Six Years From Today," *Washington Post*, July 4, 1970. In a November 1970 memo, Charles Williams of the White House had noted: "There is a pervasive crisis of confidence in America today. Surveys show that more and more average Americans are pessimistic about their personal future because they are pessimistic about the nation's future." Memo from Charles Williams, White House, to Melbourne Spector, November 17, 1970, RG 452-A1-O1, ARBC Central Classified Records, 1965–73, box 8, folder: "Horizons 76," ARBA.

40. Shirley Patterson, "Open House USA: A Definition," March 17, 1972; Eugene Skora to Jack LeVant, March 24, 1972; "ARBC, Chronology of Open House USA," March 31, 1971, RG 452-A1-O1, ARBC Central Classified Records, 1965–73, box 27, folder: "Open House, USA," ARBA.

41. American Revolution Bicentennial Administration, *The Bicentennial of the United States of America*, 1: 244.

42. John Pierson, "The U.S. Needs Help in Throwing a Party," *Wall Street Journal*, July 31, 1972; ARBC Communications Committee, "A Report on the American Revolution Bicentennial Celebration, 1976: Highlights of Progress to-date," November 1971, RG 452-A1-06, Correspondence with Federal Agencies, 1969–73, box 42, folder: "National Trust for Historic Preservation," ARBA.

43. Vermont Bicentennial Report, [n.d., ca. 1971], Boston 200 Collection, box 43, folder "Public Relations and Advertising: Brochures," Boston Public Library (hereafter cited as B200).

44. ARBC Communications Committee, "A Report on the American Revolution Bicentennial Celebration, 1976: Highlights of Progress to-date."

45. Bodnar, *Remaking America*, 13–20. Local initiatives are also described in Gordon, *The Spirit of 1976*.

46. David Goodman to Leonard Lock, November 16, 1972, RG 452-A1-O1, ARBC Central Classified Records, 1965–73, box 26, folder: "Heritage '76," ARBA.

47. For examples of media attention to the ARBC in this period, see Howard Taubman, "1976 Bicentennial Group Is Planning a Varied, Year-Long Celebration for Entire Nation," *New York Times*, August 1, 1971; "Around Town: '76'–'71=5," *Washington Post*, April 12, 1971.

48. Schulman, *The Seventies*; Cowie, *Stayin' Alive*. See also Self, *All in the Family*.

49. Matusow, *Nixon's Economy*, 214; Perlstein, *The Invisible Bridge*.

50. On Nixon's politics, see Perlstein, *Nixonland*; Farber, "The Silent Majority."

51. "Bicentennial Head," *Washington Post*, August 7, 1970.

52. Transcript of White House Press Conference with David Mahoney, released by White House Press Secretary, September 11, 1970, RG 452-A1-O1, ARBC Central Classified Records, 1965–73, box 5, folder: "White House Release, 1970," ARBA.

53. Marilyn Bender, "Will the Real Norton Simon Please Stand Up," *New York Times*, June 16, 1974; Melbourne Spector to R. Lynn Carroll: "Memo re: Purposes and Functions of Commission Itself," September 21, 1970, RG 452-A1-O1, ARBC Central Classified Records, 1965–73, box 7, folder: "Organization & Management 1970," ARBA.

54. There was a lengthy debate within ARBC about the voting rights of these ex officio members, who were often not able to attend meetings but who often sent subordinates to vote as surrogates despite the fact that regular ARBC members (both private and public) were explicitly forbidden from this practice. Patricia H. Collins to Melbourne Spector, October 24, 1969, RG 452-A1-O1, ARBC Central Classified Records, 1965–73, box 4, folder: "Organization & Management: Commission Members," ARBA.

55. Jack LeVant, "Director's Report to the Commission," December 9, 1971, RG 452-A1-O1, ARBC Central Classified Records, 1965–73, box 17, folder: "Directors Report to ARBC 12/9/71," ARBA.

56. For more on Nixon-era privatization, see Parmet, *Richard Nixon and His America*; Kotlowski, *Nixon's Civil Rights*; Matusow, *Nixon's Economy*.

57. Barry Gidley to Jack LeVant and Hugh Hall, "Memo re: Support Corporation for the Commission," December 9, 1971, RG 452-A1-O1, ARBC Central Classified Records, 1965–73, box 10, folder: "Corporation-Foundation, 1971," ARBA.

58. Eugene Skora to Jack LeVant, December 3, 1971, RG 452 A1-O1, ARBC Central Classified Records, 1965–73, box 18, folder: "Delegation of Authority," ARBA.

59. See Kindleberger, *Manias, Panics, and Crashes*; Matusow, *Nixon's Economy*.

60. Donald Janson, "Philadelphia Starts Again on 1976 Bicentennial after Government Calls Plan Too Costly," *New York Times*, December 18, 1970; Homer Bigart, "Site Dispute Dims Hopes for '76 Philadelphia Exposition," *New York Times*, January 21, 1972.

61. Donald Janson, "Black Dissent and High Cost Snag Philadelphia Bicentennial Plans," *New York Times*, November 14, 1970; Donald Janson, "Minorities Fight Plan for 1976 Bicentennial Fair," *New York Times*, January 10, 1971.

62. Donald Janson, "'76 Fair Disputed in Philadelphia," *New York Times*, April 11, 1971.

63. "Plans for Philadelphia Fair in '76 Seen Dead," *Los Angeles Times*, May 31, 1971; Donald Janson, "Philadelphia Moves to Drop 1976 World's Fair," *New York Times*, May 5, 1971.

64. Ada Louise Huxtable, "Bicentennial Panel Urges Network of Parks; Project Could Cost Up to $1.2-Billion, Commission Says," *New York Times*, February 23, 1972; Wolf Von Eckart, "To Honor a Revolution—Parks for the People," *Washington Post*, March 18, 1972.

65. Davis, Brody & Associates, "A Proposal for a National Focus Commemorating the American Revolution Bicentennial in 1976," February 10, 1972, RG 452 23A, Office of the General Counsel, Subject Files, 1969–77, box 101, folder: "Davis, Brody Associates, Bicentennial Parks Model," ARBA.

66. Horace Sutton, "Bicentennial Park in Each State," *Chicago Tribune*, May 14, 1972.

67. Eugene L. Meyer, "Bicentennial Parks Proposal Faces Barriers," *Washington Post*, December 14, 1972.

68. Eugene L. Meyer, "Panel Leaves Nation Without '76 Celebration," *Washington Post*, May 16, 1973.

69. Eugene L. Meyer, "The Big Birthday Bungle," *Washington Post*, July 2, 1972, C1; Eugene L. Meyer, "Study Raps Bicentennial Staff," *Washington Post*, July 20, 1972;

Report of Arthur D. Little, Inc., to proceedings of ARBC Executive Committee meeting, June 22, 1972, RG 452 A1-O1, ARBC Central Classified Records, 1965–73, box 20, folder: "Little, Arthur D," ARBA.

70. "Washington: For the Record," *New York Times*, June 20, 1972; Mary Russell, "Quick Bicentennial Vote Dies," *Washington Post*, June 20, 1972.

71. Eugene Mayer, "U.S. Bicentennial Unit Assailed for No Plans," *Washington Post*, December 9, 1971; Carolyn Toll, "Historians Assail Lack of Planning for the Bicentennial," *Chicago Tribune*, October 26, 1972.

72. Dworkin, "The Bicentennial: Is It Slowly Sinking into the Potomac?," 48.

73. Eugene L. Meyer, "Counter Bicentennial Group Seeks End to Exploitation," *Washington Post*, September 8, 1972.

74. William Greider, "Group Plans to Show Radical Spirit of '76," *Washington Post*, October 15, 1971.

75. Robert Gruenberg, "News for Nixon: 'People' Uniting for Bicentennial," *Tucson Daily Star*, March 24, 1974.

76. See, for example, "Nixon 'Stealing the Revolution'?" *Washington Post*, August 13, 1971.

77. Bob Arnbeck, "Expose of an Expose: Confessions of the Bicentennial Commission Spy," *Washington Post*, March 18, 1973.

78. Eugene L. Meyer, "The Big Birthday Bungle," *Washington Post*, July 2, 1972; Eugene L. Meyer, "Study Raps Bicentennial Staff," *Washington Post*, July 20, 1972.

79. Eugene L. Meyer, "Bicentennial Commission: Deeply Involved in Politics," *Washington Post*, August 14, 1972.

80. Beverly Carman, Letter to the Editor, *Washington Post*, August 22, 1972; "Bicentennial Budget Bill Withdrawn," *Los Angeles Times*, August 15, 1972; "Documents Link Politics to the '76 Fete," *New York Times*, August 20, 1972; "The Dispirit of '76," *Boston Globe*, September 3, 1972.

81. Eugene L. Meyer, "The Red, White, Blue—and Green," *Washington Post*, August 15, 1972.

82. Acting director of ARBC, Hugh A. Hall, one of the only employees who would stay until 1976, responded in a letter to the editor of the *Washington Post*, characterizing the articles as a left-wing plot and accusing the *Post* of failing to check facts. The *Post* responded that Hall had "chosen to duck" by critiquing only the *Post*'s use of the "ARBC papers" and continued to question the commission's close ties to the White House and GOP. Hugh A. Hall, "Letter to the Editor: Bicentennial Commission Director Responds," *Washington Post*, August 21, 1972; "More on the Bicentennial Commission," *Washington Post*, August 21, 1972.

83. Eugene L. Meyer, "Senator Pastore Quits Units on Bicentennial," *Washington Post*, August 17, 1972.

84. Eugene L. Meyer, "Black Caucus Criticizes 1976 Bicentennial Panel," *Washington Post*, August 24, 1972; Eugene L. Meyer, "Bicentennial 'Attacks' Decried by Republicans," *Washington Post*, August 19, 1972.

85. "Nixon 'Stealing the Revolution'?" *Washington Post*, August 13, 1971.

86. Paul J. Asciolla, "U.S. History Needs Overhaul," *Chicago Tribune*, September 5, 1973.

87. James J. Kirkpatrick, "Would You Have Joined Up in the American Revolution?" *Los Angeles Times*, July 4, 1973.

88. Eugene L. Meyer, "Did National Politics Foil the Fair?" *Washington Post*, May 18, 1972.

89. William Greider, "Group Plans to Show Radical Spirit of '76," *Washington Post*, October 15, 1971.

90. "Bicentennial Budget Bill Withdrawn," *Washington Post*, August 15, 1972; Hugh Hall to Jack LeVant, "Memo re: Telephone Call from John Aidair, General Accounting Office," July 17, 1972, RG-452-A1-06, Correspondence with Federal Agencies, 1969–73, box 41, folder: "General Accounting Office," ARBA; Eugene L. Meyer, "Bicentennial Director Quits; Management Was Criticized," *Washington Post*, August 2, 1972. Despite Mahoney's public defense, LeVant resigned the day before the HJC hearings.

91. Eugene L. Meyer, "GAO Is Mildly Critical of Bicentennial Group," *Washington Post*, December 22, 1972; Eugene L. Meyer, "Bicentennial Commission Hit in Report by House Unit Staff," *Washington Post*, December 30, 1972.

92. "Criticisms and Findings of the House Judiciary Committee Staff Report on the Operations of the ARBC," May 8, 1973, RG 452-A1-O1, ARBC Central Classified Records, 1965–73, box 19, folder: "House Judiciary Committee, Subcommittee No 2. September 1972" ARBA; Telegram from David Mahoney to Harold Donahue, August 21, 1972, RG-452-A1-O1, ARBC Central Classified Records, 1965–73, box 19, folder: "Congressman Harold D. Donohue (Mass.)," ARBA.

93. Comptroller General of the United States, General Accounting Office, "Report: Organization and Operations of the American Revolution Bicentennial Commission," December 21, 1972, RG 452 23A, Office of the General Counsel: Subject Files, 1969–77, box 105, folder: "General Accounting Office," ARBA; "House Inquiry: 1976 Commission Scored in Report," *New York Times*, December 30, 1972; "Shakeup Urged; Bicentennial Unit Scored as Failure," *Los Angeles Times*, January 1, 1973.

94. John Copley to David Mahoney, September 18, 1972, RG 452-A1-O1, ARBC Central Classified Records, 1965–73, box 25, folder: "Bicentennial Cities," ARBA.

95. "From Manhattan to Mid-America: A 'Grass Roots' Bicentennial," *U.S. News & World Report*, August 19, 1974, 65–67.

96. Eugene L. Meyer, "Diluting the Spirit of '76," *Washington Post*, August 16, 1972.

97. For accounts of the planning of the Bicentennial, see Gordon, *The Spirit of 1976*; Spillman, *Nations and Commemoration*; Zaretsky, *No Direction Home*, 143–82; Lowenthal, "The Bicentennial Landscape"; Capozzola, "It Makes You Want to Believe in the Country."

98. Statement of David J. Mahoney before the Subcommittee on Interior and Related Agencies of the Committee on Appropriations, February 21, 1973, RG 452-A1-O1, ARBC Central Classified Records, 1965–73, box 28, folder: "ARBC Appropriations Hearings for FY73, Feb 21, 1973," ARBA; Statement of Hugh A. Hall, Acting Director of the ARBC before the Subcommittee on Federal Charters, Holidays, and Celebrations of the Senate Committee on the Judiciary, July 11, 1973, RG 452-A1-O1, ARBC Central Classified Records, 1965–73, box 28, folder: "ARBC Hearings: Senate Committee on

the Judiciary, 7/11/73" ARBA; Eugene L. Meyer, "Bicentennial Panel Wants Funds Doubled," *Washington Post*, December 12, 1972.

99. "Discussion Paper #1: Use of Revenues from the Sale of the 1976 Gold Medal" (undated, December 1972–January 1973), RG 452-A1-O1, Office of the Administrator: Correspondence with Advisory Council Members, 1975–76, box 96, folder: "Discussion Paper #1: Use of Revenues from the Sale of the 1976 Gold Medal," ARBA.

100. Charles Goodspeed, "Suggested State Criteria for Use by State Bicentennial Commissions," November 14, 1972, RG 452-A1-O1, ARBC Central Classified Records, 1965–73, box 26, folder: "State and Local Bicentennial Commissions," ARBA; Hugh Hall, "Action No 2-73, Bicentennial Communities Program," RG 452-A1-O1, ARBC Central Classified Records, 1965–73, box 29, folder: "Organization & Management: Delegation of Authority, 1973," ARBA.

101. Hugh Hall to Nancy Hanks, NEA, December 21, 1972, with enclosure: "Proposed Policy for Implementation of ARBC Matching Project Grants," December 15, 1972, RG 452-A1-O1, ARBC Central Classified Records, 1965–73, box 19, folder: "Grants 1972," ARBA

102. "Bicentennial Communities: A Progress Report," *Bicentennial Times* 2, no. 1 (January 1975); "Action No 2-73, Bicentennial Communities Program," RG 452-A1-O1, ARBC Central Classified Records, 1965–73, box 29, folder: "Organization & Management: Delegation of Authority, 1973," ARBA.

103. Martha Jane Shay to Sid Eiges and Herb Hetu, "Memo re: Briefing material (prepared for *Today* show)," August 7, 1974, RG 452-A1-O1, Office of the Administrator: Correspondence with Advisory Council Members, 1975–76, box 96, folder: "ARBA Council—Miscellaneous Correspondence," ARBA.

104. American Revolution Bicentennial Administration (ARBA), *The Bicentennial of the United States of America*, 2: 142–86

105. John L. Cotter, *Above Ground Archaeology* (Washington, DC: U.S. GPO, 1975). For more examples of nationally funded programs, including those mentioned above, see RG 452-A1-70, Programs, States and Communities Division: Records Concerning Nationally Recognized Bicentennial Programs, 1972–77, boxes 253–65, ARBA.

106. Carolyn Toll, "Historians Assail Lack of Planning for Bicentennial," *Chicago Tribune*, October 26, 1972.

107. "Patriotic Groups to Restage Historic Events," *Bicentennial Times* 2, no. 3 (April 1975); Wendy Schuman, "Marching Out of the Past," *New York Times*, May 20, 1973.

108. "President Proposes a New Unit to Plan U.S. Bicentennial," *New York Times*, February 2, 1973.

109. Although the ARBC had seemingly shifted gears, there was still a close connection between the presidency and the Bicentennial, as Nixon continued to attempt to use the celebration for his own political advancement. After his landslide victory over George McGovern, Nixon arranged for a colonial marching band, the "Spirit of '76," to precede him in the January Inaugural parade. "Marching Toward '76," *Washington Post*, February 9, 1973; Joanne Omang, "12,000 to Tootle and March Up Avenue Behind Nixon," *Washington Post*, January 20, 1973.

110. Eugene L. Meyer, "House Panel Criticizes White House for Proposing a Bicentennial Czar," *Washington Post*, March 15, 1973.

111. "New Plan Urged for Bicentennial," *New York Times*, April 25, 1973. Despite the controversy surrounding the ARBC, an increasingly desperate and erratic Nixon still considered using appointments for political aims. Just weeks before his second inauguration, Nixon and Chief of Staff H. R. Haldeman discussed giving the administration position to Special Assistant Jeb Magruder as a reward for his work in the cover-up of the Watergate burglary and other "dirty tricks." It was ultimately decided that the spot was too "politically visible." Months later, Magruder would begin cooperating with the federal prosecutors in exchange for a reduced sentence. Kutler, *Abuse of Power*, 194–97.

112. On the Watergate scandals, see Ambrose, *Nixon*; Berkowitz, *Something Happened*, 12–32.

113. ARBC, "Bicentennial News" press releases, March 14, 1973, December 2, 1973, RG 452 A1-36, Communications and Public Affairs Division: Official News Release, 1970–76, box 175, folder: "Press Releases, 1972–73," ARBA.

114. Eugene L. Meyer, "Spirit of '76," *New Leader*, June 24, 1974.

115. Transcripts of speeches, box 17A, folder: "New England Life Forums," B200.

116. Kevin Phillips, "Previous Celebrations Held During Crisis," *Philadelphia Bulletin*, July 9, 1974.

117. Richard Jensen, "Grant, Nixon a Century Apart: Two Embattled Presidents," *Chicago Tribune*, November 12, 1973; Page Smith, "On the Anniversary of a Party in Boston," *New York Times*, December 15, 1973.

118. "Bicentennial Unit Created by Nixon," *Washington Post*, December 12, 1973; "Bicentennial Fete Leader Quits Post," *Chicago Tribune*, December 27, 1973.

119. Albin Krebs, "Notes on People: Navy Chief to Head Bicentennial," *New York Times*, February 12, 1974.

120. "Nixon Appoints Navy Secretary to Plan 'Truly National' Bicentennial," *Los Angeles Times*, March 11, 1974; John M. Crewdson, "Nixon Names Head of Agency for '76: Navy Secretary Warner to Coordinate Bicentennial Restoring Structures," *New York Times*, March 11, 1974; "Bicentennial Post," *Los Angeles Times*, April 12, 1974.

121. Quoted in *Bicentennial Times* 1, no. 3 [n.d., ca. January 1974], 7.

122. *The Bicentennial of the United States of America*, 2: 26–30.

123. Edward Stafford, "Memo for the Record re: Bicentennial Times," November 13, 1973, RG 452-A1-01, ARBC Central Classified Records, 1965–73, box 28, folder: "Information & Public Relations: Newsletter," ARBA.

124. "Bicentennial Celebration: Charges of Commercialism Are Expected to Proliferate as 1976 Approaches," *New York Times*, March 11, 1974; Lou Cannon, "Warner Is Named to Head '76 Agency," *Washington Post*, March 11, 1974.

125. "Negativism Stalls Bicentennial Plans," *Salt Lake Tribune*, May 29, 1974.

126. "New Light on the Bicentennial," *Washington Post*, August 13, 1974.

127. "Will Ex-Navy Man Keep Bicentennial Afloat?" *Fayetteville Observer*, June 9, 1974; Robert Karen, "New Light in the Steeple," *The Nation*, June 29, 1974, 818–19.

128. Howard, *The PBC*, 34.

129. "Commission Chief Says Bicentennial Won't Divert from Watergate," *Dennison Herald*, June 30, 1974.

130. "President Calls on Nation to Emulate Founders in Word and Deed," *Bicentennial Times* 3, no. 2 (February 1976).

131. "What They Said 200 Years Later in Philadelphia," *Bicentennial Times* 1, no. 10 (September 1974); "President Signals Bicentennial Countdown," *Bicentennial Times*, 2, no. 6 (July 1975).

132. Gaylord Shaw, "Ford Places Documents of Liberty on Display," *Los Angeles Times*, July 3, 1976.

Chapter Three

1. National Trust for Historic Preservation and ARBC, "Meeting House Preservation Act," memo, May 1973, RG 452-A1-70, Programs, States and Communities Division: Records Concerning Nationally Recognized Bicentennial Programs, 1972–77, box 260, folder: "Meeting House Preservation Act," ARBA; see also "Heritage Meeting House" [n.d., ca. December 1973], RG 452 A1-93, Programs, States and Communities Division: General Records Relating to the Heritage Program, 1971–75, box 311, folder: "Presentation for Warner," ARBA.

2. Correspondence between David Goodman, ARBC, and Howard Lancour, Michigan, November 16, 1972, Charles "Pat" Hall, Wyoming, November 18, 1972, RG 452-A1-O1, ARBC Central Classified Records, 1965–73, box 26, folder: "Heritage '76," ARBA.

3. Ibid.

4. National Trust for Historic Preservation, "Heritage '76 Meeting House Proposal: A National Preservation Plan to Commemorate the Bicentennial," December 8, 1972, RG 31, Department of Commerce Series: American Revolution Bicentennial File, box 3: General Correspondence, C-N, Pennsylvania State Archives, Harrisburg, PA.

5. On the role of artifacts in historical meaning making, see Maines and Glynn, "Numinous Objects"; Susan Stewart, *On Longing*; Ulrich, *The Age of Homespun*; Lubar and Kendrick, *Legacies*. On history and the formation of identity, see Anderson, *Imagined Communities*; Lowenthal, *The Past Is a Foreign Country*, 35–73.

6. West, *Domesticating History*, 1–38; Herbst, "Historic Houses."

7. Marling, *George Washington Slept Here*; Wallace, *Mickey Mouse History*, 3–32.

8. Barthel, *Historic Preservation*.

9. Verne E. Chatelain, "Suggested Statements of Principles and Standards Involving National Historical Areas," in J. Thomas Schneider, *Report to the Secretary of the Interior on the Preservation of Historic Sites and Buildings* (Washington, DC: Department of the Interior, 1935), 2–3, quoted in Sprinkle, *Crafting Preservation Criteria*, 26–27.

10. Shackel, "Introduction: The Making of the American Landscape"; Lindgren, "A Spirit That Fires the Imagination."

11. Meringolo, *Museums, Monuments, and National Parks*; Sprinkle, *Crafting Preservation Criteria*.

12. "Historic Shrines," *Washington Post*, October 23, 1947; "To Preserve Our Heritage," *New York Times*, September 8, 1949.

13. "Culture Trust Is Urged, Law Will Be Asked to Preserve Historic Sites and Buildings," *New York Times*, November 5, 1948.

14. Finley, *History of the National Trust for Historic Preservation, 1947–1963*, 95–97.

15. Ibid., 14–27. For more examples of buildings favored by preservationists, see Vanderbilt, *The Living Past of America*.

16. Sugrue, *The Origins of the Urban Crisis*; Zipp, *Manhattan Projects*.

17. "Preservation and Urban Renewal: Is Coexistence Possible?" *Antiques Magazine*, October 1963.

18. "Misplaced Zeal," *Chicago Tribune*, June 20, 1964.

19. William L. Slayton, letter to the editor, *Chicago Tribune*, July 16, 1964.

20. Fitch, *Historic Preservation*; Glass, *The Beginnings of a New National Historic Preservation Program, 1957 to 1969*.

21. Wolf Von Eckardt, "Freeways Run into a Blockade," *Washington Post*, June 26, 1966. See also John Pierson, "They'll Save Historic Buildings from Demolition," *Boston Globe*, December 11, 1966.

22. See Meringolo, *Museums, Monuments, and National Parks*.

23. See Udall, *The Quiet Crisis*.

24. Glass, *The Beginnings of a New National Historic Preservation Program*, 3–15.

25. See also Wellrock, *Preserving the Nation*, 151–203.

26. National Historic Preservation Act (16 USC 470). Patricia L. Parker, "What Is the National Historic Preservation Act?," National Park Service, Local Preservation, Distributed by Interagency Resources Division, Washington, DC, May 1987, National Trust for Historic Preservation Collection, University of Maryland, College Park. See also Special Committee on Historic Preservation United States Conference of Mayors, *With Heritage So Rich*.

27. Murtagh, *Keeping Time*, 25–35.

28. "Preservation Is People," *Preservation News*, October 1972.

29. National Trust for Historic Preservation, "Excerpts from Goals and Programs," 1973, Appendix 23 in Mulloy, *The History of the National Trust for Historic Preservation, 1963–1973*, 281.

30. Ziegler, *Historic Preservation in Inner City Areas*, 9.

31. National Trust for Historic Preservation, "Excerpts from Goals and Programs," 1973, Appendix 23 in Mulloy, *The History of the National Trust for Historic Preservation*, 281.

32. James Biddle, "Preface," in Mulloy, *The History of the National Trust for Historic Preservation*, xi.

33. Ibid.

34. Providence Preservation Society (hereafter cited as PPS), *Forty: 1956–1996*, commemorative booklet, 1996, Rhode Island Historical Society Library (hereafter cited as RIHS), Providence, RI.

35. PPS, *First Street Festival*, May 16, 1958, booklet, RIHS.

36. William McKenzie Woodward, *1956–1981, Providence Preservation Society 25th Anniversary*, commemorative booklet, 1981, RIHS, 4–6.

37. PPS, *First Street Festival*, May 16, 1958, booklet, RIHS. See also PPS, *Third Street Festival*, May 6, 1960, booklet, RIHS; PPS, *Seventh Annual Street Festival*, May 16, 1964, booklet, RIHS.

38. For an excellent account of the PPS's early activities, see Greenfield, "Marketing the Past: Historic Preservation in Providence, Rhode Island."

39. Salkind, "Scale, Sociality, and Serendipity in Providence, Rhode Island's Post-Industrial Renaissance."

40. PPS, "Explore Historic Providence," press release, March 1975, Collection of Providence Preservation Society (CPPS), MSS 241, box 14, folder: "Tours Past, 1975," RIHS; "Third tour: Early 19th century—Age of the China Trade," 1974, CPPS, MSS 241, box 14, folder: "Broadsides, Written Materials," RIHS.

41. "Education Committee Report, Tours Program, Analysis of Income: 1970 to date," November 12, 1975, CPPS, MSS 241, box 14, folder: "Tours Past, 1975," RIHS.

42. Johnette Isham, PPS, "City Exploration," [n.d., ca. 1972], CPPS, MSS 241, box 14, folder: "Downtown Tour," RIHS.

43. Leo Blackman, drafts for Downtown Tour [n.d., ca. 1975–76], CPPS, MSS 241, box 14, folder: "Downtown Tour," RIHS.

44. Leo Blackman, PPS, *Looking Up Downtown*, broadside, 1976, RIHS. See also, "Looking Up Downtown," *PPS News*, October 14, 1974, Antoinette Downing Papers, MSS 98, box 22, folder: "Clippings and Posters," RIHS.

45. Leo Blackman, *Explore Historic Providence*, broadside, 1976, CPPS, MSS 241, box 14, folder: "Broadsides of Historic Providence, 1976," RIHS.

46. As a result of increased funding possibilities opened up by the new legislation, newer preservation projects partnered with corporate interests and stressed functionality. By the mid-to-late 1970s, preservation groups sought to create "main streets" and commercial districts where rehabilitated buildings could be used to generate income for upkeep and further preservation. Historic preservation, with its new connections to government, commerce, and business, followed other models of neoliberal development that were becoming prevalent in political and cultural activity. See Ziegler and Kidney, *Historic Preservation in Small Towns*; Weinberg, *Preservation in American Towns and Cities*; Lee, *Past Meets Future*. On public-private partnerships in local cultural organizations, see Greenberg, *Branding New York*.

47. Katherine Kane to William Underwood Company, "Proposal for Improvement of Freedom Trail," July 24, 1974, box 40, folder: "Freedom Trail/Underwood Proposal," B200; see also Boston 200 brochures "Boston's Freedom Trail" (1975) and "The Americans Are Coming, the Americans Are Coming!" (1975), box 43, folder: "Public Relations and Advertising: Brochures," B200.

48. Ethel L. Payne, "Brothers Move Insures Black Roles in Fete," *Chicago Daily Defender*, August 24, 1971.

49. Vincent DeForest, quoted in Eugene Meyer, "The Big Birthday Bungle," *Washington Post*, July 2, 1972. See also Martin S. Goldman to Lynn Carroll, ARBC, Memo re: meeting with Vincent DeForest, September 6, 1973, RG 452-A1-70, Programs, States and Communities Division: Subject Files of the Ethnic-Racial Program Office, 1975–76, box 272, folder: "Afro-American Bicentennial Corporation," ARBA.

50. Johnsye Smith, "Bicentennial 'Time for Questions,' Official Says Blacks Should Not Be Turned Off," *Tulsa Tribune*, January 13, 1975. See also statements of Robert DeForrest in "Hearings Before Subcommittee No. 2 of the Committee of the Judi-

ciary House of Representatives, Ninety-Third Congress, First Session on H.R. 3695 and H.R. 3976 to Establish the American Revolution Bicentennial Administration, March 14 and 15, 1973" (Washington, DC: U.S. Government Printing Office, 1973), 291–307.

51. Burns, *From Storefront to Museum*, 72–128.

52. Vincent DeForest, quoted in Jacqueline Trescott, "Blacks, the Bicentennial and 'Two Souls,'" *Washington Post*, March 20, 1976.

53. Eugene Meyer, "Neglected Black Historic Sites Recorded for Bicentennial," *Washington Post*, April 14, 1973.

54. "Black Landmarks," *Washington Post*, August 11, 1975.

55. Robert DeForrest, "Afro American Bicen. Completes Survey of Historic Sites," *Sentry Post: Citizen Voice of the D.C. Bicentennial Commission* 2, no. 3 (June/July 1973): 8–9, box 86, folder: "DC Bicentennial Commission," B200.

56. See Evans and Boyte, *Free Spaces: The Sources of Democratic Change in America*; Habermas, *The Structural Transformation of the Public Sphere*.

57. On African American preservation efforts, see Barton, *Sites of Memory*.

58. Mary Ellen Perry, "Search for Black Landmarks," *Washington Star-News*, April 14, 1974; "In Search of Black History," *Chicago Daily Defender*, September 9, 1972; Claudia Levy, "Anacostia: Restoration Efforts Mounted for Historic Area of City," *Washington Post*, April 28, 1973.

59. Ellen Hoffman, "D.C. Group to Fight Avenue Bill; Opposes Private Corporation," *Washington Post*, September 30, 1970; "Whose Heavy Hand?" *Washington Post*, September 30, 1970; Wolf Von Eckardt, "A Sure Thing, It Seems: A Fingers-Crossed Urban Renewal Project Cityscape," *Washington Post*, July 3, 1971.

60. For accounts of the long battle between local and federal interests in Washington, DC, see Eugene Meyer, "Bicentennial Panel Reformed," *Washington Post*, December 18, 1971; Jack Eisen, "'76 Finish Sought for 'Triangle'; Nixon Budget Asks $126 Million," *Washington Post*, January 25, 1972; Juan M. Vasquez, "Nixon Plans Role for DC in '76 Fete," *New York Times*, February 5, 1972; Bart Barnes, "Sports Arena Fight: Progress vs. People; D.C. Area Residents, Businessmen at Odds on Sports Arena Plan," *Washington Post*, February 13, 1972.

61. Nichols, "Historic American Landscapes Survey." See also Jane Donovan, "The Meaning of Death," in Donovan, *Many Witnesses*; Lesko, Babb, and Gibbs, *Black Georgetown Remembered*.

62. Quoted in Fred Brown Jr., "Preserving America's Black Historic Landmarks," *Washington Post*, February 20, 1989.

63. Timothy S. Robinson, "Mount Zion Cemetery Is Saved by Judge," *Washington Post*, August 1, 1975; "Requiescat in Pace," *Washington Post*, August 11, 1975.

64. Emily Isberg, "Black Landmarks," *Washington Post*, July 28, 1974; Angela Terrell, "Black Landmarks," *Washington Post*, August 3, 1974; "Six Historic Sites Are Named," *Washington Post*, March 18, 1977.

65. Fred Brown Jr., "Preserving America's Black Historic Landmarks," *Washington Post*, February 20, 1989.

66. "Clues Are Found to Lost Negro Colony Here," *New York Times*, July 2, 1969.

67. Maynard, "Weeksville Revisited."

68. Wellman, *Brooklyn's Promised Land*. See also Green, "The Weeksville Heritage Center."

69. Scott, "Reimagining Freedom in the Twenty-First Century at a Post-Emancipation Site."

70. See the Weeksville Society, 1970–73, Medgar Evers Oral History Series, 5th of July Resource Center for Self-Determination and Freedom, Weeksville Heritage Center, Brooklyn, New York. See also Scott, "Reimagining Freedom."

71. Cited in Columbia University Oral History Research Office, *Annual Report*, 1975, 3.

72. For examples of histories of slavery that use WPA oral histories as evidence, see Gutman, *The Black Family in Slavery and Freedom*; Genovese, *Roll, Jordan, Roll*.

73. Terkel, *Hard Times*, and *Working*. See also Adam Cohen, "Studs Terkel's Legacy: A Vivid Window on the Great Depression," *New York Times*, November 8, 2008.

74. Fogerty, "Oral History and Archives: Documentary Context."

75. Dale Rosen, "Bi-Centennial Neighborhood History Project: A draft proposal," July 1973, box 26NI, folder: "proposals," B200; Lew Carter, "Boston 200 Press Release: Boston Neighborhood Exhibits Funded," August 22, 1974, box 26NI, folder: "Neighborhood Exhibits," B200; Eleanor K. Welch, "Hanging Out at the Jeffries Point Reading Room," *East Boston Community News*, April 15, 1975, box 30NI, folder: "East Boston," B200.

76. Washington State Oral/Aural History Program interviews, Center for Pacific Northwest Studies, Heritage Resources, Western Washington University, Bellingham, WA. See also Samantha Sunderland, "Archives Month Flashback: Oral Histories for Bicentennial," *Washington Secretary of State Blog*, October 28, 2013, blogs.sos.wa.gov/FromOurCorner/index.php/2013/10/archives-month-flashback-oral-histories-for-bicentennial/.

77. Mary T. Henry, "Esther Hall Mumford," on HistoryLink, September 9, 2008, http://www.historylink.org/index.cfm?DisplayPage=output.cfm&file_id=8781. See also Mumford, *Seven Stars and Orion* and *Seattle's Black Victorians*.

78. For early theorizations of this relationship, see Menninger, "Some Psychological Factors Involved in Oral History Interviewing." For more contemporary accounts, see Mould, "Interviewing"; and Yow, "'Do I Like Them Too Much?' Effects of the Oral History Interview on the Interviewer and Vice-Versa."

79. Ritchie, *Doing Oral History*.

80. Mumford, *Seven Stars and Orion*, ii.

81. Ibid., 48.

82. For oral history projects of the time, see Jenkins, *Past Present*; Montell, *The Saga of Coe Ridge*; Oblinger, *Interviewing the People of Pennsylvania*; Porter, *The Workers World at Hagley*.

83. Herbert Collins to Brooke Hindle, June 10, 1976, National Museum of American History, Division of Political History, 1960–82, box 1, folder: "July, 1976," Smithsonian Institution Archives.

84. See Lemisch, *Towards a Democratic History*.

85. Bicentennial Schlock Collection, Sterling Memorial Library, Department of Manuscripts and Archives, Yale University Library. For complete finding aid, see http://drs.library.yale.edu/fedora/get/mssa:ms.1262/PDF.

86. For more discussion of Bicentennial Schlock, see Gordon, *The Spirit of 1976*. The connections between citizenship and consumption have also been explored by Lizabeth Cohen in *A Consumer's Republic*.

87. Jesse Lemisch, "Bicentennial Schlock," *The New Republic*, November 6, 1976, 21–23.

88. On the souvenir, see Stewart, *On Longing*, 132–69.

89. "Bicentennial Schlock Spoofs Tradition," *New York Times*, Monday October 11, 1976.

90. Lemisch, "Bicentennial Schlock," 21.

91. "Minutes of the Ad Hoc Committee on the Meeting House Program," December 17, 1975, Helen Byrd (National Trust) to George Ebner (Pennsylvania Bicentennial Commission), December 22, 1975, Archives of the Department of Commerce, Bicentennial Commission, RG 318, box 3, folder: "Meeting Houses-ARBC," Pennsylvania State Archives.

Chapter Four

1. *Increase and Diffusion: A Brief Introduction to the Smithsonian Institution* (Smithsonian Institution Office of Public Affairs, 1975), 48; and *Increase and Diffusion*, 31, both in Office of Public Affairs Publications, 1970–98, Accession 99-054, Smithsonian Institution Archives (hereafter cited as SIA).

2. Wallace, *Mickey Mouse History*, 267. See also Bennett, *The Birth of the Museum*; Conn, *Museums and American Intellectual Life, 1876–1926*.

3. For more on postwar funding for the arts, see Harris, *Capital Culture*; Conn, *Do Museums Still Need Objects?* See also Frank Taylor, oral history, interview 3 (1979–80), Oral history interviews with Frank A. Taylor 1974, 1979–80, 1982, 2005, box 1, folder: transcripts, SIA.

4. Walker, *A Living Exhibition*, 64–65.

5. Herman Schaden, "New Smithsonian Unit to Be a Palace of Progress," *Washington Star*, May 25, 1962, A16, quoted in Walker, *A Living Exhibition*, 65.

6. See Post, *Who Owns America's Past? The Smithsonian and the Problem of History*; Museum of History and Technology, *Exhibits in the Museum of History and Technology* (Washington, DC: Smithsonian Institution Press, 1968). See also Corn, "Tools, Technologies, and Contexts," 237–61.

7. Museum of History and Technology, *Growth of the United States, 1640–1851*, brochure, 1967; Museum of History and Technology, *Exhibits in the Museum of History and Technology*.

8. On the longer history of period rooms, see Kulik, "Designing the Past."

9. Post, *Who Owns America's Past?*, 113.

10. Walker, *A Living Exhibition*, 175–79. See also Marzio, *A Nation of Nations*; Museum of History and Technology, "Nation of Nations" brochure, 1967, 97-014, National Museum of American History (hereafter cited as NMAH), Department of Exhibits, Records, ca. 1964–92, box 1, folder: ANON, SIA.

11. Jean M. White, "'Nation of Nations,' from 6,000 Perspectives," *Washington Post*, June 9, 1976, C1.

12. Anna Reed, "1876 Opens in Grand Style," *Smithsonian Torch*, June 1976.

13. *Centennial Post*, Office of Telecommunications Production Records: 1876, 1975–84, box 1, folder: "'1876' correspondence and development 2 of 2," SIA.

14. Post, *1876* (Washington, DC: Smithsonian Institution Press, 1976).

15. Rydell, Findling, and Pelle, *Fair America*. See also Lauren Rabinowitz's work on visual organization of racial and gendered hierarchy and spectatorship in the 1893 Chicago Exposition, *For the Love of Pleasure*, 47–67.

16. See Kulik, "Designing the Past," 7–17. One could argue that the Smithsonian's National Air and Space Museum, opened in the Bicentennial year and featuring a celebratory display of flight and space technology, was the last real world's fair held in the United States, but there was even a sense of history to this: by that time, the space program, linked so intrinsically to the modernist period, had begun to decline.

17. William Miner (exhibit curator) to Matthew Cantor, Philadelphia, Pennsylvania, October 4, 1978, NMAH, Office of the Director, Subject Files, ca. 1977–92, box: "Exhibits 1876," folder: "1876 Exhibition Correspondence 1978," SIA. On "patina" and aesthetic decay, see Lowenthal, *The Past Is a Foreign Country*, 148–82.

18. Correspondence between William Miner and Brooke Hindle, September 13, 22, 1976, NMAH, Office of the Director, Subject Files, ca. 1977–92, box 1, folder: "1876 Exhibition Correspondence, 1976," SIA. See also correspondence between Brooke Hindle and Paul Perrot, April 28, 1975, NMAH, Department of Collections Management Services, Exhibition Records, 1971–98, box 4, folder: "Paul N. Perrot: Correspondence, 1973–76," SIA.

19. On museum practices at the time, see Greif, "Cleaning Up the Treasures of History."

20. On the emotional currency of the object, see Maines and Glynn, "Numinous Objects"; Greenblatt, "Resonance and Wonder"; and Pearce, *Objects of Knowledge*.

21. Post, *Who Owns America's Past?*, 321–22n41.

22. *Celebrating a Century*, wr. Benjamin Lawless, dir. Karen Loveland, Smithsonian Motion Pictures Unit, National Museum of History and Technology, 1976 (28 mins). Viewed at Smithsonian Institution Archives.

23. Benjamin Lawless, "1876: Celebrating a Century," exhibition script, March 10, 1976; Smithsonian Office of Public Affairs Press Release, April 12, 1976, Office of Telecommunications, Production Records: 1876, 1975–84, box 1, folder: "1876," SIA.

24. Leila-Joyner Smith, "Smithsonian: Remnants of the '76 Centennial," *Washington Post*, January 19, 1975; Henry Mitchell, "1876: History and Hoopla," *Washington Post*, May 21, 1976; Lewis, "Exhibit Review: The Smithsonian's '1876' Exhibit."

25. Benjamin Lawless to Paul Perrot, August 13, 1975, Office of Telecommunications Production Records: 1876, 1975–84, box 2, folder: "1876 correspondence," SIA.

26. *Centennial Post*, Office of Telecommunications, Production Records: 1876, 1975–84, box 1, folder: "1876 correspondence and development 2 of 2," SIA.

27. For more on the relationship between affect and politicized realization, see Ngai, *Ugly Feelings*, 3; Gould, *Moving Politics*; Berlant, *The Female Complainte*, 1–32; Kathleen Stewart, *Ordinary Affects*; Massumi, *Parables for the Virtual*.

28. See, for example, J. Y. Smith, "100 Picket at White House against A-Weapon," *Washington Post*, July 9, 1975; Lawrence Meyer and Janis Johnson, "Protest Marches

of Past, Now a 'Walk' for Justice," *Washington Post*, October 16, 1976; Judith Valente, "29 Are Arrested at Pentagon," *Washington Post*, December 29, 1976.

29. See Harris, *Capital Culture*.

30. Betsy Earls, "Progress Report, September 20, 1972," box 8-NI, folder: "beginning efforts."

31. Katherine Kane, "Exhibit on the American Revolution Period," Grant Application, National Endowment for the Humanities, March 14, 1973, box 11-NI, folder: "Quincy Market," B200.

32. Richard Rabinowitz, "Role-Playing in the Exhibit for Boston," September 28, 1973, box 11NI, folder: "Quincy Market," B200.

33. Michael Sand & Associates, "The American Revolution Exhibit: A Progress Report, January 1974," box 11-NI, folder: "Quincy Market," B200.

34. Ibid., 5.

35. Sand left Boston 200 over a financial dispute. The final designer, DeMartin, Corona, Cranstoun, and Downes, used many of Sand's original concepts. Michael Sand & Associates, Press release announcing resignation over financial dispute, December 12, 1974, box 5B, folder: "correspondence," B200; Michael Keating to Katherine Kane, re: Dispute with Michael Sand, January 14, 1975, box 5B, folder: "Sand Contract," B200.

36. Steve Clark, Boston 200, "Recollections on Citygames," transcript, January 13, 1977, box 17, folder: "Steve Clark," B200.

37. John MacDonald, "Treatment and Script for Decisions and Audio Visual Elements in Boston 200 Exhibit," May 14, 1975, box 4, folder: "script for AV segment," B200. See also Katherine Kane to Boston 200 Board of Directors, "memo re: Recent Developments on the Revolution Exhibit," March 11, 1975, box 4, folder: "general information," B200.

38. "The Revolution in Boston," Press Release, box 5, folder: "Eighteenth Century Exhibit," B200.

39. John Macdonald, "Treatment and Script for Audio Visual Elements in Boston 200 Exhibit," May 14, 1974, box 5, folder: "Eighteenth Century Exhibit," B200.

40. Photograph from "The Revolution," box 55, folder: "18th Century Exhibit," B200.

41. Peter Sage, exhibit coordinator, to Dr. Walter Muir Whitehill, Andover, June 9, 1975, box 4, folder: "correspondence/content," B200.

42. John MacDonald, "Treatment and Script for Decisions and Audio Visual Elements in Boston 200 Exhibit," May 14, 1975, box 5, folder: "script for AV Segment," B200.

43. *You Are There*, October 2, 1955, CBS.

44. G. W. Hoffmeister, Bicentennial Coordinator, Honeywell, to Katherine Kane, May 21, 1975, box 5, folder: "computers/Honeywell," B200.

45. Wade Franklin, "Would You Have Been a Patriot or a Tory in 1776?" *Hartford Times*, November 11, 1975.

46. Sample ballot, "The Revolution," box 5, folder: "ballots"; "The Totalizer," exhibition script draft, [n.d., ca. late 1975], box 5, folder: "exhibit script," B200.

47. Peter Sage to Kathy Kane, Mike Sand, re: Mike Sand's Progress Report, April 29, 1974, box 5, folder: "correspondence/content," B200.

48. Bill Fripp, "A Simple Test of Patriotism," *Boston Globe*, December 16, 1975; Daniel Q. Haney, "Tory or Patriot? The Computer Will Tell All," *Lewiston Journal*, March 4, 1976; American Association for State and Local History, "Boston Still Turning Out Patriots and Loyalists," *History News* 3, no. 1 (March 1976): 1.

49. Guy Darst, "Boston Separates Patriots, Tories," *Kennebec Journal*, August 5, 1976; "Voting System Tests Revolutionary Fervor," *Honeywell World*, October 20, 1975; Wade Franklin, "Would You Have Been a Patriot or a Tory in 1776?" *Chicago Sun-Times*, November 11, 1975; Margot Hornblower, "Revolutionizing the Revolution: Would You Have Dumped the Tea?" *Washington Post*, December 9, 1975.

50. In March of 1976, 70,000 visitors to "The Revolution" had taken the test: the tallies were 47 percent Patriots and 27 percent Loyalists, with 26 percent undecided. Margot Hornblower, "47% Support Patriots in Loyalty Quiz," *Los Angeles Times*, March 26, 1976.

51. Richard Battista and Doug Bell to Boston 200, December 12, 1975, box 5B, folder: "correspondence," B200. See folder for similar.

52. Lalor Cadley, "Memo re: Meeting with History Task Force," November 15, 1974, box 4, folder: "18c exhibit/Michael Sand," B200; Peter Sage to Katherine Kane and Michael Sand on opinions of William Osgood and Byron Rushing, April 1, 1974, box 4, folder: "arbitration on Revolution," B200.

53. For more on Disney and history, see Wallace, *Mickey Mouse History*.

54. Venturi, *Learning from Las Vegas*.

55. Greiff, *Independence*, 194–228.

56. Among the exhibitions I write about, this one is unique because, until January of 2012, it was still entirely intact and without significant modifications. While I have reconstructed other exhibits from published accounts and archival records, Franklin Court testifies to the staying power of the new direction that museum exhibition took in this period. In 2010, at the time of my visit, it appeared dated (and, in fact, was subsequently closed and renovated), but at its inception, it represented the cutting edge of museum exhibition.

57. Deetz, "The Changing Historic House Museum."

58. Greiff, *Independence Hall*, 222.

59. Exhibit signage, "Franklin Exchange," Franklin Court, Philadelphia, PA.

60. "Franklin Court Telephone Exchange: Script and Guide for Directing Telephone Calls," Library and Archives of Independence National Historical Park, Philadelphia, PA.

61. For more on telephony and spectrality, see Ronell, *The Telephone Book*; Jeffrey Sconce, *Haunted Media*.

62. John Secondari Productions, *Portrait of a Family*, 1976. Script held in Library and Archives of Independence National Historical Park, Philadelphia, Pennsylvania.

63. See Turner, *From Counterculture to Cyberculture*.

64. See McCarthy and Wright, *Technology as Experience*.

65. Jay Anderson, *Time Machines*; Snow, *Performing the Pilgrims*.

66. Wallace, *Mickey Mouse History*, 3–32.

67. Snow, *Performing the Pilgrims*, 21–48; Handler and Gable, *The New History in an Old Museum*, 28–77; Colby, *Plimoth Plantation Then and Now*, 106–9; Abing, "Old Sturbridge Village."

68. "Life-Sized Replicas: Plymouth Is Rebuilding Early Pilgrim Village," *Boston Globe*, August 21, 1948; Ward Allan Howe, "Pilgrim Holiday," November 6, 1949; Wallace, *Mickey Mouse History*, 3–32; Rosen, *Change Mummified*.

69. Swigger, *History Is Bunk*; Greenspan, *Creating Colonial Williamsburg*, 76–94.

70. Abing, "Old Sturbridge Village," 161–63.

71. See, for example, Colonial Williamsburg Incorporated, *An Official Guidebook*, 1957.

72. Carson, "Living Museums of Everyman's History," 25. See also *Colonial Williamsburg Official Guidebook*; Joe Harrington, "Pilgrim Village Replica, Mayflower II at Plimoth," *Boston Globe*, June 24, 1960.

73. See, for example, Tilden, *Interpreting Our Heritage*, 68–83.

74. Carson, "Living Museums of Everyman's History," 29.

75. "Old Sturbridge Village Honored," *Massachusetts Spy and Village Courier*, May 30, 1964, quoted in Abing, "Old Sturbridge Village," 126.

76. Quoted in Snow, *Performing the Pilgrims*, 26.

77. On the longer history of living history farms, see Schlebecker, *Living Historical Farms*, 5–16.

78. Kelsey, "Outdoor Museums and Historical Agriculture."

79. Schlebecker and Peterson, *Living Historical Farms Handbook*, 1–59; Kelsey, "Harvests of History"; Hawes, "The Living Historical Farm in North America."

80. Carson, "Living Museums of Everyman's History," 22. See also Richard Rabinowitz, *Curating America*.

81. Handler and Gable, *The New History in an Old Museum*, 28–77.

82. Carson, "Living Museums of Everyman's History," 23.

83. For profiles of living history museums in the 1970s, see Anderson, *Time Machines*.

84. Snow, *Performing the Pilgrims*, 183–212.

85. Deetz, "The Changing Historic House Museum," 51.

86. Deetz and Deetz, *The Times of Their Lives*, 273–92.

87. Deetz, "The Changing Historic House Museum," 52.

88. Ibid.

89. Ibid., 54.

90. Kirshenblatt-Gimblett, *Destination Culture*, 189–200.

91. Snow, *Performing the Pilgrims*, 120–82.

92. Carson, "Living Museums of Everyman's History," 29.

93. Ronsheim, "Is the Past Dead?," 16–17.

94. See, for example, Schlereth, "It Wasn't That Simple," 39–40.

95. For more on these debates, see Magelssen, *Living History Museums*.

96. For defenses of first-person interpretation, see Anderson, *Time Machines*; Roth, *Past Into Present*; Hilker, *The Audience and You*, 28–34.

97. Kay, *Keep It Alive*, 22–23.

98. National Park Service, Environmental Living Program brochure, 1975, box 40, folder: "National Park Service," B200.

99. National Park Service, Environmental Living Program brochure, 1975, "Getting There," box 40, folder: "National Park Service," B200.

100. "Pupils Dress the Part to Recreate Colonial Classroom," *Christian Science Monitor*, April 14, 1976.

Chapter Five

1. William Worthington, Smithsonian Institution, "1876" docent, e-mail to author, March 13, 2012.

2. On the use of "hegemony" to describe the reinforcement of dominant meaning, rather than something closer to "ideology" or even "social control," I take inspiration from T. J. Jackson Lears's excellent discussion on the topic in *No Place of Grace*, 10.

3. For critical analyses of reenactment as a form, see Schneider, *Performing Remains*; Magelssen, *Simming*; and McCalman and Pickering, *Historical Reenactment*.

4. "The Gaudy Show at Manassas, VA," *Washington Post*, July 30, 1961. See also Allan Nevins, "The Glorious and the Terrible," *Saturday Review*, September 2, 1961; Brooks Atkinson, "Air of Celebration Attached to Civil War Centennial Belies Tragedy of Conflict," *New York Times*, September 19, 1961.

5. For histories of reenactment, especially Civil War reenactment, see Cook, *Troubled Commemoration*; Tony Horowitz, *Confederates in the Attic*; Cullen, *The Civil War in Popular Culture (A Reusable Past)*.

6. "Goals Cited for Bicentennial of Revolution," *Los Angeles Times*, April 4, 1968; Edward Brooke to Carlisle Humelsine, March 31, 1967, RG 452-A1-O1, ARBC Central Classified Records, 1965–73, box 1, folder: "Meeting: Theme Committee, 1967," ARBA.

7. Stanton, *Reenactors in the Parks*, 15–16.

8. See McCollough, *Living Pictures on the New York Stage*; Chapman, "Living Pictures"; Fisher, "Interperformance."

9. Glassberg, *American Historical Pageantry*.

10. Ibid.

11. Turner, *From Counterculture to Cyberculture*; Frank, *The Conquest of Cool*; Evans, "Beyond Declension."

12. Binkley, *Getting Loose*.

13. Marilyn Stout, "Fort Ticonderoga: A Bicentennial Replay," *New York Times*, May 4, 1975; Peter Anderson, "Spirit of '76 to Live Again on Weekend," *Boston Globe*, April 13, 1975; Ann Marie Currier, "Couriers Relate News of Concord on South Shore," *Boston Globe*, April 19, 1975.

14. Margaret Carroll, "Chicagoland Drums up a Revolutionizing Spirit of '76," *Chicago Style*, September 6, 1974; Jo Martin, "Stage Revolutionary Battle," *New York Daily News*, October 18, 1974; "State Bicentennial Endorses O'Neill Minutemen," *Frontier and Holt County Independent*, May 4, 1974; Barbara Archer, "Delaware Crossing Reenacted," *Newark Star-Ledger*, January 22, 1975; Paul Jablow, "Revolutionary Rider Makes a Comeback," *Philadelphia Inquirer*, April 28, 1975; Anne Bishop, "The

Western Spirit of '76," *Literary Tabloid*, June 1975; "Historical Figures to Make a Comeback," *Seattle Daily News*, August 6, 1975; James Tuite, "Vintage Cars Crank Up for Rerun of 1908 Race," *New York Times*, September 11, 1975; Henry Darling, "Caravan Will Reenact Expedition by Benedict Arnold," *Philadelphia Sunday Bulletin*, September 28, 1975; "Pilot to Re-Enact 1926 Flight in April," *Caldwell, Idaho News Tribune*, January 19, 1976; Lucrecia Steiger, "Fronteras '76 Links the Past to the Future," *San Diego Union*, January 11, 1976; "The Knox Trail Reenactment," *Worcester Evening Gazette*, January 12, 1976.

15. John Burgess, "Historic Ride Reenacted on Its Bicentennial," *Washington Post*, June 18, 1975.

16. "Historic Trail Being Traced," *Arizona Republic*, August 17, 1975.

17. "Hawaii-Tahiti Voyagers Set for Bicentennial Journey," *San Jose Mercury News*, September 28, 1975; "Crew Members Named for Tahiti Canoe Trip," *Honolulu Star-Bulletin*, February 9, 1976.

18. On America and mobility, see Belasco, *Americans on the Road*; McShane, *Down the Asphalt Path*; Volti, *Cars and Culture*.

19. Miller, *The 60s Communes*.

20. Jon Van, "Bicentennial Takes Bikers for a Long, Fulfilling Ride," *Chicago Tribune*, July 11, 1976; Judy Moore, "Pedaling among American Trails," *Los Angeles Times*, June 27, 1976.

21. See Matusow, *Nixon's Economy*; Kotlowski, *Nixon's Civil Rights*.

22. Report of Tucson Bicentennial Committee, April 28, 1975, RG 452-A1-O1, Office of Administrator Records, ARBA Advisory Council 75-6, box 96, folder: "April 7 1975 Council Meeting (Tucson)," ARBA.

23. Melvin T. Smith, "Bicentennial Report," December 2, 1976, RG 452-A1-70, Programs, States and Communities Division: Records Concerning Nationally Recognized Bicentennial Programs, 1972–77, box 257, folder: "Dominguez-Escalante," ARBA.

24. See Lassiter, *The Silent Majority*; McGirr, *Suburban Warriors*; Wilentz, *The Age of Reagan*.

25. Margot Hornblower, "Spanish Heritage Recalled," *Washington Post*, November 19, 1975.

26. "Canoeists Recreate Voyage by LaSalle," *Los Angeles Times*, September 7, 1976; Michael Sneed, "LaSalle Explorers Paddle to Success," *Chicago Tribune*, April 4, 1977.

27. Cherrie Hall, "Horizons '76, memo for the record," March 18, 1975, RG 452-A1-70, Programs, States and Communities Division: Records Concerning Nationally Recognized Bicentennial Programs, 1972–77, box 260, folder: "LaSalle Expedition II," ARBA; Jon Van, "LaSalle's Journey—Elgin Style," *Chicago Tribune*, October 26, 1975; Jon Van, "A-paddling they will go—for 3,000 Miles," *Chicago Tribune*, August 4, 1976.

28. William Crawford Jr., "Imagine LaSalle Exhorting His Crew, 'Stay Cool, Men,'" *Chicago Tribune*, December 2, 1976.

29. Mark Starr, "LaSalle Voyage Is Put on Ice," *Chicago Tribune*, December 9, 1976; Seth S. King, "Civilization Slows LaSalle Expedition II," *New York Times*, February 5, 1977.

30. Reid Lewis, project proposal to ARBA, June 28, 1975, RG 452-A1-70, Programs, States and Communities Division: Records Concerning Nationally Recognized Bicentennial Programs, 1972–77, box 260, folder: "LaSalle Expedition II," ARBA.

31. Agnew and Lamb, "Introduction: What Is Re-enactment?"; Agnew, "History's Affective Turn"; Cook, "The Use and Abuse of Historical Reenactment"; d'Oro, "Reenactment and Radical Interpretation."

32. Reid Lewis, quoted in Spurr, *River of Forgotten Days*, 154.

33. Lynne Baranski, "Sacre Bleu! An Illinois Teacher and His Students Retrace La Salle's 1682 Expedition," *People*, April 18, 1977; Tiffany Ray, "Elgin Teacher Wins Award from France," *Chicago Tribune*, October 16, 2002; Boissoneault, "Always Further."

34. "Mississippi River Trip Proves Point," *Los Angeles Times*, May 25, 1977.

35. See also Frederick Lowe, "LaSalle Trek Presses South," *Chicago Tribune*, December 13, 1976; "Canoeists to Go on, Despite Crash," *Chicago Tribune*, January 14, 1977.

36. Reid Lewis recollections in Boissoneault, "Always Further."

37. "Bicentennial Wagon Train Pilgrimage to Pennsylvania," *Columbia City Commercial Mail*, October 8, 1975; "Bicentennial Wagon Train to Recall Pioneer Spirit," *Virginia Bulletin-Democrat*, July 24, 1975; Nick Gardner, "Wagons Will Roll Through our Valley," *Skagit Valley Herald*, January 18, 1975.

38. See Slotkin, *Gunfighter Nation*.
I view the fact that the Wagon Train's trip was *in reverse* as significant for several reasons. From a logistical perspective, the types of volunteers (trail riders, wagon enthusiasts, and so on) that had the skills necessary to participate were more easily found in the western states, which had a more developed network of club organizations. At the same time, one could make the observation that, ideologically, the backward trip can be read as a further confusion of history and temporality such as those we have seen in this chapter and chapter 4, or as an assertion of the political dominance of Sunbelt states.

39. Aitkin-Kynett press release draft, October 5, 1976, RG 31, Secretary of Commerce, series 14: Wagon Train File, box 7, folder: "Aitkin Kynett Co.: Planning, Supervision, Execution of Wagon Train Project"; T. Gray Associates, promotional brochure, "The Bicentennial Wagon Train Pilgrimage," 1975, RG 31, Secretary of Commerce, series 17: Wagon Train File, box 1, folder: "misc.," both in Bicentennial Wagon Train Collection, State Archives of Pennsylvania, Harrisburg, Pennsylvania (hereafter cited as BWT); Enos Pennington, "Ford Invited to Join Wagon Train," *Cincinnati Post*, April 30, 1976; Linda Rosenblatt, "Conestogas Plod on Toward Valley Forge," *Albany Times-Union*, May 31, 1976.

40. "Pledge of Rededication," [n.d., ca. 1975], RG 31, Secretary of Commerce, series 14: Wagon Train File, box 6, folder: "Pledge," BWT; Monica Hesse, "Bicentennial Wagon Train Signatures Are Lost Pieces of the American Past," *Washington Post*, July 3, 2011.

41. Aitkin-Kynett press release draft, October 5, 1976, RG 31, Secretary of Commerce, series 14: Wagon Train File, box 7, folder: "Aitkin Kynett Co, Inc, File, Planning, Supervision, Execution of Wagon Train Project," BWT.

42. For more on the relationship between the Bicentennial and commerce, see Gordon, *The Spirit of 1976*.

43. Letters from wagoneers to Aitkin-Kynett: Mr. and Mrs. John Keeler, New Brighton, PA, to Lieutenant Governor Kline, February 26, 1975; Thelma Gray to Richard Read, December 13, 1975; Kathy Baird to T. Gray Associates, November 17, 1975, RG 31, Secretary of Commerce, series 14: Public Relation File, box 4, folder: "Thelma Gray Correspondence," BWT.

44. Thelma Gray to George Ebner, February 22, 1977; RG 31, Secretary of Commerce, series 14: Public Relation File, box 4, folder: "Thelma Gray Correspondence," BWT.

45. Thelma Gray, "Bicentennial Wagon Train Pilgrimage to Pennsylvania," undated publicity brochure, RG 31, Secretary of Commerce, series 14: Public Relation File, box 4, folder: "publicity," BWT.

46. Aitkin-Kynett, Report on the Bicentennial Wagon Train Pilgrimages to Pennsylvania, June 8, 1975 to March 1, 1976, RG 31, Secretary of Commerce, series 14: Planning, Supervision, Execution of Wagon Train Project, box 7, folder: "Wagon Train Participation," BWT; see also Official Souvenir Program, 1976, RG 31, Secretary of Commerce, series 14: Public Relations File, box 4, folder: "Publicity," BWT.

47. For more on the potential of embodied performance, see Schneider, *Performing Remains*; Dinshaw, *Getting Medieval*.

48. "Membership Application," list of participants, August 1976, RG 31, Secretary of Commerce, series 17: Public Relations File, box 6, folder: "Participants," BWT. See also George Ebner (Pennsylvania Bicentennial Commission) to Creed Black (*Philadelphia Inquirer*), July 16, 1976, RG 31, series 17: Public Relations File, box 7, folder: "press," BWT.

49. Compare these Wagon Train articles: Andrew Malcolm, "Wagon Train Gets Underway on Year's Trip to Valley Forge," *New York Times*, June 15, 1975; "Wagon Train Now in Utah on Eastward Journey," *Salt Lake Tribune*, August 1, 1975; "Storm Drenches Bicen Wagoneers," *Portland Oregon Journal*, July 30, 1975; "Bicentennial Wagon Train to Recall Pioneer Spirit," *Virginia Bulletin-Democrat*, July 24, 1975, with these Bikecentennial articles: James Rees, "Biking Couple Are Now Wedded Couple," *Newport News Daily Press*, September 8, 1974; Mary Bralove, "On the Trail, Bikers Have Ups and Downs Plus Aches and Pains," *Wall Street Journal*, October 6, 1976; Judy Moore, "Biking for the Bicentennial," *Washington Post*, April 25, 1976.

50. Bill Collins, "Wagon Train's Appetites, Tales Are Both Tall," *Philadelphia Inquirer*, August 8, 1976. See also participation request letters: Dick Tomlinson to T. Gray and Associates, August 3, 1975, RG 31: Secretary of Commerce, series 14: Public Relations File, box 7, folder: "Wagon Train Certificates," BWT; Mr. and Mrs. John Keeler to Lieutenant Governor Kline, February 26, 1975; Franklin McCollim to Thelma Gray, November 15, 1975; Kathy Baird to T. Gray Associates, November 17, 1975, Record Group 31: Department of Commerce, Bicentennial Commission, series 14: Public Relations File, box 4, folder: "Thelma Gray Correspondence," BWT.

51. Tom Allen, "Shelton Shelters Trail Mules," *Omaha World-Herald*, October 18, 1975.

52. George Foster, "Bicentennial Wagon Train Rolls First Cabin," *Seattle Post-Intelligencer*, June 11, 1975.

53. See Kate Jackson letter in Earl Reinhalter, ed., *The WagoNews: A Newsletter for those who travelled with the Great Lakes Route of the Bicentennial Wagon Train*, Issue 5, April 1977, RG 31, Secretary of Commerce, series 14: Public Relations File, box 2, folder: "Aitkin-Kynett (general) July–December 1976," BWT.

54. Eddie and Louise Relph, "The Great Lakes Wagon Train Trek to Valley Forge," in Reinhalter, *The WagoNews*, Issue 5, April 1977, RG 31: Secretary of Commerce, series 14: Public Relations File, box 2, folder: "Aitkin-Kynett (general) July–December 1976," BWT.

55. Keith Gates, "Memories from the Gates," in Reinhalter, *The WagoNews*, Issue 5, April 1977, RG 31, Secretary of Commerce, series 14: Public Relations File, box 2, folder: "Aitkin-Kynett (general) July–December 1976," BWT.

56. In recent years, significant work on embodied history has been done in the field of cultural studies and performance studies. See, for example, Agnew and Lamb, "Introduction: What Is Re-enactment?"; Magelssen, *Simming*; Schneider, *Performing Remains*; Landsberg, *Engaging the Past*; DeGroot, *Consuming History*; and Magelssen and Justice-Malloy, *Enacting History*.

57. "Mrs. R. G." to Eddie and Louise Relph, reprinted in *The WagoNews*, Issue 4, February–March 1977, RG 31, Secretary of Commerce, series 14: Public Relations File, box 2, folder: "Aitkin-Kynett (general) July–December 1976," BWT.

58. Parkman, quoted in "Wagons East," *Philadelphia News*, June 12, 1975.

59. "Bicentennial Wagon Train to Roll Though Parish," *Denham Springs News*, December 29, 1975; Gary Taylor, "Wagon Train Readied Here for Trip East," *Houston Post*, December 26, 1975; Joseph Lucia, "LA Wagon Train Heads for Norco," *New Orleans Times-Picayune*, February 19, 1976; "Wagon Trains Recreate West, Rekindle Patriotism," *Birmingham News*, March 7, 1976; Thomas Hill, "Wagon Train Brings Pioneer Days to Life," *Tennessee Star*, March 10, 1976; Chambers Williams, "Wagon Train Show Draws 5,000 to Milan City Park," *Jackson Tennessee Sun*, April 8, 1976; Mark Talbert, "Begin Trek to Rekindle Spirit of America," *Cedar Valley Times*, April 7, 1976.

60. Photographs from Wagon Train, RG 31, Secretary of Commerce, series 15, box 5: "Bicentennial Wagon Train Photograph Album," BWT. See also Reinhalter, *The WagoNews*, Issue 4, February–March 1977; Issue 5, April 1977, RG 31, Secretary of Commerce, series 14: Public Relations File, box 2, folder: "Aitkin-Kynett (general) July–December 1976," BWT.

61. Hedgepeth, *The Alternative*.

62. Jack Hurst, "Indian Threat Reported on Caravan," *Philadelphia Inquirer*, June 11, 1975. See also *Wagon Train Weekly* (newsletter) 1, no. 10 (June 21, 1976), RG 31, Secretary of Commerce, series 14: Wagon Train File, box 6, folder: "File, Planning, Supervision, Execution of Wagon Train Project," BWT.

63. Ward Welsh, "Newsletter" (internal Pennsylvania Bicentennial Commission), [n.d., ca. early 1976], RG 31, Secretary of Commerce, series 17: Wagon Train File, box 1, folder: "misc.," BWT; "Indians Bar Train Attack," *New York Times*, June 22, 1975; "Tribe Plans Ambush," *Chicago Defender*, June 12, 1975; "Indians Besiege '76 Wagon Train," *Chicago Tribune*, June 13, 1975; Hurst, "Indian Threat Reported on Caravan."

64. Steve Judd, quoted in Gary Taylor, "Wagon Train Readied Here for Trip East," *Houston Post*, December 26, 1975.

65. "Indians Want Hard Look at Nation in Bicentennial," *Scottsdale Progress*, February 5, 1975.

66. "American Indians Snub Bicentennial Celebration," *San Antonio Express*, March 9, 1975; "A Statue of Sitting Bull," *Pawtucket Times*, February 28, 1975; "Bicentennial: Another Meaning for Indians," *Newtown Bee*, May 30, 1975; "Indians May Shun Parade," *Kansas City Times*, September 30, 1975.

67. Robert Olmos, "Indians Divided on Bicentennial," *Portland Oregonian*, August 24, 1975.

68. For more on the American Indian Movement, see Warrior and Smith, *Like a Hurricane*.

69. "No Rough Stuff for Bicentennial," *Sioux Falls Argu-Leader*, April 24, 1975; "AIM Bicentennial Position Is Vicious," *Rochester Post-Bulletin*, May 6, 1975; Walt Murray, "Indians to Stage Protests During Bicentennial," *Long Beach Press-Telegram*, November 2, 1975; Len Lear, "Indian Leader Urges Blacks to 'Disrupt Bicentennial,'" *Philadelphia Tribune*, December 3, 1974.

70. Means and Wolf, *Where White Men Fear to Tread*, 174–78; Banks and Erdoes, *Ojibwa Warrior*, 111–13.

71. This incident is recounted slightly differently in the two memoirs. While the quote as cited is according to Banks's account, Means remembers it as "we're not going to eat this shit!" In his memoir, James Deetz, who was then assistant director at Plimoth Plantation, mentions the "day of mourning," but not the Thanksgiving incident. Banks and Erdoes, *Ojibwa Warrior*, 113; Means and Wolf, *Where White Men Fear to Tread*, 176; Deetz and Deetz, *The Times of Their Lives*, 22–23.

72. "Mourning Indians Dump Sand on Plymouth Rock," *New York Times*, November 27, 1970, 26.

73. Banks and Erdoes, *Ojibwa Warrior*, 113.

74. Tom Wicker, "Manhattan Tea Party," clipping provenance and date unknown [ca. May 1974], found in RG 452-A1-34, box 169, folder: "May," ARBA; Tom Tiede, "The Birthday Everyone Has Ignored," *Point Pleasant Register*, March 28, 1974; "Nation Ready to Celebrate the Fourth," *Lexington Herald*, July 4, 1974; Peter Anderson, "73 Minutemen Cried Wolf, People's Group Says," *Boston Globe*, January 13, 1974; "Boston Tea Party Reenactment Is Scheduled Here," *Baton Rouge State Times*, December 13, 1973.

75. "Taxpayers Group Plans Tea Party Reenactment," *San Diego Union*, December 14, 1973; "One Man Sacramento Tea Party," *San Jose Mercury News*, December 18, 1973; "2 Pueblo Groups List Gripes on Anniversary of Boston Tea Party," *Pueblo Star-Journal*, December 15, 1973; "Dump Food as Protest," *Davenport Times-Democrat*, December 16, 1973; Viola Osgood, "NOW Stages Hub March on Eve of Tea Party," *Boston Globe*, December 16, 1976.

Chapter Six

1. Dorothy McGhee, "20,000 Rebels Rise Up at Boston Oil Party—Dump King, Exxon," *Common Sense* 2, no. 1 (January 1974); "Tea Party Kicks Off the Bicentennial," *Jamaica Plain Citizen*, December 13, 1973.

2. Betty Mills, "Protests Add Flavor to Boston Tea Party," *Norfolk Virginia, Ledger-Star*, December 17, 1973; Robert Jones, "Plan for Plain Tea Party Goes Over the Rail," *Los Angeles Times*, December 16, 1973.

3. Dick Solito, "Crashers May Provide Additional Excitement at Boston Tea Party," *Concord Journal*, November 22, 1973; John Kifner, "1973's Boston Tea Party Brews a Protest: Anti-Nixon Movement Steals Stage," *Philadelphia Bulletin*, December 17, 1973; Don Oakley, "Blow for Liberty, or Rash Radicalism," *Union Pennsylvania Standard*, December 17, 1973.

4. Warren Talbot, "Boston Oil Party Hopes to Upstage Tea Party," *Boston Globe*, December 13, 1973; Bruce Bowman, "Revolution at the Boston Tea Party," *Ipswich Hamilton-Chronicle*, December 12, 1973; "Protestors Blast Nixon at Boston Oil Party," *Marion, Illinois Republican*, December 17, 1973; "Reenactment of Boston Tea Party Turns to Protest Against 'Tyrant Pres.,'" *Eldorado Journal*, December 17, 1973; "A Wild Tea Party," *Racine Journal Times*, December 17, 1973.

5. Tom Goff (AP), "Revolutionists Tar Nixon Effigy," *Beverly, Massachusetts Times*, December 17, 1973; Stephen Isaacs, "Boston Tea Party Restaged," *Washington Post*, December 17, 1973.

6. Howard, *The PBC*.

7. See Berger, *The Hidden 70s*.

8. See Reed, *The Art of Protest*; Gosse, *Rethinking the New Left*; Farber, *The Sixties*.

9. Elbaum, *Revolution in the Air*.

10. Rossen, "Revolutionary Nationalism and the American Left."

11. Ibid., 153.

12. The concept of "revolutionary nationalism" was subsequently taken up by several groups on the reconfiguring Left, most prominently the New American Movement, a Marxist initiative dedicated to both education and electoral politics. Victor Cohen, "The New American Movement and the Los Angeles Socialist Community School"; Oliver, "American Socialist Strategy in Transition."

13. Rifkin, "The Red, White, and Blue LEFT."

14. William Greider, "Group Plan to Show Radical Spirit of '76," *Washington Post*, October 15, 1971.

15. Rifkin, "Whose Bicentennial?," 12.

16. Ibid., 18.

17. In fact, one of the PBC's first acts was to apply to the ARBC for official recognition as a Bicentennial program under the "Heritage" rubric. See Martha Jane Shay to George Lang, ARBC, July 12, 1972; Martha Jane Shay to Deborah Lawrence, July 11, 1972, reprinted in *"The Attempt to Steal the Bicentennial": Report of the Subcommittee to Investigate the Administration of the Internal Security Act and Other Internal Security Laws of the Committee on the Judiciary*, U.S. Senate, 94th Cong., 2d sess. (May 1976), 101–2. Washington DC: U.S. Government Printing Office.

18. For a framework and other examples of resistance at the site of memory, see Lipsitz, *Time Passages*.

19. See Eugene L. Meyer, "Counter Bicentennial Group Seeks End of Exploitation," *Washington Post*, September 8, 1972; Eugene L. Meyer, "The Big Birthday Bungle," *Washington Post*, July 2, 1972; Eugene L. Meyer, "The Red, White, Blue—and

Green," *Washington Post*, August 15, 1972; Eugene L. Meyer, "GAO Is Mildly Critical of Bicentennial Group," *Washington Post*, December 22, 1972; Eugene Meyer, "Bicentennial Commission Hit in Report by House Unit Staff," *Washington Post*, December 30, 1972.

20. Phil Gailey, "Plans Are Traditional, Inventive," *The New Leader*, June, 24, 1974; William May, "Unofficial Panel Suggests Revolutionary Celebration," *Winston-Salem Journal and Sentinel*, July 28, 1974; "Old Time Americanism," *Miami News*, December 31, 1974; James Perry, "Bicentennial Planners on Collision Course," *Sharon, Pennsylvania Herald*, December 6, 1974; "Non-Organized Group Hopes to Form Bicentennial Units," *Decatur Herald*, February 11, 1975.

21. James J. Kilpatrick, "A Conservative View: Bicentennial Shaping Up as Glorious Fizzle of '76," *Washington Star Syndicate*, May 9, 1974.

22. Charlie Jones, People's Bicentennial Commission, *Common Sense: Special Supplement* [n.d., ca. 1973], box 48, folder: "PBC," Boston 200 Collection, Boston Public Library (hereafter cited as B200); People's Bicentennial Commission, *Voices of the American Revolution*.

23. People's Bicentennial Commission, *America's Birthday: A Planning and Activity Guide for Citizen Participation during the Bicentennial Years*, 10–11.

24. Ibid., 48, 120–39.

25. Charlie Jones, People's Bicentennial Commission, "Our Rights and Our Liberties," *Common Sense: Special Supplement* [n.d., ca. 1973], box 48, folder: "PBC," B200.

26. Rifkin, "The Red, White, and Blue LEFT," 122.

27. Sheila O'Brien, "Tories, Patriots Fighting," *Flint Journal*, March 31, 1974.

28. People's Bicentennial Commission, *Common Sense* 2, 3.

29. Rifkin, "Whose Bicentennial?," 9–20.

30. People's Bicentennial Commission, *America's Birthday*, 9.

31. People's Bicentennial Commission, "Is This What America's 200th Birthday Is All About?," [n.d., ca. Spring 1975], box 48, folder: "PBC," B200.

32. See for example, Sam Adams, "Guest Opinion," *Common Sense* 2, no. 2 (April 1974): 3; Samuel Thatcher, "Before Going On . . . A Revolutionary Oration, July 4, 1776–style," *Common Sense*, Special Supplement, [n.d., ca. 1973].

33. Letters from Dorothy Matkins, Harriet C. Machine, and John P. Goggin, "Committee of Correspondence," *Common Sense* 2, no. 1 (January 1974): 13.

34. William May, "Unofficial Panel Suggests Revolutionary Celebration," *Salem Journal & Sentinel*, July 28, 1974; Dan Daniel, "Bi-Centennial," *Stuart, Virginia Enterprise*, July 31, 1974; Milton Jaques, "Unofficial People's Group Adds Spark to Bicentennial," *Pittsburgh Post-Gazette*, January 22, 1975.

35. People's Bicentennial Commission, "Sons and Daughters of Liberty," posters and handbills, box 48, folder: "PBC," B200.

36. Tom Mathews and Jane Whitmore, "Up-to-the-Minutemen," *Newsweek*, May 19, 1975, 29; John Kifner, "Wary Citizens at Lexington and Concord Await," *New York Times*, April 17, 1975; Margot Hornblower, "Concord Faces an Invasion," *Washington Post*, April 17, 1975; Howard, *The PBC*, 50–53.

37. "45,000 Patriots Gather at PBC Rally for Economic Democracy," "The Second Midnight Ride to Concord," *Common Sense* 3, no. 2 (May 1975): 8–10; Joan Merrick

Naider, "New Concord Alert: Town Fears Bicentennial Heard 'Round the World,'" *Chicago Daily News*, March 22, 1975.

38. Ernest B. Furguson, "The Uglification of the Bicentennial," *Baltimore Sun*, April 22, 1975; Tom Matthews, "Up-to-the-Minutemen," *Newsweek*, May 19, 1975, 29; Bud Vestal, "Bicentennial People Warn of the Wrong Kind of Revolutionary Spirit," *Grand Rapids Press*, May 4, 1975.

39. Victor Riesel, "Radicals Make Bicentennial Bloody," *Milwaukee Sentinel*, April 25, 1975.

40. "From Manhattan to Mid-America: A 'Grass Roots' Bicentennial," *U.S. News & World Report*, August 19, 1974, 65–67.

41. "Growing Controversy over the Bicentennial: Two Views," *U.S. News & World Report*, March 18, 1975, 35–38.

42. By this time, the OPEC embargo had ended, Nixon had resigned, and the PBC had changed its message, moving from a reproach of the state to a condemnation of business. The Concord rally inaugurated PBC's new approach: a plan called "New Economic Democracy" that applied the ideals of the Declaration of Independence to economic, rather than political, principles. The rally coincided with a new book called *Common Sense* 2. Continuing to use the language of Revolutionary nationalism and encouraging affective connections to simulate understanding the inequalities of the past and the present, *Common Sense* 2 charged contemporary corporations with working against the freedom of the small entrepreneur, arguing that legislative changes must be made to the organization of capital and the ownership of the means of production. "New Patriots Unanimously Adopt Declaration of Economic Independence," *Common Sense* 3, no. 2 (May 1975); People's Bicentennial Commission, *Common Sense* 2, 2–9.

43. *"The Attempt to Steal the Bicentennial."*

44. Nicholas von Hoffman, "All the Corruption That's Fit to Tattle on the Boss," *Washington Post*, May 19, 1976; Henry Clay Gold, "Bicentennial Faction a 'Tool of New Left,'" *Kansas City Times*, May 6, 1976.

45. Stephen J. Lynton and Eugene L. Meyer, "Peaceful Protest Covers a Wide Range of Issues," *Washington Post*, July 5, 1976.

46. On archives, silencing, and memory, see Trouillot, *Silencing the Past*.

47. "Dellums Backs 'People's' Bicentennial of Fourth of July Coalition," *Black Panther*, June 5, 1976, 5. For an account of the Puerto Rican Independence Movement, another significant part of the Fourth of July Coalition, see Starr, "'Hit Them Harder'"

48. See Liberation News Service, "People's Bicentennial," Liberation News Service, July 10, 1976, www.lns-archive.org/packets/1976-07-10_LNS_packet_800.pdf, accessed December 12, 2011; Southern Africa Solidarity Coalition, "Demonstrate July 4th for Bicentennial Without Colonies—Freedom for All Oppressed Nations," Berkeley, 1976, in Social Protest Collection, Bancroft Library, University of California-Berkeley.

49. "July 4th Coalition Appeal to Black Communities," *Black Panther*, June 26, 1976.

50. Ericka Huggins speech, quoted in "7,000 Rally at S.F.'s People's Bicentennial," *Black Panther*, July 10, 1976, 1, 14–15.

51. Kelland, "Clio's Foot Soldiers," 106–21.

52. See, for example, Carmichael and Hamilton, *Black Power*. See also Theoharis and Woodard, *Groundwork*; McClymer, *Mississippi Freedom Summer*, 199–200.

53. Black Panther Party, "Ten Point Plan," http://www.blackpanther.org/TenPoint .htm, accessed February 12, 2011.

54. "This Week in Black History," *Black Panther*, July 27, 1974, March 1, 1975, July 22, 1971, August 10, 1974, August 3, 1974.

55. Smethurst, *The Black Arts Movement*; Sell, "The Black Arts Movement"; Elam, *The Past as Present*.

56. Baraka, *Slave Ship* (1967), in *The Motion of History and Other Plays*, 129–50.

57. Elam, *Taking It to the Streets*, vi.

58. Baraka, *Slave Ship*, 132. See also Colbert, *The African American Theatrical Body*.

59. Elam, *Taking It to the Streets*, 73–106.

60. Bentsen, "Vision and Form in *Slave Ship*."

61. Other critics have noted that Black Arts–inflected literature like that of Octavia Butler, Gayl Jones, and Toni Morrison likewise explored questions of memory, intersubjectivity, and affective identification. See Rushdy, *Remembering Generations*.

62. The long history and ongoing memory of racist blackface performance such as the minstrel show's depictions of antebellum life may have caused African Americans to avoid reenactments, which had already been used against them as a strategy of domination and oppression. For histories of minstrelsy, see Toll, *Blacking Up*; Lott, *Love and Theft*; Smulyan, *"Popular Ideologies*, 16–40. On later reenactments of enslavement, see Woolfork, *Embodying American Slavery in Contemporary Culture*.

63. See, for example, U.S. News Staff, "From the Archives: A Bicentennial Guide to Black History," *U.S. News & World Report*, February 24, 1976.

64. See Ruffins, "Mythos, Memory, and History"; Stewart and Ruffins, "A Faithful Witness"; Horton and Crew, "Afro-American Museums," in *History Museums in the United States*, 215–36; Romano and Raiford, "Introduction: The Struggle Over Memory," in *The Civil Rights Movement in American Memory*; Dagbovie, *African American History Reconsidered*.

65. See Burns, *From Storefront to Monument*; Aldrige and Young, *Out of the Revolution*; Rojas, *From Black Power to Black Studies*; Marable, *Living Black History*.

66. For a survey of Bicentennial activities by state, see ARBA, *The Bicentennial of the United States of America*, vol. 2. See also Leon Pitt, "TV Bicentennial Minutes Hit for Ignoring Blacks," *Chicago Sun-Times*, November 10, 1975; Len Lear, "Millions for Flowers, Nothing for Blacks, BEDC Leaders Say of Bicentennial Planning," *Philadelphia Tribune*, April 27, 1974; Acel Moore, "Black Bicentennial Role Is Termed Inadequate," *Philadelphia Inquirer*, October 25, 1974; "Bicentennial Role Blasted," *Washington Afro-American*, November 2, 1974.

67. "The Bicentennial Blues," photo editorial, *Ebony*, June 1976, 152–53.

68. Earl Byrd, "Bicentennial: Blacks' Views Dim," *Washington Star*, December 21, 1975.

69. John Teets, "PhotOpinion: Is the Bicentennial Ignoring Black People? Asked Near the Wrigley Building," *Chicago Sun Times* [n.d., ca. January 1976].

70. For other examples of this critique, see Wes Albers, "Blacks View Differently Meaning of Bicentennial," *Lincoln Star*, February 11, 1976; Bea L. Hines, "Should Blacks Celebrate the Bicentennial?," *Miami Herald*, February 1, 1976; Al Johnson, "Yes I'm Angry, Says Black Congressman," *Richmond News Leader*, March 13, 1976; "Blacks' Role," *Bridgeport Telegram*, March 5, 1976; Carol Dumas, "Black People and the Bicentennial," *Cleveland Post*, April 3, 1976; David Chartrand, "Minority Groups Conspicuous in Bicentennial Absence," *Lawrence, Kansas Journal World*, March 29, 1976; Thomas A. Johnson, "Few Blacks Inspired by Bicentennial," *Wall Street Journal*, July 8, 1976; Margot Hornblower, "Bicentennial: A Black Perspective," *Washington Post*, March 27, 1975.

71. William Braden, "Bicentennial Boycotting for the Du Sable Museum," *Chicago Sun-Times*, November 30, 1975.

72. "Widow of Dr. W. E. B. Du Bois Cites Stake in Bicentennial," *Chicago Daily Defender*, November 10, 1975.

73. For more on "grassroots" participation, see Gordon, *The Spirit of 1976*; Bodnar, *Remaking America*, 206–44; Capozzola, "It Makes You Want to Believe in the Country"; Lowenthal, "The Bicentennial Landscape."

74. Jeanne Saddler, "Citizens Support Exhibition Plans," *Baltimore Sun*, August 12, 1974.

75. Bert Wade, "She Puts Black History Up Front for Bicentennial," *Providence Journal*, December 9, 1975.

76. See also June Brown Garner, "The Blacks' Role in the Revolution," *Detroit News*, September 27, 1974; Chuck Stone, "Color US History Honest," *Philadelphia News*, October 22, 1974; Betty James interview with Betty Shabazz, "Malcolm X's Widow Tells of Pilgrimage," *Washington Star*, March 10, 1975; Bayard Rustin, "View on the News: Why Should Blacks Observe Bicentennial? An Open Letter to My Godson Michael," *New York Voice*, February 13, 1976; Bob Ahronheim, " 'Accentuate Heritage' Historian Tells Blacks," *Jacksonville Journal*, February 10, 1976; Vernon Jordan, "The Year Ahead," *Sacramento Observer*, January 8, 1976.

77. Fundraising Feasibility study for Black American Museum & Cultural Center, Plubell Company, Buffalo, NY, 1973; Application for National Bicentennial Program, November 7, 1973, Frank Mesiah, Project Director, to William Butler, October 4, 1974, RG 452-A1-75, Programs, States and Communities Division: Program Files of the Ethnic-Racial Program Office, 1975–76, box 267, folder: Black American Museum & Cultural Center, Niagara Falls, NY, ARBA.

78. Phillip Jeter, "Museum, Cultural Center Slated for '76 Opening in Niagara Falls," *Afro-American*, August 18, 1973, 6.

79. Seth M. Scheiner to Martin Goldman, program officer, ARBC, December 1, 1973; Martin Goldman to Frank Mesiah, January 3, 1974, RG 452-A1-75, Programs, States and Communities Division: Program Files of the Ethnic-Racial Program Office, 1975–76, box 267, folder: Black American Museum & Cultural Center, Niagara Falls, NY, ARBA.

80. Fundraising Feasibility study for Black American Museum & Cultural Center, Plubell Company, Buffalo, NY, 1973; Application for National Bicentennial Program, November 7, 1973, RG 452-A1-75, Programs, States and Communities Division:

Program Files of the Ethnic-Racial Program Office, 1975–76, box 267, folder: Black American Museum & Cultural Center, Niagara Falls, NY, ARBA.

81. Robert DeForrest, quoted in Eugene Meyer, "The Big Birthday Bungle," *Washington Post*, July 2, 1972. See also Statement of Robert DeForrest in "Hearings Before Subcommittee No. 2 of the Committee of the Judiciary House of Representatives, Ninety-Third Congress, First Session on H.R. 3695 and H.R. 3976 to Establish the American Revolution Bicentennial Administration, March 14 and 15, 1973" (Washington, DC: U.S. Government Printing Office, 1973), 291–307.

82. See Martin S. Goldman to Lynn Carroll, ARBC, Memo re: meeting with Vincent DeForest, September 6, 1973, RG 452 A1-70, Programs, States and Communities Division: Subject Files of the Ethnic-Racial Program Office, 1975–76, box 272, folder: "Afro-American Bicentennial Corporation," ARBA.

83. Burns, *From Storefront to Monument*, 41–71, 106–28.

Conclusion

1. "Kid Politics," *This American Life*, episode 424, originally aired January 14, 2011. Podcast and transcript available at www.thisamericanlife.org/radio-archives/episode /424/kid-politics. See also Web site of Air Force One Discovery Center, Reagan Library and Museum, www.reaganfoundation.org/education-class-visit-overview .aspx, accessed April 1, 2012.

2. Fawcett, "Presidential Libraries."

3. Web site of John F. Kennedy Presidential Library and Museum, http://www .jfklibrary.org/, accessed April 2, 2012.

4. "The New Presidential Library Showcases Legacy of Abraham Lincoln," *PBS Newshour*, aired April 15, 2005, transcript available at www.pbs.org/newshour/bb /media/jan-june05/lincoln_4-15.html.

5. For a theorization of reenactment in the context of media convergence and cross-platform interactions, see King, *Networked Reenactments*.

6. See Wark, *Gamer Theory*; Dyer-Witheford, *Games of Empire*; Raley, *Tactical Media*, 65–108; Penny Von Eschen, "Rebooting the Cold War from Films to Video Games," presentation at Annual Meeting of the American Studies Association, Baltimore, MD, 2011.

7. The National Archives Experience, www.digitalvaults.org, accessed March 28, 2012.

8. Archival Research Catalog, National Archives and Records Administration, arcweb.archives.gov/arc/action/BasicSearchForm?jScript=true, accessed March 28, 2012.

9. 911digitalarchive.org/. On digital archives, see Diana Taylor, "Save As . . . Knowledge and Transmission in the Age of Digital Technologies," Keynote Address, Imagining America Conference, 2010. PDF available at imaginingamerica.org/wp-content /uploads/2011/05/Foreseeable-Futures-10-Taylor.pdf, accessed April 4, 2012; Hansen, *Bodies in Code*; Uricchio, "The Future of a Medium Once Known as Television."

10. Magelssen, *Simming*; Woolfork, *Embodying American Slavery in Contemporary Culture*; Bartov, "Chambers of Horror"; Bentley Boyd, "Colonial Williamsburg Auctions

Slaves: Re-enactment Provokes Emotional Debates," *Newport News Daily Press*, October 11, 1994.

11. Rymsza-Pawlowska, "Frontier House."

12. For a more detailed reading of this exhibit, see Lonetree, *Decolonizing Museums*; Atalay, "No Sense of the Struggle."

13. Post, *Who Owns America's Past?*, 113–14, 273–84.

14. National Museum of American History, *Broad Stripes and Bright Stars*, short documentary, January 2011, www.youtube.com/watch?v=S-qcpROHI3Y.

15. Stanton, *The Lowell Experiment*; Filene, "Passionate Histories."

16. Agnew and Lamb, "What Is Reenactment? An Introduction"; Agnew, "History's Affective Turn"; Cook, "The Use and Abuse of Historical Reenactment."

17. Lepore, *The Whites of Their Eyes*, 68.

18. Ibid. See also Gordon S. Wood, "No Thanks for the Memories," *New York Review of Books*, January 13, 2011.

19. "Kid Politics," *This American Life*.

Bibliography

Archives and Collections

American Revolution Bicentennial Collection, Records of the American Revolution Bicentennial Administration, National Archives and Records Administration II, College Park, MD.

Black Panther Collection, Hoover Institution Library and Archives, Stanford University, Palo Alto, CA.

Boston 200 Collection, Boston Public Library, Boston, MA (now at City of Boston Archives).

Franklin Court Collection, Library and Archives of Independence National Historical Park, Philadelphia, PA.

Hall-Hoag Collection of Extremist Propaganda, Brown University, Providence, RI.

Jesse Lemisch Bicentennial Schlock Collection, Sterling Memorial Library, Department of Manuscripts and Archives, Yale University, New Haven, CT.

National Trust for Historic Preservation Collection, University of Maryland, College Park.

Fulton Oursler Jr. Papers, Special Collections Research Center, Georgetown University, Washington, DC.

Pennsylvania Bicentennial Collection, State Archives of Pennsylvania, Harrisburg.

Providence Preservation Society Collection, Rhode Island Historical Society Library, Providence.

Rhode Island Bicentennial Collection, Rhode Island Historical Society Library, Providence.

Smithsonian Institution Archives, Washington, DC.

Social Protest Collection, Bancroft Library, University of California-Berkeley, Berkeley.

Television Archive, the Paley Center for Media, New York, NY.

David J. Wolper Collection, University of Southern California, Los Angeles.

Newspapers and Popular Periodicals

The Afro-American
Albany Times-Union
American Heritage
Antiques Magazine
Arizona Republic
Baltimore Sun
Baton Rouge State Times

Beverly Times (MA)
Bicentennial Times
Birmingham News
Black Panther
The Black Scholar
Boston Globe
Bridgeport Telegram

Caldwell News Tribune (ID)
Cedar Valley Times
Chicago Daily Defender
Chicago Daily News
Chicago Style
Chicago Sun-Times
Chicago Tribune
Christian Science Monitor
Cincinnati Post
Cleveland Post
Columbia City Commercial Mail
Concord Journal
Davenport Times-Democrat
Decatur Herald
Denham Springs News
Dennison Herald
Detroit News
East Boston Community News
Eldorado Journal
Fayetteville Observer
Flint Journal
Frontier and Holt County Independent
Grand Rapids Press
Hartford Times
History News
Honeywell World
Honolulu Star-Bulletin
Houston Post
Ipswich Hamilton-Chronicle
Jackson Tennessee Sun
Jacksonville Journal
Jamaica Plain Citizen
Kansas City Times
Kennebec Journal
Lawrence Journal-World (KS)
Ledger-Star (Norfolk, VA)
Lewiston Journal
Lexington Herald
Liberation News Service
Life
Lincoln Star
Literary Tabloid
Long Beach Press-Telegram
Los Angeles Times
Marion Republican (IL)

Massachusetts Spy and Village Courier
Miami Herald
Miami News
Milwaukee Sentinel
Ms.
Museum News
The Nation
Newark Star-Ledger
New Leader
New Orleans Times-Picayune
Newport News Daily Press
The New Republic
Newsweek
Newtown Bee
New York Amsterdam News
New York Daily News
New York Times
New York Voice
Omaha World-Herald
Pawtucket Times
People
Philadelphia Bulletin
Philadelphia Inquirer
Philadelphia News
Philadelphia Tribune
Pittsburgh Post-Gazette
Point Pleasant Register
Portland Oregonian
Portland Oregon Journal
Preservation News
The Progressive
Providence Journal
Pueblo Star-Journal (CO)
Racine Journal Times
Reader's Digest
Richmond News Leader
Rochester Post-Bulletin
Sacramento Observer
Salem Journal & Sentinel
Salt Lake Tribune
San Antonio Express
San Diego Union
San Jose Mercury News
Saturday Review
Scottsdale Progress

Seattle Post-Intelligencer
Sharon Herald (PA)
Sioux Falls Argus Leader
Skagit Valley Herald
Smithsonian Torch
Stuart Enterprise (VA)
Tennessee Star
Time
Tucson Daily Star
Tulsa Tribune

Union Pennsylvania Standard
U.S. News & World Report
Virginia Bulletin-Democrat
Wall Street Journal
Washington Afro-American
Washington Post
Washington Star-News
Winston-Salem Journal and Sentinel
Worcester Evening Gazette

Published Sources

Abing, Laura. "Old Sturbridge Village: An Institutional History of a Cultural Artifact." Ph.D. diss., Marquette University, 1997.

Agnew, Vanessa. "History's Affective Turn: Historical Reenactment and Its Work in the Present." *Rethinking History* 11 (2007): 299–312.

Agnew, Vanessa, and Jonathan Lamb. "Introduction: What Is Re-enactment?" *Criticism* 46, no. 3 (Summer 2004): 327–39.

Alderson, William T., and Shirley Payne Low. *Interpretation of Historical Sites*. Nashville, TN: American Association for State and Local History, 1976.

Aldrige, Delores P., and Carlene Young, eds. *Out of the Revolution: The Development of Africana Studies*. New York: Lexington Books, 2003.

Allen, Steve. *Meeting of Minds*. New York: Crown Publishers, 1978.

Ambrose, Stephen. *Nixon: Ruin and Recovery, 1973–1990*. New York: Simon & Schuster, 1991.

American Association of State and Local History. *101 Ideas From History News*. Nashville, TN: American Association of State and Local History, 1975.

American Revolution Bicentennial Administration (ARBA). *The Bicentennial of the United States of America: A Final Report to the People*. 5 vols. Washington, DC: U.S. Government Printing Office, 1977.

Ames, Kenneth, Barbara Franco, and L. Thomas Frye, eds. *Ideas and Images: Developing Interpretive History Exhibits*. Nashville, TN: American Association of State and Local History, 1992.

Anderson, Benedict. *Imagined Communities*. London: Verso, 1991.

Anderson, Jay, ed. *A Living History Reader*. Nashville: American Association of State and Local History, 1991.

———. *Time Machines: The World of Living History*. Nashville, TN: American Association for State and Local History, 1984.

Anderson, Martin. *The Federal Bulldozer: A Critical Analysis of Urban Renewal: 1949–1962*. Cambridge, MA: MIT Press, 1964.

Anderson, Steve. "Loafing in the Garden of Knowledge: History TV and Popular Memory." *Film & History* 30, no. 1 (March 2000): 14–23.

Ang, Ien. *Watching Dallas: Soap Opera and the Melodramatic Imagination*. London: Methuen, 1985.

Ashton, Paul, and Hilda Kean, eds. *People and Their Pasts: Public History Today*. London: Palgrave Macmillan, 2009.

Atalay, Sonya. "No Sense of the Struggle: Creating a Context for Survivance at the NMAI." *American Indian Quarterly* 30, no. 3 (Summer/Fall 2006): 597–618.

Baldwin, James, and Margaret Mead. *A Rap on Race*. Philadelphia: J.B. Lippincott and Company, 1971.

Banks, Dennis, and Richard Erdoes. *Ojibwa Warrior: Dennis Banks and the Rise of the American Indian Movement*. Norman: University of Oklahoma Press, 2011.

Baraka, Amiri. *The Motion of History and Other Plays*. New York: William Morrow and Company, 1978.

Barnouw, Erik. *Tube of Plenty: The Evolution of American Television*. New York: Oxford University Press, 1990.

Barta, Tony, ed. *Screening the Past: Film and the Representation of History*. Westport, CT: Praeger, 1998.

Barthel, Diane. *Historic Preservation: Collective Memory and Historical Identity*. New Brunswick, NJ: Rutgers University Press, 1996.

Barton, Craig Evan, ed. *Sites of Memory: Perspectives on Architecture and Race*. Princeton, NJ: Princeton Architectural Press, 2001.

Bartov, Omer. "Chambers of Horror: Holocaust Museums in Israel and the United States." *Israel Studies* 2, no. 2 (1997): 66–87.

Baudrillard, Jean. *Selected Writings*. Edited by Mark Poster. Palo Alto, CA: Stanford University Press, 1988.

———. *Simulacra and Simulation*. Ann Arbor: University of Michigan Press, 1990.

Belasco, Warren James. *Americans on the Road: From Autocamp to Motel, 1910–1945*. Cambridge, MA: MIT Press, 1979.

Belk, Russell W. *Collecting in a Consumer Society*. Routledge: London, 1995.

Bellah, Robert. *Beyond Belief: Essays on Religion in a Post-Traditional World*. New York: HarperCollins, 1970.

Benjamin, Walter. "Theses on the Concept of History." In *Illuminations*, edited by Hannah Arendt, translated by Harry Zohn, 255–64. New York: Shocken Books, 1968.

Bennett, Tony. *The Birth of the Museum: History, Theory, Politics*. London: Routledge Press, 1995.

Benson, Susan Porter, Steven Brier, and Roy Rosenzweig. *Presenting the Past: Critical Perspectives on History and the Public*. Philadelphia: Temple University Press, 1986.

Bentsen, Kimbery W. "Vision and Form in *Slave Ship*." In *Imamu Amiri Baraka (Leroi Jones): A Collection of Critical Essays*, edited by Kimberly W. Bentsen, 174–85. Englewood Cliffs, NJ: Prentice Hall, 1978.

Berger, Dan, ed. *The Hidden 70s: Histories of Radicalism*. New Brunswick, NJ: Rutgers University Press, 2010.

Berkowitz, Edward D. *Something Happened: A Political and Cultural Overview of the Seventies*. New York: Columbia University Press, 2006.

Berlant, Lauren. *The Female Complaint: On the Unfinished Business of Sentimentality in American Culture*. Durham, NC: Duke University Press, 2008.

Berman, Marshall. *All That Is Solid Melts Into Air: The Experience of Modernity*. London: Verso, 1983.

Bernstein, Robin. "Dances with Things: Material Culture and the Performance of Race." *Social Text* 27 (2009): 67–94.

Binkley, Sam. *Getting Loose: Lifestyle Consumption in the 1970s*. Durham, NC: Duke University Press, 2007.

Boddy, William. *Fifties Television: The Industry and Its Critics*. Urbana: University of Illinois Press, 1990.

Bodnar, John. *Remaking America: Public Memory, Commemoration, and Patriotism in the Twentieth Century*. Princeton, NJ: Princeton University Press, 1992.

Bodroghkozy, Aniko. "Is This What You Mean by Color TV? Race, Gender, and Contested Meanings in NBC's *Julia*." In *Private Screenings: Television and the Female Consumer*, edited by Lynn Spigel and Denise Mann, 143–68. Minneapolis: University of Minnesota Press, 1992.

Boissoneault, Lorraine. "Always Further: Following in the Footsteps of La Salle." Senior Thesis, Miami University Honors Program, Miami University of Ohio, 2012.

Borstelmann, Thomas. *The 1970s: A New Global History from Civil Rights to Economic Inequality*. Princeton, NJ: Princeton University Press, 2012.

Brooks, Tim, and Earle Marsh. *The Complete Directory to Prime Time Network and Cable TV Shows, 1946–Present*. New York: Ballantine Books, 2007.

Burke, Peter. *What Is Cultural History?* Cambridge: Polity Press, 2004.

Burns, Andrea A. *From Storefront to Museum: Tracing the Public History of the Black Museum Movement*. Amherst: University of Massachusetts Press, 2013.

Capozzola, Christopher. "It Makes You Want to Believe in the Country: Celebrating the Bicentennial in an Age of Limits." In *America in the Seventies*, edited by Beth Bailey and David Farber, 29–49. Lawrence: University of Kansas Press, 2004.

Carmichael, Stokely, and Charles V. Hamilton. *Black Power: The Politics of Liberation*. New York: Vintage Books, 1967.

Carroll, Peter. *It Seemed Like Nothing Happened: America in the 1970s*. New Brunswick, NJ: Rutgers University Press, 1990.

Carson, Cary. "Living Museums of Everyman's History." *Harvard Magazine* 83 (July–August 1981).

Chapman, Mary Megan. "Living Pictures: Women and Tableaux Vivant in Nineteenth-Century American Fiction and Culture." Ph.D. diss, Cornell University, 1992.

Charlton, Thomas L., Lois E. Myers, and Rebecca Sharpless, eds. *Handbook of Oral History*. Lanham, MD: Alta Mira Press, 2006.

Christiansen, Erik. *Channeling the Past: Politicizing History in Postwar America*. Madison: University of Wisconsin Press, 2013.

Clark, Elizabeth C. *History, Theory, Text: Historians and the Linguistic Turn*. Cambridge, MA: Harvard University Press, 2004.

Cohen, Lizabeth. *A Consumer's Republic: The Politics of Mass Consumption in Postwar America*. New York: Knopf, 2003.

Cohen, Victor. "The New American Movement and the Los Angeles Socialist Community School." *Minnesota Review* 69 (Fall/Winter 2007): 139–151.

Colbert, Soyica Diggs. *The African American Theatrical Body: Reception, Performance, and the Stage*. Cambridge: Cambridge University Press, 2011.

Colby, Jean Poindexter. *Plimoth Plantation Then and Now*. New York: Hastings House, 1972.

Colonial Williamsburg Incorporated. *An Official Guidebook*. Williamsburg, VA: Colonial Williamsburg Inc., 1957.

Conn, Steven. *Do Museums Still Need Objects?* Philadelphia: University of Pennsylvania Press, 2010.

———. *Museums and American Intellectual Life, 1876–1926*. Chicago: University of Chicago Press, 2000.

Cook, Alexander. "The Use and Abuse of Historical Reenactment: Thoughts on Recent Trends in Public History." *Criticism* 46, no. 3 (2004): 487–96.

Cook, Robert J. *Troubled Commemoration: The American Civil War Centennial, 1961–1965*. Baton Rouge: Louisiana State University Press, 1997.

Corn, Joseph J. "Tools, Technologies, and Contexts: Interpreting the History of American Technics." In *History Museums in the United States: A Critical Assessment*, edited by Warren Leon and Roy Rosenzweig, 237–61. Urbana: University of Illinois Press, 1989.

Cotter, John L. *Above Ground Archaeology*. Washington, DC: U.S. Government Printing Office, 1975.

Cowie, Jefferson R. *Stayin' Alive: The 1970s and the Last Days of the Working Class*. New York: New Press, 2012.

Creeber, Glen. *Serial Television: Big Drama on the Small Screen*. London: British Film Institute, 2004.

Cruse, Harold. *Rebellion or Revolution?* New York: William Morrow & Company, 1968.

Cullen, Jim. *The Civil War in Popular Culture (A Reusable Past)*. Washington, DC: Smithsonian Institution Press, 1995.

Cuno, James. *Museums Matter: In Praise of the Encyclopedic Museum*. Chicago: University of Chicago Press, 2007.

Curtin, Michael. *Redeeming the Wasteland: Television Documentary and Cold War Politics*. New Brunswick, NJ: Rutgers University, 1995.

Dagbovie, Pero Gaglo. *African American History Reconsidered*. Urbana: University of Illinois Press, 2010.

Dayan, Daniel, and Elihu Katz. *Media Events: The Live Broadcasting of History*. Cambridge, MA: Harvard University Press, 1992.

Dean, David, Yana Meerzon, and Kathryn Prince, eds. *History, Memory, Performance*. London: Palgrave Macmillan, 2015.

Deetz, James. "The Changing Historic House Museum: Can It Live?" *Historic Preservation* 23, no. 1 (1971): 50–54.

———. *In Small Things Forgotten: An Archaeology of Early American Life*. New York: Anchor Books, 1977.

Deetz, James, and Patricia Scott Deetz. *The Times of Their Lives: Life, Love and Death in Plymouth Colony*. New York: W. H. Freeman and Company, 2000.

DeGroot, Jerome. *Remaking History*. London: Routledge, 2015.

Delmont, Matthew F. *Making Roots: A Nation Captivated*. Berkeley: University of California Press, 2016.

Dinshaw, Carolyn. *Getting Medieval: Sexual Communities Pre- and Postmodern*. Durham, NC: Duke University Press, 1999.

Doane, Mary Ann. "Information, Crisis, Catastrophe." In *Logics of Television: Essays in Cultural Criticism*, edited by Patricia Mellencamp, 222–39. Bloomington: Indiana University Press, 1990.

Doctorow, E. L. *Ragtime*. New York: Random House, 1975.

Donovan, Jane, ed., *Many Witnesses: A History of Dumbarton United Methodist Church 1772–1990*. Washington, DC: Dumbarton United Methodist Church, 1998.

d'Oro, Giusseppa. "Reenactment and Radical Interpretation." *History and Theory* 43 (May 2004): 198–208.

Doss, Erika. *Memorial Mania: Public Feeling in America*. Chicago: University of Chicago Press, 2010.

Dudziak, Mary. *Cold War Civil Rights: Race and the Image of American Democracy*. Princeton, NJ: Princeton University Press, 2000.

Dyer-Witheford, Nick. *Games of Empire: Global Capitalism and Video Games*. Minneapolis: University of Minnesota Press, 2009.

Edgerton, Gary. "Television as Historian: A Different Kind of History Altogether." In *Television Histories: Shaping Collective Memories*, edited by Gary Edgerton and Peter C. Rollins, 1–18. Lexington: University Press of Kentucky, 2001.

Ehrlich, Paul. *The Population Bomb*. New York: Ballantine Books, 1968.

Elam, Harry J., Jr. *The Past as Present in the Drama of August Wilson*. Ann Arbor: University of Michigan Press, 2006.

———. *Taking It to the Streets: The Social Protest Theatre of Luis Valdez and Amiri Baraka*. Ann Arbor: University of Michigan Press, 1997.

Elam, Harry J., Jr., and David Krasner, eds. *African American Performance and Theater History: A Critical Reader*. Oxford: Oxford University Press, 2001.

Elbaum, Max. *Revolution in the Air: Sixties Radicals Turn to Lenin, Mao, and Che*. London: Verso, 2002.

Evans, Sara M. "Beyond Declension: Feminist Radicalism in the 1970s and 1980s." In *The World the Sixties Made: Politics and Culture in Recent America*, edited by Van Gosse and Richard Moser, 52–66. Philadelphia: Temple University Press, 2003.

Evans, Sara M., and Harry C. Boyte. *Free Spaces: The Sources of Democratic Change in America*. New York: Harper & Row, 1986.

Farber, David. *The Age of Great Dreams: America in the 1960s*. New York: Hill & Wang, 1994.

———. "The Silent Majority." In *The Sixties: From Memory to History*, edited by David Farber, 291–316. Chapel Hill: University of North Carolina Press, 1994.

———, ed. *The Sixties: From Memory to History*. Chapel Hill: University of North Carolina Press, 1994.

Faust, Drew Gilpin. *This Republic of Suffering: Death and the American Civil War*. New York: Alfred A. Knopf, 2008.

Fawcett, Sharon K. "Presidential Libraries: A View from the Center." *Public Historian* 28, no. 3 (Summer 2006): 13–36.

Feldman, Anita Clair. *Little House, Long Shadow: Laura Ingalls Wilder's Impact on American Culture*. Columbia: University of Missouri Press, 2008.

Felski, Rita. *Doing Time: Feminist Theory and Postmodern Culture*. London: Routledge, 2000.

Feuer, Jane. "The Concept of Live Television: Ontology as Ideology." In *Regarding Television*, edited by E. Ann Kaplan, 12–21. Frederick, MD: American Film Institute, 1983.

Feuer, Jane, Paul Kerr, and Tise Vahimagi, eds. *MTM: "Quality Television."* London: British Film Institute, 1984.

Filene, Benjamin. "Passionate Histories: 'Outsider' History-Makers and What They Teach Us." *Public Historian* 34, no. 1 (Winter 2012): 11–33.

Finley, David E. *History of the National Trust for Historic Preservation, 1947–1963*. Washington, DC: National Trust for Historic Preservation, 1965.

Fishbein, Leslie. "*Roots*: Docudrama and the Interpretation of History." In *Why Docudrama: Fact/Fiction on Film and TV*, edited by Alan Rosenthal, 271–95. Carbondale: Southern Illinois University Press, 1999.

Fisher, Jennifer. "Interperformance: The Live Tableaux of Suzanne Lacy, Janine Antoni, and Marina Abramovic." *Art Journal* 56, no. 4 (Winter 1997): 28–33.

Fitch, James Marson. *Historic Preservation: Curatorial Management of the Built World*. Charlottesville: University of Virginia Press, 1990.

Fitzpatrick, Ellen. *History's Memory: Writing America's Past; 1880–1980*. Cambridge, MA: Harvard University Press, 2002.

Fogerty, James E. "Oral History and Archives: Documentary Context." In *Handbook of Oral History*, edited by Thomas L. Charlton, Lois E. Myers, and Rebecca Sharpless, 197–226. Lanham, MD: Alta Mira Press, 2006.

Foner, Eric, ed. *The New American History*. Philadelphia: Temple University Press, 1990.

Foucault, Michel. *The Archaeology of Knowledge*. New York: Pantheon Books, 1972.

Frank, Thomas. *The Conquest of Cool: Business Culture, Counterculture, and the Rise of Hip Consumerism*. Chicago: University of Chicago Press, 1997.

Freeman, Elizabeth. *Time Binds: Queer Temporalities, Queer Histories*. Durham, NC: Duke University Press, 2010.

Fried, Richard M. *The Russians Are Coming! The Russians Are Coming: Pageantry and Patriotism in Cold-War America*. New York: Oxford University Press, 1998.

Friedan, Betty. *The Feminine Mystique*. New York: Dell, 1963.

Friedman, Jeff. "Muscle Memory: Performing Embodied Knowledge." In *Art and the Performance of Memory: Sounds and Gestures of Recollections*, edited by Richard Candida Smith, 156–80. London: Routledge, 2011.

Gabler, Neal. *Walt Disney*. New York: Vintage, 2006.

Genovese, Eugene D. *Roll, Jordan, Roll: The World the Slaves Made*. New York: Vintage Books, 1973.

Gillis, John R., ed. *Commemorations: The Politics of National Identity*. Princeton, NJ: Princeton University Press, 1994.

Glass, James A. *The Beginnings of a New National Historic Preservation Program, 1957 to 1969*. Nashville, TN: American Association for State and Local History, 1990.

Glassberg, David. *American Historical Pageantry: The Uses of Tradition in the Early Twentieth Century*. Chapel Hill: University of North Carolina Press, 1990.

———. *Sense of History: The Place of the Past in American Life*. Amherst: University of Massachusetts Press, 2001.

Glassie, Henry. "Meaningful Things and Appropriate Myths: The Artifact's Place in American Studies." *Prospects* 3 (1977): 1–49.

Gonzales, Jennifer A. *Subject to Display: Reframing Race in Contemporary Installation Art*. Cambridge: Massachusetts Institute of Technology Press, 2008.

Gordon, Tammy. *The Spirit of 1976: Commerce, Community, and the Politics of Commemoration*. Amherst: University of Massachusetts Press, 2013.

Gosse, Van. *Rethinking the New Left: An Interpretative History*. New York: Palgrave Macmillan, 2005.

Gosse, Van, and Richard Moser, eds. *The World the Sixties Made: Politics and Culture in Recent America*. Philadelphia: Temple University Press, 2003.

Gould, Deborah. *Moving Politics: Emotion and ACT UP's Fight against AIDS*. Chicago: University of Chicago Press, 2009.

Gray, Herman. *Watching Race: Television and the Struggle for "Blackness."* Minneapolis: University of Minnesota Press, 1995.

Green, Pamela. "The Weeksville Heritage Center." In *Case Studies in Cultural Entrepreneurship*, edited by Gretchen Sullivan Sorin and Lynne A. Sessions, 11–22. New York: Rowman & Littlefield, 2015.

Greenberg, Miriam. *Branding New York: How a City in Crisis Was Sold to the World*. New York: Routledge, 2008.

Greenblatt, Stephen. "Resonance and Wonder." In *Exhibiting Cultures: The Poetics and Politics of Museum Display*, edited by Ivan Karp and Steven D. Lavine, 42–56. Washington, DC: Smithsonian Institution Press, 1990.

Greenfield, Briann. "Marketing the Past: Historic Preservation in Providence, Rhode Island." In *Giving Preservation a History: Histories of Historic Preservation in the United States*, edited by Max Page and Randall Mason, 163–84. New York: Routledge, 2004.

———. *Out of the Attic: Inventing Antiques in Twentieth-Century New England*. Amherst: University of Massachusetts Press, 2009.

Greenspan, Anders. *Creating Colonial Williamsburg: The Restoration of Virginia's Eighteenth-Century Capital*. Chapel Hill: University of North Carolina Press, 2002.

Greif, Lucien R. "Cleaning Up the Treasures of History." *Curator* 13, no. 4 (December 1970): 290–99.

Greiff, Constance M. *Independence: The Creation of a National Park*. Philadelphia: University of Pennsylvania Press, 1987.

Gurian, Elaine Heumann. *Civilizing the Museum*. London: Routledge, 2006.

Gutman, Herbert. *The Black Family in Slavery and Freedom*. New York: Vintage Books, 1977.

Habermas, Jurgen. *The Structural Transformation of the Public Sphere: An Inquiry into a Category of Bourgeois Society*. Cambridge, MA: MIT Press, 1989.

Haley, Alex. *Roots: The Saga of an American Family*. New York: Doubleday, 1976.

Handler, Richard, and Eric Gable. *The New History in an Old Museum: Creating the Past at Colonial Williamsburg*. Durham, NC: Duke University Press, 1997.

Hansen, Mark B. N. *Bodies in Code: Interfaces with Digital Media*. New York: Routledge, 2006.

Harris, Neil. *Capital Culture: J. Carter Brown, the National Gallery of Art, and the Reinvention of the Museum Experience*. Chicago: University of Chicago Press, 2013.

Hartje, Robert G. *Bicentennial U.S.A.: Pathways to Celebration*. Nashville, TN: American Association for State and Local History, 1973.

Harvey, David. *The Condition of Postmodernity: An Enquiry into the Origins of Cultural Change*. Malden, MA: Wiley-Blackwell Press, 1991.

Hass, Kristin Ann. *Carried to the Wall: American Memory and the Vietnam Veterans Memorial*. Berkeley: University of California Press, 1998.

Hawes, Edward. "The Living Historical Farm in North America: New Directions in Research and Interpretation." *ALHFAM Annual* (1976): 33–39.

Hedgepeth, William. *The Alternative: Communal Life in New America*. New York: Macmillan, 1970.

Herbst, John A. "Historic Houses." In *History Museums in the United States: A Critical Assessment*, edited by Warren Leon and Roy Rosenzweig, 98–114. Urbana: University of Illinois Press, 1989.

Hilker, Gordon. *The Audience and You: Practical Dramatics for the Park Interpreter*. Washington, DC: Office of Publication, National Park Service, 1974.

Himmelstein, Hal. *Television Myth and the American Mind*. Westport, CT: Praeger, 1994.

Hofstadter, Richard. *The Progressive Historians: Turner, Beard, Parrington*. New York: Alfred A. Knopf, 1968.

hooks, bell. "Performance Practice as a Site of Opposition." In *Let's Get It On: The Politics of Black Performance*, edited by Catherine Ugwu, 210–21. New York: Bay Press, 1995.

Horowitz, Daniel. *The Anxieties of Affluence: Critiques of American Consumer Culture, 1939–1979*. Amherst: University of Massachusetts Press, 2004.

Horowitz, Tony. *Confederates in the Attic: Dispatches from the Unfinished Civil War*. New York: Vintage Press, 1999.

Horton, James Oliver, and Spencer R. Crew. "Afro-American Museums: Towards a Policy of Inclusion." In *History Museums in the United States: A Critical Assessment*, edited by Warren Leon and Roy Rosenzweig, 215–36. Urbana: University of Illinois Press, 1989.

Howard, Ted. *The PBC: A History*. Washington, DC: People's Bicentennial Commission, 1976.

Hughes-Warrington, Marjorie. *The History on Film Reader*. London: Routledge, 2009.

Hutcheon, Linda. *A Poetics of Postmodernism: History, Theory, Fiction*. New York: Routledge, 1988.

Huyssen, Andreas. *Twilight Memories: Marking Time in a Culture of Amnesia*. New York: Routledge, 1994.

Isserman, Maurice, and Michael Kazin. *America Divided: The Civil War of the 1960s*. New York: Oxford University Press, 2000.

Jacobs, Jane. *The Death and Life of Great American Cities*. New York: Random House, 1961.

Jacobson, Matthew Frye. *Roots Too: White Ethnic Revival in Post–Civil Rights America*. Cambridge, MA: Harvard University Press, 2006.

Jameson, Fredric. *Postmodernism, or the Cultural Logic of Late Capitalism*. Durham, NC: Duke University Press, 1990.

———. *The Seeds of Time*. New York: Columbia University Press, 1996.

Jenkins, Sara. *Past Present: Recording Life Stories of Older People*. Washington, DC: St. Alban's Parish, 1978.

Jimerson, Randall C. *Archives Power: Memory, Accountability, and Social Justice*. Chicago: Society of American Archivists, 2009.

Kachun, Mitch. *Festivals of Freedom: Memory and Meaning in African American Emancipation Celebrations, 1808–1915*. Amherst: University of Massachusetts Press, 2003.

Kaiser, David E. *American Tragedy: Kennedy, Johnson, and the Origins of the Vietnam War*. Cambridge, MA: Harvard University Press, 2000.

Kammen, Michael. *Mystic Chords of Memory: The Transformation of Tradition in American Culture*. New York: Knopf, 1991.

———, ed. *The Past Before Us*. Ithaca, NY: Cornell University Press, 1980.

Kaplan, Amy. *The Social Construction of American Realism*. Chicago: University of Chicago Press, 1988.

Kay, William Kennon. *Keep It Alive: Tips on Living History Demonstrations*. Washington, DC: U.S. Department of the Interior, 1970.

Kazin, Michael. *American Dreamers: How the Left Changed a Nation*. New York: Vintage Books, 2011.

Kelland, Lara. "Clio's Foot Soldiers: Twentieth-Century U.S. Social Movements and the Uses of Collective Memory." Ph.D. diss, University of Illinois at Chicago, 2013.

Kelsey, Darwin. "Harvests of History." *Historic Preservation* 28, no. 3 (1976): 20–24.

———. "Outdoor Museums and Historical Agriculture." *Agricultural History* 46 (1972): 105–27.

Killen, Andreas. *1973 Nervous Breakdown: Watergate, Warhol, and the Birth of Post-Sixties America*. New York: Holtzbrinck Publishers, 2006.

Kindleberger, Charles P. *Manias, Panics, and Crashes: A History of Financial Crises*. New York: Wiley Investment Classics, 2005.

King, Katie. *Networked Reenactments: Stories Transdisciplinary Knowledges Tell*. Durham, NC: Duke University Press, 2011.

Kirshenblatt-Gimblett, Barbara. *Destination Culture: Tourism, Museums, and Heritage*. Berkeley: University of California Press, 1998.

Kotlowski, Dean. *Nixon's Civil Rights: Politics, Principles, and Policy*. Cambridge, MA: Harvard University Press, 2002.

Knell, Simon J., ed. *Museums in the Material World*. London: Routledge, 2007.

Kuhn, Annette. "Women's Genres: Melodrama, Soap Opera, and Theory." In *Feminist Television Criticism: A Reader*, 2nd ed., edited by Charlotte Brundson and Lynn Spigel, 225–34. Berkshire: Open University Press, 2008.

Kulik, Gary. "Designing the Past: History Museum Exhibition from Peale to the Present." In *History Museums in the United States*, edited by Warren Leon and Roy Rosenzweig, 3–37. Urbana: University of Illinois Press, 1989.

Kutler, Stanley I., ed. *Abuse of Power: The New Nixon Tapes*. New York: Free Press, 1995.

Landsberg, Alison. *Engaging the Past: Mass Culture and the Production of Historical Knowledge*. New York: Columbia University Press, 2015.

——. *Prosthetic Memory: The Transformation of American Remembrance in the Age of Mass Culture*. New York: Columbia University Press, 2004.

Lasch, Christopher. *The Culture of Narcissism: American Life in an Age of Diminishing Expectations*. New York: W.W. Norton, 1977.

Lassiter, Matthew. *The Silent Majority: Suburban Politics in the Sunbelt South*. Princeton, NJ: Princeton University Press, 2006.

Lawless, Benjamin. *The Color of Dust: And Other Dirty Little Secrets from Our Nation's Attic*. Indianapolis: Dog Ear Publishing, 2010.

Lears, T. J. Jackson. *No Place of Grace: Antimodernism and the Transformation of American Culture*. Chicago: Chicago University Press, 1981.

Lee, Antoinette J., ed. *Past Meets Future: Saving America's Historic Environments*. Washington, DC: Preservation Press, 1992.

Lembcke, Jerry. *The Spitting Image: Myth, Memory, and the Legacy of Vietnam*. New York: New York University Press, 1998.

Lemisch, Jesse. *Towards a Democratic History*. Detroit: Radical Education Project, 1967.

Lentz, Kirsten Marthe. "Quality vs. Relevance: Feminism, Race, and the Politics of the Sign in 1970s Television." *Camera Obscura* 15, no. 1 (2000): 45–93.

Leon, Warren, and Roy Rosenzweig, eds. *History Museums in the United States: A Critical Assessment*. Urbana: University of Illinois Press, 1989.

Lepore, Jill. *The Whites of Their Eyes: The Tea Party's Revolution and the Battle Over American History*. Princeton, NJ: Princeton University Press, 2010.

Lesko, Kathleen M., Valerie Babb, and Carroll R. Gibbs. *Black Georgetown Remembered: A History of Its Black Community from the Founding of "The Town of George" in 1751 to the Present Day*. Washington, DC: Georgetown University Press, 1999.

Levine, Lawrence C. "The Unpredictable Past: Reflections on Recent American Historiography." *American Historical Review* 94, no. 3 (June 1989): 671–79.

Levinson, Sanford. *Written in Stone: Public Monuments in Changing Societies*. Durham, NC: Duke University Press, 1990.

Lewis, W. David. "Exhibit Review: The Smithsonian's '1876' Exhibit." *Technology and Culture* 18, no. 4 (October 1977): 670–84.

Lifton, Robert Jay. *Home From the War: Learning from Vietnam Veterans*. New York: Other Press, 1973.

Lindgren, James M. "A Spirit That Fires the Imagination: Historic Preservation and Cultural Regeneration in Virginia and New England, 1850–1950." In *Giving Preservation a History: Histories of Historic Preservation in the United States*, edited by Max Page and Randall Mason, 107–30. New York: Routledge, 2004.

Lipsitz, George. "The Meaning of Memory: Family, Class and Ethnicity in Early Network Television Programs." In *Private Screenings: Television and the Female Consumer*, edited by Lynn Spigel and Denise Mann, 71–110. Minneapolis: University of Minnesota Press, 1992.

———. *Time Passages: Collective Memory and American Popular Culture*. Minneapolis: University of Minnesota Press, 2001.

Logevall, Fredrik. *Choosing War: The Lost Chance for Peace and the Escalation of War in Vietnam*. Berkeley: University of California Press, 1999.

Lonetree, Amy. *Decolonizing Museums: Representing Native America in National and Tribal Museums*. Chapel Hill: University of North Carolina Press, 2012.

Lott, Eric. *Love and Theft: Blackface Minstrelsy and the American Working Class*. New York: Oxford University Press, 1995.

Lowenthal, David. "The Bicentennial Landscape: A Mirror Held up to the Past." *Geographical Review* 67, no. 3 (July 1977): 253–67.

———. *The Heritage Crusade and the Spoils of History*. Cambridge: Cambridge University Press, 1998.

———. *The Past Is a Foreign Country*. Cambridge: Cambridge University Press, 1985.

Lubar, Steven, and Kathleen Kendrick. *Legacies: Collecting America's History at the Smithsonian*. Washington, DC: Smithsonian Institution Press, 2001.

Lyotard, Jean-Francois. *The Postmodern Condition: A Report on Knowledge*. Geoff Bennington and Brian Massumi, trans. Minneapolis: University of Minnesota Press, 1984.

Lytle, Mark. *America's Uncivil Wars: The Sixties Era from Elvis to the Fall of Richard Nixon*. New York: Oxford University Press, 2006.

MacDonald, J. Fred. *One Nation Under Television: The Rise and Decline of Network TV*. New York: Pantheon Books, 1990.

———. *Who Shot the Sherriff? The Rise and Fall of the Television Western*. New York: Praeger, 1986.

Magelssen, Scott. *Living History Museums: Undoing History through Performance*. New York: Rowman & Littlefield, 2007.

———. *Simming: Participatory Performance and the Making of Meaning*. Ann Arbor: University of Michigan Press, 2014.

Magelssen, Scott, and Rhona Justice-Malloy, eds. *Enacting History*. Tuscaloosa: University of Alabama Press, 2011.

Maines, Rachel P., and James J. Glynn. "Numinous Objects." *Public Historian* 15, no. 1 (Winter 1993): 8–25.

Marable, Manning. *Living Black History: How Reimagining the African American Past Can Remake America's Racial Future*. New York: Basic Civitas, 2006.

Marcus, Daniel. *Happy Days and Wonder Years: The Fifties and the Sixties in Contemporary Cultural Politics*. New Brunswick, NJ: Rutgers University Press, 2004.

———. "Profiles in Courage: Televisual History on the New Frontier." In *Television Histories: Shaping Collective Memory in the Media Age*, edited by Gary R. Edgarton and Peter C. Rollins, 79–102. Lexington: University Press of Kentucky, 2001.

Marling, Karal Ann. *George Washington Slept Here: Colonial Revivals and American Culture, 1876–1986.* Cambridge, MA: Harvard University Press, 1988.

Marzio, Peter C., ed. *A Nation of Nations: The People Who Came to America as Seen through Objects and Documents Exhibited at the Smithsonian Institution.* New York: Harper & Row, 1976.

Massumi, Brian. *Parables for the Virtual: Movement, Affect, Sensation.* Durham, NC: Duke University Press, 2002.

Matusow, Allen J. *Nixon's Economy: Booms, Busts, Dollars, and Votes.* Lawrence: University Press of Kansas, 1998.

———. *The Unraveling of America: A History of Liberalism in the 1960s.* New York: Harper Torch Books, 1986.

May, Elaine Tyler. *Homeward Bound: American Families in the Cold War Era.* New York: Basic Books, 1988.

———. "The Radical Roots of American Studies—Presidential Address." *American Quarterly* 48, no. 2 (1996): 179–200.

Maynard, Joan. "Weeksville Revisited." In *An Introduction to the Black Contribution to the Development of Brooklyn*, edited by Robert Swan, 85–90. New York: New Muse Community Museum of Brooklyn, 1977.

McCalman, Ian, and Paul A. Pickering, eds. *Historical Reenactment: From Realism to the Affective Turn.* London: Palgrave Macmillan, 2010.

McCarthy, John, and Peter Wright. *Technology as Experience.* Cambridge, MA: MIT Press, 2004.

McCauley, Mary Seibert. "Alex Haley, A Southern Griot: A Literary Biography." Ph.D. diss., Vanderbilt University, 1983.

McClymer, John F. *Mississippi Freedom Summer.* Belmont, CA: Thomson/Wadsworth Press, 2004.

McCollough, Jack W. *Living Pictures on the New York Stage.* Ann Arbor: University of Michigan Press, 1983.

McGirr, Lisa. *Suburban Warriors: The Origins of the New American Right.* Princeton, NJ: Princeton University Press, 2001.

McKenzie, A. Calvin, and Robert Westbrot. *The Liberal Hour: Washington and the Politics of Change in the 1960s.* New York: Penguin Press, 2008.

McShane, Clay. *Down the Asphalt Path: The Automobile in the American City.* New York: Columbia University Press, 1994.

Means, Russell, and Marvin J. Wolf. *Where White Men Fear to Tread: The Autobiography of Russell Means.* New York: Saint Martin's Press, 1995.

Menninger, Robert. "Some Psychological Factors Involved in Oral History Interviewing." *Oral History Review* (1975): 68–75.

Meringolo, Denise E. *Museums, Monuments, and National Parks: Toward a New Genealogy of Public History.* Amherst: University of Massachusetts Press, 2012.

Miller, Timothy. *The 60s Communes: Hippies and Beyond.* Syracuse, NY: Syracuse University Press, 1999.

Mires, Charlene. *Independence Hall in American Memory*. Philadelphia: University of Pennsylvania Press, 2002.

Mittell, Jason. *Television and American Culture*. New York: Oxford University Press, 2010.

Modeleski, Tania. "The Search for Tomorrow in Today's Soap Operas: Notes on a Feminine Narrative Form." In *Feminist Television Criticism: A Reader*, 2nd ed., edited by Charlotte Brundson and Lynn Spigel, 29–40. Berkshire: Open University Press, 2008.

Montell, William Lunwood. *The Saga of Coe Ridge: A Study in Oral History*. Knoxville: University of Tennessee Press, 1970.

Mould, David H. "Interviewing." In *Catching Stories: A Practical Guide to Oral History*, edited by Donna M. Deblasio, Charles F. Ganzert, et al., 82–103. Athens: University of Ohio Press, 2009.

Muensterberger, Werner. *Collecting: An Unruly Passion*. Princeton, NJ: Princeton University Press, 1994.

Mulloy, Elizabeth D. *The History of the National Trust for Historic Preservation, 1963–1973*. Washington, DC: Preservation Press, 1976.

Mumford, Esther Hall. *Seattle's Black Victorians*. Seattle, WA: Anase Press, 1980.

———. *Seven Stars and Orion: Reflections of the Past*. Seattle, WA: Anase Press, 1986.

Murray, Rolland. "Black Crisis Shuffle: Fiction, Race, and Simulation." *African American Review* 42, no. 2 (2008): 1–19.

Murtagh, William J. *Keeping Time: The History and Theory of Preservation in America*. Hoboken, NJ: John Wiley & Sons, 2006.

Museum of History and Technology. *Exhibits in the Museum of History and Technology*. Washington, DC: Smithsonian Institution Press, 1968.

Newcombe, Horace. "From Old Frontier to New Frontier." In *The Revolution Wasn't Televised: Sixties Television and Social Conflict*, edited by Lynn Spigel and Michael Curtin, 287–304. New York: Routledge, 1997.

Ngai, Sianne. *Ugly Feelings*. Cambridge, MA: Harvard University Press, 2007.

Nichols, Bill. *Representing Reality: Issues and Concepts in Documentary*. Bloomington: Indiana University Press, 1991.

Nichols, Wende. "Historic American Landscapes Survey: Mount Zion Cemetery/ Female Union Band Cemetery," Historic American Landscapes Survey, National Park Service, 2008.

Nora, Pierre. "Between Memory and History: Les Lieux de Memoire." *Representations* 26 (Spring 1989): 7–24.

Novick, Peter. *That Noble Dream: The 'Objectivity Question' and the American Historical Profession*. Cambridge: Cambridge University Press, 1988.

Oblinger, Carl. *Interviewing the People of Pennsylvania: A Conceptual Guide to Oral History*. Harrisburg: Pennsylvania Historical and Museum Commission, 1978.

Oliver, Arnold James, Jr. "American Socialist Strategy in Transition: The New American Movement and Electoral Politics, 1972–1982." Ph.D. diss., University of Colorado, 1983.

Page, Max, and Randall Mason, eds. *Giving Preservation a History: Histories of Historic Preservation in the United States*. New York: Routledge, 2004.

Parmet, Herbert. *Richard Nixon and His America*. Boston: Little, Brown, 1990.

Peacock, John. *Fashion Sourcebooks: The 1970s*. London: Thames and Hudson, 1997.

Pearce, Susan. *Museums, Objects, and Collections: A Cultural Study*. Washington, DC: Smithsonian Institution Press, 1992.

———, ed. *Objects of Knowledge*. London: Athlone Press, 1990.

Pease, Donald E., and Robyn Wiegman, eds. *The Futures of American Studies*. Durham, NC: Duke University Press, 2002.

People's Bicentennial Commission. *America's Birthday: A Planning and Activity Guide for Citizen Participation during the Bicentennial Years*. New York: Simon & Schuster, 1973.

———. *Common Sense 2: The Case against Corporate Tyranny*. New York: Bantam, 1975.

———. *Voices of the American Revolution*. New York: Bantam, 1975.

Perks, Robert, and Alistair Thomson, eds. *The Oral History Reader*. New York: Routledge, 1998.

Perlstein, Rick. *The Invisible Bridge: The Fall of Nixon and the Rise of Reagan*. New York: Simon & Schuster, 2015.

———. *Nixonland: The Rise of a President and the Fracturing of America*. New York: Scribner, 2008.

Porter, Glenn. *The Workers World at Hagley*. Wilmington, DE: Hagley Foundation, 1981.

Post, Robert C., ed. *1876: A Centennial Exhibition*. Washington, DC: Smithsonian Institution Press, 1976.

———. *Who Owns America's Past? The Smithsonian and the Problem of History*. Baltimore, MD: Johns Hopkins University Press, 2013.

Rabinowitz, Lauren. *For the Love of Pleasure: Women, Movies, and Culture in Turn-of-the-Century Chicago*. New Brunswick, NJ: Rutgers University Press, 1998.

Rabinowitz, Richard. *Curating America: Journeys through Storyscapes of the American Past*. Chapel Hill: University of North Carolina Press, 2016.

Radar, Karen A., and Victoria Cain. *Life on Display: Revolutionizing U.S. Museums of Science and Natural History in the Twentieth Century*. Chicago: University of Chicago Press, 2014.

Radstone, Susannah. *The Sexual Politics of Time: Confession, Nostalgia, Memory*. London: Routledge, 2007.

Raley, Rita. *Tactical Media*. Minneapolis: University of Minnesota Press, 2009.

Rapping, Elayne. *The Movie of the Week: Private Stories, Public Events*. Minneapolis: University of Minnesota Press, 1992.

Reed, T. V. *The Art of Protest: Culture and Activism from the Civil Rights Movement to the Streets of Seattle*. Minneapolis: University Press of Minnesota, 2005.

Reich, Charles. *The Greening of America*. New York: Random House, 1970.

Reynolds, Simon. *Retromania: Pop Culture's Addition to Its Own Past*. New York: Faber & Faber, 2011.

Rifkin, Jeremy. "The Red, White, and Blue LEFT." *The Progressive* (November 1971): 14–19.

———. "Whose Bicentennial?" In *How to Commit Revolution American Style*, edited by John Rossen and Jeremy Rifkin, 9–20. Secaucus, NJ: Lyle Stuart, Inc., 1973.

Riggs, Marlon. *Color Adjustment.* California Newsreel, 1991.

Ritchie, Donald A. *Doing Oral History: A Practical Guide.* Oxford: Oxford University Press, 2003.

Rodgers, Daniel T. *Age of Fracture.* Cambridge, MA: Belknap Press, 2011.

Rojas, Fabio. *From Black Power to Black Studies: How a Radical Social Movement Became an Academic Discipline.* Baltimore, MD: Johns Hopkins University Press, 2010.

Romano, Renee, and Leigh Raiford, eds. *The Civil Rights Movement in American Memory.* Athens: University of Georgia Press, 2006.

Ronell, Avital. *The Telephone Book: Technology, Schizophrenia, Electric Speech.* Lincoln: University of Nebraska Press, 1989.

Ronsheim, Robert. "Is the Past Dead?" *Museum News* 53, no. 3 (November 1974): 16–17.

Rosen, Philip. *Change Mummified: Cinema, Historicity, Theory.* Minneapolis: University of Minnesota Press, 2001.

Rosenstone, Robert. *Visions of the Past: The Challenges of Film to Our Idea of History.* Cambridge, MA: Harvard University Press, 1995.

Rosenzweig, Roy, and David Thelen. *The Presence of the Past: Popular Uses of History in Everyday Life.* New York: Columbia University Press, 1998.

Rossen, John. "Revolutionary Nationalism and the American Left." In *How to Commit Revolution American Style,* edited by John Rossen and Jeremy Rifkin, 146–61. Secaucus, NJ: Lyle Stuart, Inc., 1973.

Rossen, John, and Jeremy Rifkin, eds. *How to Commit Revolution American Style.* Secaucus, NJ: Lyle Stuart, Inc., 1973.

Roth, Stacy F. *Past Into Present: Effective Techniques for First-Person Historical Interpretation.* Chapel Hill: University of North Carolina Press, 1998.

Ruffins, Fath Davis. "Mythos, Memory, and History: African American Preservation Efforts, 1820–1990." In *Museums and Their Communities: The Politics of Public Culture,* edited by Ivan Karp, Christine Mullen Kreamer, and Steven D. Lavine, 506–611. Washington, DC: Smithsonian Institution Press, 1992.

Rushdy, Ashraf H. A. *Remembering Generations: Race and Family in Contemporary African American Fiction.* Chapel Hill: University of North Carolina Press, 2001.

Rydell, Robert. *All the World's a Fair: Visions of Empire at American International Expositions, 1876–1916.* Chicago: Chicago University Press, 1984.

———. *World of Fairs: The Century-of-Progress Expositions.* Chicago: University of Chicago Press, 1993.

Rydell, Robert, John Findling, and Kimberly Pelle. *Fair America: World's Fairs in the United States.* Washington, DC: Smithsonian Institution Press, 2000.

Rymsza-Pawlowska, Malgorzata J. "Frontier House: Reality TV and the Historical Experience." *Film & History: An Interdisciplinary Journal of Film and Television Studies* 37, no. 1 (2007): 35–42.

Salkind, Micah. "Scale, Sociality, and Serendipity in Providence, Rhode Island's Post-Industrial Renaissance." In *Creative Economies in Post-Industrial Cities: Manufacturing a (Different) Scene,* edited by Myrna Margulies Breitbart, 33–57. Farnham, Surrey: Ashgate, 2013.

Samuel, Lawrence. *The End of the Innocence: The 1964–1965 New York World's Fair.* New York: Syracuse University Press, 2007.

Savage, Kirk. *Standing Soldiers, Kneeling Slaves: Race, War, and Monument in Nineteenth-Century America.* Princeton, NJ: Princeton University Press, 1997.

Schlebecker, John T. *Living Historical Farms: A Walk into the Past.* Washington, DC: Smithsonian Institution Press, 1968.

Schlebecker, John T., and Gale E. Peterson. *Living Historical Farms Handbook.* Washington, DC: Smithsonian Institution Press, 1972.

Schlereth, Thomas J. "It Wasn't That Simple." *Museum News* 56, no. 1 (January–February 1978): 39–40.

Schneider, Rebecca. *Performing Remains: Art and War in Times of Theatrical Reenactment.* London: Routledge, 2011.

Schulman, Bruce J. *Lyndon B. Johnson and American Liberalism.* Boston: Bedford Books, 1995.

———. *The Seventies: The Great Shift in American Culture, Society, and Politics.* New York: Da Capo Press, 2001.

Sconce, Jeffrey. *Haunted Media: Electronic Presence from Telegraphy to Television.* Durham, NC: Duke University Press, 2000.

———. "The 'Outer Limits' of Oblivion." In *The Revolution Wasn't Televised: Sixties Television and Social Conflict*, edited by Lynn Spigel and Michael Curtin, 21–46. New York: Routledge, 1996.

Scott, Jennifer. "Reimagining Freedom in the Twenty-First Century at a Post-Emancipation Site." *The Public Historian* 37, no. 2 (May 2015): 73–88.

Seelye, John D. *Memory's Nation: The Place of Plymouth Rock.* Chapel Hill: University of North Carolina Press, 1998.

Self, Robert O. *All in the Family: The Realignment of American Democracy Since the 1960s.* New York: Hill & Wang, 2012.

Sell, Mike. "The Black Arts Movement: Performance, Neo-Orality, and the Destruction of the 'White Thing.'" In *African American Performance and Theater History: A Critical Reader*, edited by Harry J. Elam Jr. and David Krasner, 56–80. Oxford: Oxford University Press, 2001.

Shackel, Paul A. "Introduction: The Making of the American Landscape." In *Myth, Memory, and the Making of the American Landscape*, edited by Paul A. Shackel, 1–16. Gainesville: University Press of Florida, 2001.

Skinner, Tina, ed. *Fashionable Clothing from the Sears Catalogs: Mid-1970s.* New York: Schiffer Book for Collectors and Designers, 1999.

Slotkin, Richard. *Gunfighter Nation: The Myth of the Frontier in Twentieth-Century America.* New York: Maxwell Macmillan, 1992.

Smethurst, James Edward. *The Black Arts Movement: Literary Nationalism in the 1960s and 70s.* Chapel Hill: University of North Carolina Press, 2005.

Smith, Michael L. "Making Time: Representations of Technology at the 1964 World's Fair." In *The Power of Culture: Critical Essays on American History*, edited by Richard Wrightman Fox and T. J. Jackson Lears, 223–46. Chicago: University of Chicago Press, 1993.

Smulyan, Susan. *Popular Ideologies: Mass Culture at Mid-Century*. Philadelphia: University of Pennsylvania Press, 2007.

Snow, Stephen Eddy. *Performing the Pilgrims: A Study of Ethnohistorical Role-Playing at Plimoth Plantation*. Jackson: University Press of Mississippi, 1993.

Sobchack, Vivian, ed. *The Persistence of History: Cinema, Television, and the Modern Event*. New York: Routledge, 1996.

Special Committee on Historic Preservation United States Conference of Mayors. *With Heritage So Rich*. New York: Random House, 1966.

Spigel, Lynn. "From Domestic Space to Outer Space: The 1960s Fantastic Family Sitcom." In Spigel, *Welcome to the Dreamhouse*, 107–40.

———. *Make Room for TV: Television and the Family Ideal In Postwar America*. Chicago: University of Chicago Press, 1992.

———. *Welcome to the Dreamhouse: Popular Media and Postwar Suburbs*. Durham, NC: Duke University Press, 2001.

Spigel, Lynn, and Michael Curtin, eds. *The Revolution Wasn't Televised: Sixties Television and Social Conflict*. New York: Routledge, 1997.

Spillman, Lyn. *Nations and Commemoration: Creating National Identities in the United States and Australia*. Cambridge: Cambridge University Press, 1997.

Sprinkle, John H., Jr. *Crafting Preservation Criteria: The National Register of Historic Places and American Historical Preservation*. New York: Routledge, 2014.

Spurr, Daniel. *River of Forgotten Days: A Journey Down the Mississippi in Search of La Salle*. New York: Henry Holt and Company, 1998.

Stanton, Cathy. *The Lowell Experiment: Public History in a Postindustrial City*. Amherst: University of Massachusetts Press, 2006.

———. *Reenactors in the Parks: A Study of External Revolutionary War Reenactment Activity at National Parks*. Boston: National Park Service Northeast Ethnography Program, November 1999. http://www.nps.gov/revwar/reenactors/, accessed June 2009.

Starr, Meg. "'Hit Them Harder': Leadership, Solidarity, and the Puerto Rican Independence Movement." In *The Hidden 70s: Histories of Radicalism*, edited by Dan Berger, 135–54. New Brunswick, NJ: Rutgers University Press, 2010.

Stein, Judith. *Pivotal Decade: How the United States Traded Factories for Finance in the Seventies*. New Haven, CT: Yale University Press, 2011.

Stewart, Jeffrey C., and Fath Davis Ruffins. "A Faithful Witness: Afro-American Public History in Historical Perspective, 1828–1984." In *Presenting the Past: Critical Perspectives on History and the Public*, edited by Susan Porter Benson, Steven Brier, and Roy Rosenzweig, 307–36. Philadelphia: Temple University Press, 1986.

Stewart, Kathleen. *Ordinary Affects*. Durham, NC: Duke University Press, 2007.

Stewart, Susan. *On Longing: Narratives of the Miniature, the Gigantic, the Souvenir, the Collection*. Durham, NC: Duke University Press, 1993.

Stocking, George W., ed. *Objects and Others: Essays on Museums and Material Culture*. Madison: University of Wisconsin Press, 1985.

Sturken, Marita. *Tangled Memories: The Vietnam War, the AIDS Epidemic, and the Politics of Remembering*. Berkeley: University of California Press, 1997.

Sugrue, Thomas J. *The Origins of the Urban Crisis: Race and Inequality in Postwar Detroit*. Princeton, NJ: Princeton University Press, 1996.

Swigger, Jessie. *History Is Bunk: Assembling the Past at Henry Ford's Greenfield Village*. Amherst: University of Massachusetts Press, 2014.

Taylor, Diana. *The Archive and the Repertoire: Performing Cultural Memory in the Americas*. Durham, NC: Duke University Press, 2003.

Terkel, Studs. *Hard Times: An Oral History of the Great Depression*. New York: Pantheon Books, 1970.

———. *Working: People Talk About What They Do All Day and How They Feel About What They Do*. New York: Pantheon Books, 1974.

Theoharis, Jeanne, and Komozi Woodard, eds. *Groundwork: Local Black Freedom Movements in America*. New York: New York University Press, 2005.

Tilden, Freeman. *Interpreting Our Heritage: Principles and Practices for Visitor Services in Parks, Museums, and Historic Places*. Chapel Hill: University of North Carolina Press, 1957.

Toffler, Alvin. *Future Shock*. New York: Random House, 1970.

Toll, Robert C. *Blacking Up: The Minstrel Show in Nineteenth-Century America*. New York: Oxford University Press, 1977.

Torres, Sasha. *Black, White, and In Color: Television and Black Civil Rights*. Princeton, NJ: Princeton University Press, 2003.

Trouillot, Michel. *Silencing the Past: Power and the Production of History*. Boston: Beacon Press, 1995.

Turner, Fred. *The Democratic Surround: Multimedia and American Liberalism from World War II to the Psychedelic Sixties*. Chicago: University of Chicago Press, 2013.

———. *From Counterculture to Cyberculture: Stewart Brand, the Whole Earth Network, and the Rise of Digital Utopianism*. Chicago: University of Chicago Press, 2010.

Tyler, Norman. *Historic Preservation: An Introduction to Its History, Principles, and Practice*. New York: W.W. Norton, 2000.

Tyrell, Ian. *Historians in Public: The Practice of American History, 1890–1970*. Chicago: University of Chicago Press, 2005.

Tyson, Amy S. *The Wages of History: Emotional Labor on Public History's Front Lines*. Amherst: University of Massachusetts Press, 2013.

Udall, Stewart. *The Quiet Crisis*. New York: Hold, Rinehart and Winston, 1963.

Ulrich, Laurel Thatcher. *The Age of Homespun: Objects and Stories in the Creation of an American Myth*. New York: Knopf, 2001.

Unrau, Harlan D. *Here Was the Revolution: Historic Sites of the War for American Independence*. Washington DC: U.S. Department of the Interior, 1976.

Uricchio, William. "The Future of a Medium Once Known as Television." In *The YouTube Reader*, edited by Pelle Snickars and Patrick Vonderau, 24–39. Stockholm: National Library of Sweden, 2009.

Vagnone, Franklin D., and Deborah E. Ryan. *Anarchist's Guide to Historic House Museums*. London: Routledge, 2015.

Vanderbilt, Cornelius, Jr. *The Living Past of America: A Pictorial Treasury of Our Historic Houses and Villages That Have Been Preserved and Restored*. New York: Crowne Publishers, 1955.

Venturi, Robert. *Learning from Las Vegas*. Cambridge, MA: MIT Press, 1977.

Volti, Rudi. *Cars and Culture: The Life Story of a Technology*. Baltimore, MD: Johns Hopkins University Press, 2004.

Von Eschen, Penny M. *Satchmo Blows Up the World: Jazz Ambassadors Play the Cold War*. Cambridge, MA: Harvard University Press, 2004.

Walker, William S. *A Living Exhibition: The Smithsonian and the Transformation of the Universal Museum*. Amherst: University of Massachusetts Press, 2013.

Wallace, Mike. *Mickey Mouse History and Other Essays on American Memory*. Philadelphia: Temple University Press, 1996.

Wark, MacKenzie. *Gamer Theory*. Cambridge, MA: Harvard University Press, 2007.

Warrior, Robert, and Paul Chaat Smith. *Like a Hurricane: The Indian Movement from Alcatraz to Wounded Knee*. New York: New Press, 1996.

Watson, Mary Ann. *The Expanding Vista: American Television in the Kennedy Years*. New York: Oxford University Press, 1990.

Weinberg, Nathan. *Preservation in American Towns and Cities*. Boulder, CO: Westview Press, 1979.

Wellman, Judith. *Brooklyn's Promised Land: The Free Black Community of Weeksville, New York*. New York: New York University Press, 2014.

Wellrock, Thomas R. *Preserving the Nation: The Conservation and Environmental Movements, 1870–2000*. New York: Harlan Davison, 2007.

West, Patricia. *Domesticating History: The Political Origins of America's House Museums*. Washington, DC: Smithsonian Institution Press, 1999.

White, Mimi, "Television: A Narrative—A History." *Cultural Studies* 3, no. 3 (October 1989): 282–300.

Whitrow, G. J. *Time in History: The Evolution of Our General Awareness of Time and Temporal Perspective*. Oxford: Oxford University Press, 1988.

Whyte, William. *Organization Man*. New York: Simon & Schuster, 1956.

Wilder, Laura Ingalls. *Little House on the Prairie*. New York: Harper Brothers, 1935.

Wilentz, Sean. *The Age of Reagan: A History, 1974–2008*. New York: Harper, 2008.

Williams, Raymond. *Television: Technology and Cultural Form*. London: Fontana, 1974.

Wise, Gene. "'Paradigm Dramas' in American Studies: A Cultural and Institutional History of the Movement." *American Quarterly* 31, no. 3 (1979): 293–337.

Wolfe, Tom. "The Me Decade and the Third Great Awakening." In *Mauve Gloves & Madmen, Clutter & Vine*, 117–56. New York: Farrar, Straus & Giroux, 1976.

Wood, Elizabeth, and Kiersten F. Latham. *The Objects of Experience: Transforming Visitor-Object Encounters in Museums*. Walnut Creek, CA: Left Coast Press, 2014.

Woodard, Komozi. *A Nation within a Nation: Amiri Baraka (LeRoi Jones) and Black Power Politics*. Chapel Hill: University of North Carolina Press, 1999.

Woolfork, Lisa. *Embodying American Slavery in Contemporary Culture*. Urbana: University of Illinois Press, 2009.

Yow, Valerie. "'Do I Like Them Too Much?' Effects of the Oral History Interview on the Interviewer and Vice-Versa." In *The Oral History Reader*, edited by Robert Perks and Alistair Thomson, 54–72. New York: Routledge, 1998.

Zaretsky, Natasha. *No Direction Home: The American Family and the Fear of National Decline, 1968–1980.* Chapel Hill: University of North Carolina Press, 2007.

Ziegler, Arthur P., Jr. *Historic Preservation in Inner City Areas: A Manual of Practice.* Pittsburgh, PA: Ober Park Associates, 1974.

Ziegler, Arthur P., Jr. and Walter C. Kidney. *Historic Preservation in Small Towns.* Nashville, TN: American Association for State and Local Histories, 1980.

Zipp, Samuel. *Manhattan Projects: The Rise and Fall of Urban Renewal in Cold War New York.* Oxford: Oxford University Press, 2010.

Zukin, Sharon. *Landscapes of Power: From Detroit to Disney World.* Berkeley: University of California Press, 1991.

Index

ABC television network, 28, 33–34, 35
Above Ground Archaeology, 59
Abraham Lincoln Presidential Library and Museum, 166
Abyssinian Daughters of Esther, 82
Adams, Abigail, 149
Adams, Samuel, 102, 146, 148
African American Museum of Philadelphia, 162
African Americans, 74; Bicentennial and, 9, 11, 55, 76–81, 142, 153–62, 163–64, 207 (n. 62); museums and, 158, 159, 160–61, 162; oral histories and, 82–83, 84–85, 157; preservation projects and, 77–82, 160. *See also* Haley, Alex; *Roots* (miniseries, 1970s)
Afro-American Bicentennial Corporation (ABC), 9, 76–81, 157, 160, 161–62, 164
Afro-American Institute for Historic Preservation and Community Development, 81
Agnew, Vanessa, 5, 169
Air Force One Discovery Center, 165–66
Allen, Steve, 23
All in the Family (television program, 1970s), 24
American exceptionalism, 90, 110, 129
American Indian Movement (AIM), 135–37, 153
American Revolution, 42, 49, 100, 138, 169; battles and, 123, 149–51; ideals and, 41, 43, 54, 61, 130, 146, 149
American Revolution Bicentennial (1976): African Americans and, 9, 11, 55, 76–81, 142, 153–62, 163–64, 207 (n. 62); battle reenactments and, 43, 120, 123, 149–51, 180 (n. 17); Bicenten-

nial Schlock collection and, 69, 85–87; Boston Tea Party and, 138, 139–41, 143, 148–49, 169; commercialization and, 55, 56, 62, 86, 129, 139; federal planning and, 8–9, 10–11, 64–65; immersive historical activities and, 5, 75–76, 87, 88; individual state plans and, 128, 160; instigation of, 39–40, 51, 64; international exposition and, 44, 45–47, 48, 95, 144; museum exhibits and, 49, 92, 93–94, 95–109, 117, 194 (n. 16); Native Americans and, 135–36, 138, 140, 163; planning for, 8–9, 40–45, 47–54; preservation projects and, 87, 88; reenactments and, 10, 60, 116, 118–19, 123–35, 137–38, 139–41, 156–57, 162–63, 169, 207 (n. 62); resistance to, 10–11, 141–42, 143–52, 153–55, 163; television and, 12, 13–15, 38, 172–73 (n. 2); transportation reenactments and, 10, 123–35, 200 (n. 38); urban renewal and, 52, 79; Wagon Train and, 10, 128–35, 200 (n. 38). *See also* American Revolution Bicentennial Administration (ARBA); American Revolution Bicentennial Commission (ARBC); Bicentennial Era; People's Bicentennial Commission (PBC)
American Revolution Bicentennial Administration (ARBA): African Americans and, 78, 159–62; Bicentennial Communities and, 58, 60, 63, 150–51; decision to reflect on past and, 61; formation of, 60–62, 145, 186 (n. 109); programming and, 60, 62, 65, 87, 88; reenactments and, 126–27, 129, 132, 150–51; running of, 62–64

Galloway, Cap, 132
Garvey, Marcus, 83
Genealogical research, 37–38
General Accounting Office (GAO), 56, 145
Glassberg, David, 121
Grange, the, 27, 146
Grant, Ulysses S., 61, 97
Greenfield Village, 4, 110
Grenada, 165–66, 170

Haldeman, H. R., 50, 187 (n. 111)
Haley, Alex, 8, 30–31, 32–33, 34, 35, 36, 37, 63, 82, 159, 177 (n. 72)
Happy Days (television program, 1970s), 22
Harley, William, 81, 83
Harris, Fred, 55
Haynes, Joseph, 81
Historic Preservation in Inner City Areas (Ziegler), 73
Historic Sites Act of 1935, 69
History: 1950s and 60s perceptions and, 15–22; African Americans and, 9, 11, 154–62; changing perceptions of, 6, 7–8, 14–15, 32–33, 65, 87, 89–90, 116, 117, 143–44, 170; direct experience of the past and, 67–68, 87, 88, 90, 92; "Disney" qualities of presenting and, 87, 104; emotional impact of, 35–36, 96–97, 98, 100, 102, 104, 118–19, 133; interactive engagement in, 96–98, 101–3, 114, 115–16, 117, 122–23, 124, 164, 196 (n. 50); oral histories and, 82–85, 157; the state and, 10–11, 40–41, 45–46, 64–65, 86, 88, 110–11, 145; technology and, 167. *See also* Museums; Preservation; Reenactments; Social history; Television
History, past as present, 73, 84, 109, 139; Bicentennial and, 39, 43, 48–49, 59, 61, 64, 65–66, 147–48; living history exhibits and, 115, 119; museum exhibits and, 100, 105, 106–7; reenact-

ments and, 6–7, 122, 134–35; television and, 15, 23–24, 35–37, 38
House Judiciary Committee (HJC), 56, 145
Huggins, Ericka, 154
Humelsine, Carlisle, 42, 43, 45, 50, 120, 180–81 (n. 25)
Humphrey, Hubert, 44
Hurley, James, 81, 82–83
Hutchinson, Thomas, 102
Huxtable, Ada Louise, 46

Increase and Diffusion: A Brief Introduction to the Smithsonian Institution (pamphlet), 89–90
In Small Things Forgotten: An Archaeology of Early American Life (Deetz), 106
I Remember Mama (television program, 1950s), 16–17
Isaacs, Stephen, 141

Jack, James, 123
Jacobs, Jane, 71
Jacobson, Matthew Frye, 37
Jefferson, Thomas, 149
John F. Kennedy Library, 166
Johnson, Charles, 135
Johnson, Lyndon B., 43, 52, 64, 65, 71, 72; Bicentennial Commission and, 41–42, 45, 48, 63
Jones, LeRoi, 31, 156

Katz, Elihu, 35
Kennedy, John F., 71, 72, 166
Kennedy, Ted, 55
Kilpatrick, James J., 145
Kine, Starlee, 165–66, 169–70
King, Martin Luther, Jr., 79

Landon, Michael, 25, 26, 27
Landsberg, Alison, 5
Lang, George, 45
La Salle, Robert de, 125, 126, 127–28
Lasch, Christopher, 3

National Organization for Women, 139, 140

National Park Service, 69–70, 72, 77, 78–79, 87, 105, 106, 116, 120

National Patriotic-Civic Organizations Coordination Committee, 60

National Register of Historic Places, 77, 78, 81

National Science Foundation, 58

National Trust for Historic Preservation, 42, 67, 69–70, 71, 72–73, 82

Native Americans, 134–37, 138, 140, 154, 163, 168, 203 (n. 71)

NBC, 24

New Deal, 26, 70, 83

Newton, Huey, 154

New York City, 95, 98

New York City Landmarks Commission, 82

New York Housing Authority, 81

New York Times, 46, 47, 54

1970s nostalgia culture, 1–3; interactive engagement with history and, 4–7, 13–14, 23–26, 27–28, 92, 138, 172 (n. 18); lack of reality and, 3, 171–72 (n. 15); living history exhibits and, 114–16; museum exhibits and, 98, 100–101, 118, 119; reenactments and, 122–23; television and, 1, 8, 13–14, 22–28

1960s "future" culture, 2; living history exhibits and, 111–14; museum exhibits and, 89–92, 95, 98; television and, 8, 13, 15–22, 25, 29, 101, 121

Nixon, Richard M., 97, 166; Bicentennial Administration and, 60–63; Bicentennial and, 10, 39, 40, 44–46, 48, 55–56, 65, 141, 149, 186 (n. 109); Bicentennial Commission and, 47, 49–52, 53–54, 55, 57, 60–61, 144, 145–46, 147, 187 (n. 111); election and, 44, 45; international exposition and, 47, 49, 52; reelection bid and, 54, 55, 186 (n. 109); resignation and, 64, 206 (n. 42); urban renewal and,

79, 111; Watergate and, 61, 146, 187 (n. 111)

Norstad, Lauris, 42

Oakland Community School, 154

Oil, 140–41, 149, 206 (n. 42)

Old Sturbridge Village, 99, 110, 111, 112, 113

Operation Urgent Fury, 165–66, 170

Oral-Aural History of Washington State, 84

Oral histories, 82–85, 157

Oral History Association, 83

Organization of Petroleum Exporting Countries (OPEC), 140, 206 (n. 42)

Otis, James, 102

"Our Peoples and Our Lives" (National Museum of the American Indian exhibit), 168

Pageants, 4, 10, 120–22, 156, 172 (n. 26)

Paine, Thomas, 146, 147, 148

Parkman, Francis, 133

Pastore, John O., 42, 55, 56

Patriotism, 40, 52, 59, 60, 97, 119, 145, 146, 148; Wagon Train and, 129, 130, 133

Pennsylvania Bicentennial Commission, 128, 132

Pentagon Papers, 54

People's Bicentennial Commission (PBC), 55, 57, 62, 76, 86, 153, 164; activities and, 10–11, 56, 63, 142, 144–48, 157, 163, 204 (n. 17); Boston Tea Party and, 140–41, 143, 148–49; counter-culture and, 150–52; formation of, 53–54, 143, 144–45; Lexington and Concord reenactment and, 149–51, 152, 206 (n. 42)

Personal transformation, 122–23

Philadelphia, 9, 44, 46–47, 52, 95, 105–9, 119, 162

Philadelphia Centennial World Exposition of 1876, 44, 56, 93–94, 97, 118

CASON → Teller?
Hess Knis

* Deb + Many Doris Forer
(Let Dem know I'm lew

(Millennium evenys at
White House)

Conference on
media + history?
(representation

TV
Film?
(Theatre?)
(Art?)

Leverage interest
in history, arts